Corporations and the Third Way

Corporations and the Third Way

SALLY WHEELER
Birkbeck College, University of London

·HART·
PUBLISHING

OXFORD AND PORTLAND, OREGON
2002

Hart Publishing
Oxford and Portland, Oregon

Published in North America (US and Canada) by
Hart Publishing
c/o International Specialized Book Services
5804 NE Hassalo Street
Portland, Oregon
97213-3644
USA

Distributed in Netherlands, Belgium and Luxembourg by
Intersentia, Churchillaan 108
B2900 Schoten
Antwerpen
Belgium

Hart Publishing is a specialist legal publisher based in Oxford, England. To order further copies of this book or to request a list of other publications please write to:

Hart Publishing, Salters Boatyard, Folly Bridge, Abingdon Rd,
Oxford, OX1 4LB
Telephone: +44 (0)1865 245533 Fax: +44 (0) 1865 794882
email: mail@hartpub.co.uk
WEBSITE: http//:www.hartpub.co.uk

British Library Cataloguing in Publication Data
Data Available

ISBN 1-84113-063-9 (paperback)

John Saunders Design & Production. Reading UK
Printed and bound in Great Britain by
Lightning Source UK Ltd

Preface

This book is the product of several years of serious thought about the place that corporations can hold in modern society. For me, it represents a personal journey from the narrow confines of the study of doctrinal law to a more multidisciplinary perspective which shapes our understanding of the place of law.

I gave a number of papers on these issues at the Institute of Citizenship Studies, at the Corporate Law Teachers Association in Flinders University, Adelaide, and Griffith University, Brisbane, both in Australia, and at the SPTL company law section meeting in Leeds. I have come to regard Griffith University as a second intellectual home and I am very grateful for the support and hospitality that I have enjoyed there over the years. Michael Freeman kindly invited me to give a Current Legal Problems lecture, and this was my first expedition into Aristotelian ethics. I gave a similar lecture at the Citizenship Conference in Leeds in 1999.

I am hugely indebted to my new colleagues (and in many my oldest friends) at Birkbeck for the welcome that they have given me and for the support and friendship they have shown me in my attempts to complete this project at what was a very difficult time.

Various colleagues and friends have read some or all of the manuscript in draft, and offered comments: John Bell, Tony Bradney, Fiona Cownie, Paddy Ireland, Jo Shaw and Gary Wilson. I am particularly grateful to both Gary Wilson and John Bell for the extended academic support they gave me during my time at Leeds.

It is ten years or so since I wrote anything of this sort of substance. I am extremely fortunate to have had during this period a very supportive family and the intellectual and emotional support of Jo Shaw.

Finally, I would like to thank Richard Hart for being the best, most supportive publisher in the world.

Sally Wheeler
Leeds, June 2001

Contents

Introduction

In recent years domestic political environments have undergone seismic changes. I think here particularly of the Eastern block on the left of the political spectrum and of the UK and the US with their move away from the right flank of the political spectrum. The result is a convergence of more centrist politics. There are obviously exceptions to this such as Italy and Austria but in very general terms what seems to be emerging is a politics with a small "p": a politics of issues rather than ideologies, a politics with questions for the individual. The most significant of these questions is how does the individual interface with the complexities of preserving and enhancing their personal identity but still being part of an emerging global edifice and a pre-existing localism. Right and left political positions have traditionally struggled to recognise the concepts of collectivity and difference respectively, that was part of their very nature. What we are left with in their wake it seems is a politics of pragmatism but nevertheless a politics with values and a politics that recognises the individual and that individual's need for connectivity. In politics with a large "P" this translates itself into the Third Way.

In chapter one I examine the events which gave birth to the Third Way in the UK and look at what expressions of it[1] might mean for the corporate sector in particular. My engagement with the Third Way is for the purposes of examining what this pragmatic politics advocates and it is not a concern of mine to address where it stands or what it is as a political system. I leave those critiques to others, with the rider that what I find difficult is that in the main a critique of the Third Way is exactly what is offered, what is missing is an alternative beyond deconstruction.[2] A main concern of mine is the possibility of synchronicity between the individual and the collective. This is a dilemma that underscores human existence and daily life. These dilemmas are

[1] Discussion of the political background in this book draws on the speeches of several Government Ministers and Ex-ministers. All these speeches can be found by consulting the relevant departmental page on the website for the Government, <www.opengov.org>. No separate references are given.

[2] For this I commend A Callinicos, *Against the Third Way* (Cambridge: Polity, 2001).

recreated for us by the entertainment media in form of popular television shows such as *Big Brother* and *The Weakest Link*. Their exact rules of engagement may differ slightly but their framework is broadly the same – how to preserve individuality for the purposes of ultimate fulfilment when survival depends on integration into the collective body.

The separation between individuality and community has lead us to the brink of a new age. The age we are leaving behind is one in which the practices of moral judgement were being taken away from the individual and instead routinised as systems of rules and laws made by "others". The age of postmodernity gives us a chance to recover individual choice and at the same time participate in a collective ethical life. My reference points here, as chapters two and three demonstrate, are to an unlikely pairing of Bauman and MacIntyre. My intellectual project is best summarised thus:

> "we are . . . having to rebalance the values of the individual and the communal. We are having to acknowledge more adequately the individual's necessary interdependence with the whole earth community . . . . [W]e are moving from individualism toward the incorporation of a more communal, interdependent conviction . . . . [F]rom this basic, critical shift flow four consequent shifts: the shift from property rights toward the rights of membership, from competition-consumer desire toward the recognition of community need, from the limited state toward the state as planner and coordinator, and from scientific specialization toward holism".[3]

Prime Minister Blair and indeed New Labour appear to hang much of their thinking on individual choice and collective ethical life on a strong sense of duty and responsibility to be borne by the individual which will lead seamlessly to the creation of "community", the building of a society in which there is participation. It is difficult to see how a more socially aware collective which also recognises individuality can be built on this idea of rights and responsibilities. There is no pre-existing equal distribution of rights in an economic and social sense, thus there can be no corresponding pattern of responsibilities and, in my view, nor should there be. A much more constructive way to approach this goal is to adopt an approach which centres on virtue – traits of character or disposition of a benevolent nature which are

[3] My debt is to S Daloz Parks, "Professional Ethics, Moral Courage, and the Limits of Personal Virtue" in B Darling-Smith (ed), *Can Virtue be Taught?* (Notre Dame, IN: University of Notre Dame Press, 1993) p 175 at p 178, herself drawing on G Lodge, *The New American Ideology* (New York, NY: Knopf, 1976).

employed by each person in the construction of the above. Failure to employ our virtues is not accompanied by a sanction from elsewhere as we might expect in the world of duty and responsibility but by an account of ourselves to ourselves. My idea of the virtues is taken from Aristotelian ethics. In chapter two I expand upon this to show how the idea of character, individuality and pursuit of the virtues can achieve some of the pragmatic politics of the Third Way. I also devote some of that chapter to explaining what I see as the contemporary importance of Aristotle, by this I mean the way in which Aristotelian ethics appeals to the fashions of life in the third millennium.

The central concern of this volume is with the position of the corporate sector. My interest is in how it should behave to be included in the search for a collective ethical existence. Formulated in this way, this proposition sounds as if it too contains a choice – the choice to be part of the Third Way or not. In chapter one I look at how corporations behave currently with respect to the social world that exists outside the matrix of profit accumulation and dividend return to shareholders. The political and social discourses in and around the Third Way make it clear that corporations have no choice but to seek to belong. Encapsulated there is a legitimacy crisis for the corporate sector. In stark terms it is no longer acceptable for this sector to assert that pursuit of profit is its sole legitimate aim in an epoch which looks for both individuality and the collective interest to be addressed.

My text does not dwell to any extent on a model of legitimacy, such engagement as there is is set out here.[4] The audience for legitimacy in this context is the collective social polity. Legitimacy links the actions of the entity or entities in question to the values of the polity to determine whether there is a match. A match registers as legitimacy. The polity is key in this setting because legitimacy is not imperilled by deviance in an individual's eyes, it depends on approval or not within the wider audience. Likewise an isolated fall from the legitimacy standard may or may not result in a legitimacy crisis depending on how it is viewed by the polity. Alternatively one or two apparently isolated incidents may result in the whole sector being considered to be in breach of current values. As I explain in chapter one the problem for the corporate sector in 2001 is that the model of pragmatic legitimacy on which it relied and helped to promulgate through the tools of

[4] For an overview of legitimacy theories in organisational studies literature on which I have drawn for the above discussion see M Suchman, "Managing Legitimacy: Strategic and Institutional Approaches" (1995) 30 *Acad of Manag Rev* 571.

self-regulation such as submitting to audit and the discipline of the market, has broken down. Assertions of social action through donations to charitable causes can be evaluated as at most enlightened self-interest which is insufficient to meet the requirements of the social polity. The replacement for this model of pragmatic legitimacy is one of moral legitimacy that demands that the corporate sector address questions of profit distribution and social intervention in accordance with the concerns of the polity. In chapter three I suggest a variety of ways in which corporations might do this.

How then do the shifts in political ideology mentioned above impact on the model of the corporation? What is the significance of individuality and community in this sector of the economy? What is needed in my view is a new theoretical grounding for corporate behaviour and in particular the interaction between the corporate sector and society. The need for this new model comes precisely from the fact that current models do not reflect the questions posed above, never mind the answers. There is a particular sterility and poverty of thought around the models of corporate structure and behaviour suggested by the legal academy. The present position is that at one end of the spectrum there is the Law and Economics School which sees individuals, such as employees, trading partners and other groups connected with the corporation as free actors able to negotiate a *contract* with the corporation. The corporation in this scheme is not an entity in itself but is constituted as a collection of such contracts. The market reigns supreme as a governance mechanism; disenchanted shareholders exit using the market, other contractors take their labour, goods and services elsewhere, negotiating for themselves a contract with more favourable terms. There is no room for wider considerations as competition dictates that self-interest equates to collective interest.[5] This model – or variations upon it – has dominated academic debate in the US in particular for the last 30 years or so.[6] While Law and Economics

[5] For a further discussion of this point see P Cox ,"The Public, The Private and The Corporation" (1997) 80 *Marquette Law Rev* 391 at 415f.

[6] There is an enormous literature on this. Among the "classics" are M Jensen and W Meckling, "Theory of the Firm: Managerial Behaviour, Agency Costs, and Ownership Structure" (1976) 3 *Journal of Financial Economics* 305 and F Easterbrook and D Fischel, *The Economic Structure of Corporate Law* (Cambridge, MA: Harvard University Press, 1991). For a more comprehensive list see M O'Sullivan, "Sustainable Prosperity, Corporate Governance, and Innovation in Europe" in J Michie and J Grieve Smith (eds), *Globalization, Growth and Governance* (Oxford: Oxford University Press, 1998) p 180 at p 193. Interestingly the contours of debate are shifting as there is now a

analyses have never held the same position of pre-eminence in the UK, their legacy can be seen in the preoccupation of many UK scholars with internal governance and accountability issues within the corporation to the detriment of a wider view of the corporate role in society.[7]

At the other end of the spectrum real radicalism and innovation from the legal academy are in short supply.[8] There are those, notably from within the domain of political science, who advocate the dismantling of large concentrative corporate structures and the creation of smaller mutualised vehicles centered on a core business to service a regional economy tied to regional investment banks.[9] Although I take issue with the reality of this project as an achievable goal, the issue of regional involvement by corporations is something that I think has more potential than it has hitherto been credited with. I look at the issues surrounding this in chapter one and in rather more detail in chapter three. Lawyers who have looked at an agenda wider than internal governance (and here I do not exempt myself from criticism)[10] have tried to focus on the importance of the cultural, economic and social contexts of corporate practices usually through the matrix of a rights based approach such as stakeholding. This would involve a dismantling of the privileges accorded to property-owning shareholders and a creation of structures to allow other groups (stakeholders) to share in the establishment and realisation of corporate goals. These goals then become, by definition, more than profit maximisation.[11] In

rising interest in communitarianism. See for example see D Branson, "The Death of Contractarianism and the Vindication of Structure and Authority in Corporate Governance and Corporate Law" and D Millon, "Communitarianism in Corporate Law: Foundation and Law Reform Strategies" in Mitchell (ed), *Progressive Corporate Law* (Boulder, CO: Westview Press, 1995) pp 93 and 1 respectively.

[7] I would include here most of the standard texts on Company/Corporate Law and the majority of articles offered up for debate by those within the legal academy.

[8] C Graham, "Regulating the Company" in L Hancher and M Moran, *Capitalism Culture and Economic Regulation* (Oxford: Oxford University Press, 1989) p 199.

[9] P Hirst, *Associative Democracy* (Cambridge: Polity, 1994). See pp 144–55 in particular. This is what I see as Hirst's "classic" position. More recently he has offered modifications to accommodate stakeholding, see ch 1 n 9.

[10] See my comments in S Wheeler, "Works Councils: Towards Stakeholding" (1997) 24 *JLS* 44 where I paint a reasonably positive picture of the contribution stakeholding could make as a grounding theory.

[11] J Parkinson, "Company Law and Stakeholder Governance" in G Kelly et al (eds), *Stakeholder Capitalism* (Basingstoke: Macmillan, 1997) p 142. I would not want this to be taken as a criticism of John Parkinson's work which I regard as being of the very

this book I advance the argument that that rights based approach of stakeholding has little resonance with present political and social discourse and that the reality of what is presented under the umbrella of stakeholding is a collection of much weaker approaches divorced from any real theoretical underpinning. These include, for example, the informal widening of corporate governance participants through the gradual absorption of business culture from the more social democratic European economies such as Germany. Piecemeal measures such as these cannot found an operating culture. What results tends to look more like social responsibility. The disappointment of social responsibility is that it does not create the platform for improved and uniform standards of behaviour, legal or ethical, amongst its proponents in the corporate sector:

> "the term is a brilliant one; it means something, but not always the same thing, to everybody. To some it conveys the idea of legal responsibility or liability; to others it means socially responsible behaviour in an ethical sense; to still others, the meaning transmitted is that of "responsible for", in a causal mode; many simply equate it with a charitable contribution". [12]

One might think that the field of business ethics which is beginning to impact to a greater degree on legal models of the corporation would be of assistance in constructing a theory of behaviour but, as I explain in this book, my experience of this literature has been that it provides little by way of a holistic theory of business life and culture. Its strength lies in dealing with more micro issues such as the behaviour of individual business executives in particular situations. My approach to providing a theoretical grounding for corporate behaviour is to use Aristotelian virtue ethics as a grounding for the aspirations and hopes of individuals and I view corporations as individuals for these purposes. In chapter three I draw upon the work of MacIntyre in an attempt to bridge the gap between the life of universal community that Aristotle advocates and the reality of the life of torment that is individual choice within postmodernity. I use the images of history, hope

highest quality within this particular genre. See my comments on his text *Corporate Power and Responsibility* (Oxford: Oxford University Press, 1993) in S Wheeler, "Company Law" in P Thomas (ed), *Socio-Legal Studies* (Aldershot: Dartmouth, 1997) p 279 at pp 283–5.

[12] D Votaw, "Genius becomes Rare" in D Votaw and S Sethi (eds), *The Corporate Dilemma: Traditional values versus contemporary problems* (Englewood Cliffs, NJ: Prentice Hall, 1973) at p 11.

in the form of aspiration, community and individuality to advocate a form of corporate social intervention. This is distinct from corporate social responsibility and corporate community involvement in that it is a strategic intervention for the benefit of those outside the legally constructed categories of recipients of corporate profit. It is an intervention predicated on an analysis of needs following an audit of needs. Sustainability of the intervention is guaranteed as far as is possible within the fluctuations of a market economy by the drafting and issuing of a care plan. As I explain in chapter three the use of the term "care" is itself of strategic significance. I use it to reinforce the basic tenet of the Third Way – the importance of the relation between the individual and the larger collective.

1

Towards a New Capitalism

1. THE IMPORTANCE OF NATIONAL DISCOURSE

The Irrelevance of Globalisation for Corporations

A constant refrain of the 1990s has been that we are in an "information age" and in, or progressing towards, a "globalised economy". Advances in technology have allowed capital markets to vary the price of stocks across the world in a matter of seconds.[1] Large and complex global financial transactions can be undertaken without the need for face-to-face interaction.[2] The opening up of the former planned economies, the rapid industrialisation of China and the desire of developing countries to attract inward investment have created a global playing field for corporations in terms of the opportunities to reduce labour costs and find more favourable taxation and employment regimes.[3] Evidence for globalisation is often presented in terms of larger corporations having a greater income in terms of annual revenue than many nation states have in terms of GDP.[4] There is obviously a difference in terms of the share of market capitalisation

[1] R Reich, *The Work of Nations: Preparing Ourselves for 21st Century Capitalism* (New York, NY: Vintage, 1991) at pp 3, 8.

[2] However face-to-face interaction is still regarded as being significant in terms of doing business deals. In their contribution to R Friedland and D Boden (eds), *Nowhere: Space, Time and Modernity*, (Berkeley, CA: UCLA Press, 1994) D Boden and H Molotch explain the utility of co-presence in these circumstances, see "The Compulsion of Proximity" 257 at pp 268–70 and 274.

[3] A Guardian Newspaper article in June 1997 pointed out that 3 European firms had announced sufficient job cuts in Europe, often followed by job creation in East Asia, in 3 days to compare with British and French Government announcements on jobs to be delivered by their job creation programmes: M Woollacott, *The Guardian*, 14 June 1997 at 20.

[4] Hitachi for example is at 16th position in the Fortune 500 with an annual revenue of $75m, the Philippines is the 40th largest country in GDP terms with a GDP of $72m. This is taken from D Logan, "Corporate Citizenship in a Global Age" (1998) 146 *Royal Society of Arts Journal* 64 at 66.

that these corporations have in each state and so their level of potential influence varies from huge in some developing countries to more marginal in more established economies.[5] The possibilities for transferability of corporate presence in and out of national economies and larger trading blocks such as the EU means that no economy is entirely immune from corporate activities.[6] There is a tendency for this one fact to be given almost mythical status in that it is used to argue that every facet of life is now dominated by the exercise or not of corporate power. This is just too simplistic a proposition. It does not explain why Microsoft has had its position of dominance curbed by successful challenges in the US courts or perhaps more pertinently why the South African government has been able to persuade leading drugs companies to supply drugs to combat AIDS at a significantly lower than quoted price.

What it is possible to assert is that large corporations do enjoy a position of some power and influence over economic life. Following on from this assertion the next question is why should corporations in this position feel the need to shape their behaviour to fit with the contemporary discourse around social existence and political life in any particular nation state. We might expect the answer to lie within legal controls at the national level in relation to issues such as taxation regimes for the corporate sector. However the approach of both the legal academy and legislative science towards large corporations has been that they exist at a level beyond that of national law.[7] In some macro senses, this is true as the references to forum shopping opportunities in the preceding paragraph makes clear. One of the more unfortunate consequences of forum shopping between legal regimes, is the opportunity it creates for social dumping; different modes of corporate behaviour occur in different locales and are driven down to the lowest level acceptable in each location. However this is an issue that lends itself to social reporting and ethical grounding. Social reporting is

[5] This is something of a generalisation; national economies, even established ones, can be dependent on the presence of one or several national champions. The effect of large corporations is less the greater the size of the national economy.

[6] For discussions of the relationship between state and corporation see P Dicken, "Global–Local Tensions: Firms and States in the Global Space-Economy" (1994) 70 *Economic Geography* 101 at 112–21 and H Wai-Chung Yeung, "The Political Economy of Transnational Corporations: A Study of the Regionalization of Singaporean Firms" (1998) 17 *Political Geography* 389.

[7] F Johns, "The Invisibility of the Transnational Corporation: An Analysis of International Law and Legal Theory" (1994) 19 *Melbourne Univ Law Rev* 893.

looked at later in this chapter. Ethical grounding is a theme developed in more detail in the two chapters which follow.

Theoretical paradigms within legal science[8] to deal with the reality of multinational enterprise have not emerged.[9] The disciplinary focus of law is to consider its relationship with globalisation and its consequences as an adversarial one. Several difficulties have stood in the way of advancement towards adequate theorisation of the large multinational. One is the debate between the interests of legal formalism encompassing respect for national differences in legal culture and economic reality. Allied to this last point is the perceived importance of relatively unencumbered multinational growth in the interests of economic development. Concentration on globalisation as an adversarial issue of control at national level pays no attention to the cultural background of capitalism[10] in different locations and misses the economic link between globalisation and localism. It ignores the changes wrought by post-Fordism to local and regional governance and development.[11] Post-Fordism as the catalyst for change in the ordering of individuals' social and working lives is something that I consider later in this section. Its significance here is that it draws attention to the relationship between localised economies and global existence.[12] Post-Fordism is not an uncontroversial term in this context. I use it as a much more general term, than, for example, many geographers would,[13] to describe

[8] Unlike for example economics, see A Rugman, "Forty Years of the Theory of the Transnational Corporation" (1999) 8 *Transnational Corporations* 51.

[9] Responses to issues that arise as a result of EU economic and social policy such as merger control and competition rules have been rather better but of course this is to use law as a technical device rather than as a tool of conceptual analysis.

[10] See the arguments of Doremus et al in *The Myth of the Global Corporation* (Princeton, NJ: Princeton University Press, 1998), P Hirst and G Thompson, *Globalization in Question* (Cambridge: Polity Cambridge, 1996) at pp 186–7 and *infra* the text accompanying nn 32–46.

[11] Thrift points out the absence of a theoretical dimension to the issue of globalisation and social regulation and also, more importantly for this book, little theoretical "tradition" (his words, my emphasis) to link "global economic processes with more local forms of . . . regulation": N Thrift, "Globalisation, Regulation, Urbanisation: the Case of the Netherlands" (1994) 31 *Urban Studies* 365 at 379.

[12] For the view that the importance of national and regional economies to firms is somewhat underplayed in current economic discourse which concentrates unduly on internationalisation see, R Whitley, "The Internationalisation of Firms and Markets: Its Significance and Institutional Structuring" (1994) 1 *Organisation* 101.

[13] See for example the work of Mark Goodwin and Joe Painter who eschew post-Fordism as a theoretical paradigm and favour instead a process based regulation theory drawing on systems theory to explain the transitions that have taken place and move

the transition from central, state based government to localised governance.

Since the late 1980s the establishment of bodies such as locally based Training and Enterprise Councils, Enterprise Zones, Urban Development Corporations and Regional Development agencies mark the move towards corporate involvement in urban regeneration. There has been a drive at the level of the EU to encourage corporations to create networks (ie non-adversarial relationships based on sharing or pooling of resources or innovative capacity) in order to push forward policies of developing regional economies and forging European integration.[14] A potential difficulty with these types of policies is, that, to the extent that they depend on the existence of local industry, implementation may be problematic. Traditional heavy industry (sunset industries) has been in decline for some time and has been replaced by an expanding service sector and new high technology industries (sunrise industry). These sunrise industries have not necessarily followed the same location pattern and thus some areas find themselves without a local industry presence.[15] Some areas such as parts of Scotland and Wales have always been in this position. This accounts for incentive schemes that exist from time to time to persuade corporations to relocate to particular areas.[16] It is important to distinguish in this context between "industry presence" in terms of headquarters or large plant base and industry presence in terms of back-office, often out-sourced, functions or put more colloquially call centres. These centres are usually to be found close to pools of flexible and low cost labour. However they do not provide the same type of industry/locality link that more traditional heavy industry or even new sunrise industry does.

For corporations there are financial incentives for participating in urban regeneration and publicity opportunities. There is also the danger that by non-involvement there is the loss of a competitive

them forward: "Local Governance, the Crises of Fordism and the Changing Geographies of Regulation" (1996) 21 *Transactions: An International Journal of Geographical Research* 635 at 638.

[14] P Cooke and K Morgan, "The Network Paradigm: New Departures in Corporate and Regional Development" (1993) 11 *Environment and Planning D: Society and Space* 543 at 552.

[15] H Hurd et al, "The Geography of Corporate Philanthropy in the United Kingdom" (1998) 16 *Environment and Planning C: Government and Policy* 3.

[16] R Bennet et al, "The Location and Concentration of Businesses in Britain: Business Clusters, Business Services, Market Coverage and Local Economic Development" (1999) 24 *Trans Inst Br Geogr* 393 at 399–405.

advantage such as the opportunity to share the training costs of potential employees with other regionally based actors. Business elites have never been as welcome in urban local governance since business elites *were* urban local government[17] during the latter years of the nineteenth century. The moving down of policy-making to the localised level gives business elites an opportunity for participation that does not exist at higher levels.[18] As I explain in section 2, other consequences of post-Fordism, such as the legitimacy crisis that profit-making enterprise finds itself in, play into this idea of economic regeneration to ensure the importance to corporations not just of national discourse[19] but also regional commitment.

2. SOCIAL AND POLITICAL CONTEXT

Post Post-Fordism: Trajectories of Capitalism

The social background against which corporations provide employment and make profits has undergone phenomenal change in the last 20 years or so. First there was the transition from Fordism to post-Fordism. It was clear by the 1970s that older industrial economies needed to restructure radically in order to remain as players in the global market.[20] What has resulted is a recasting of the social phenomenon of

[17] D Valler et al, "Local Governance and Local Business Interests: a Critical Review" (2000) 24 *Progress in Human Geog* 409.

[18] I Strange, "Directing the Show? Business Leaders, Local Partnership, and Economic Regeneration in Sheffield" (1997) 15 *Environment and Planning C: Government and Policy* 1.

[19] The link between establishing a more social democratic economic policy, the formulation of long term business strategy by business and the adoption of an industrial policy based on regionalism is identified and set out by Colin Hay in "Anticipating Accommodations, Accommodating Anticipations: The Appeasement of Capital in the 'Modernization' of the British Labour Party, 1987–1992" (1997) 25 *Politics and Society* 234. This is also a link made by Hirst in the context of the stakeholding debate. Indeed, Hirst is the only commentator to attempt to link the economic sphere and the political sphere together within the stakeholding model (see the text accompanying nn 93–112, *infra*). For Hirst the reduction of economic governance to the local level to achieve goals similar to Hay's would be accompanied by similar reforms to political governance. While this might be more achievable than the position taken in *Associative Democracy* his maintenance within this model of an anti-concentrative argument means that it is still likely to be one step too far for policy makers.

[20] The same forces that are behind globalisation were at work earlier to underpin the transition to post-Fordism; the opening up of new markets, the development of new

employment. Workplaces are no longer characterised by the Taylorist[21] virtues of de-skilling, job demarcation and the importance of production over market. Instead the market drives production with a consequent switch to just-in-time delivery,[22] requiring flexible working practices and schedules and a high level of skilling for those in employment. Unskilled employment, with the exception of the service sector, is hard to come by as machines replace the unskilled.[23] Empirical evidence of these changes is at hand in the form of statistics to show that less than 60 per cent of the employed workforce in the UK have full time jobs and that less than a third of the workforce have a conventional "nine-to-five" day.[24]

This period also saw the rise and fall of the New Right. Values such as possessive individualism and an adherence to the importance of the market necessitating a preference for individual rights over individual duties[25] held sway for much of the 1980s and early 1990s. Capital accumulation became the principal goal and anything which threatened to hold back individual advancement in this sense was demonised as a risk

economies such as China and advancements in technological innovation. There is little agreement between commentators as to the contributory value of each of these events. Compare for example the review provided by S Lash and J Urry in *The End of Organised Capitalism* (Cambridge: Policy, 1987), who focus on the sectoral imbalances in the British economy that existed from before WW1 and the weakness of capitalism at the level of top-down industrial organisation, with H Perkin, *The Third Revolution* (London: Routledge, 1996), whose analysis is based on the failure of the aspiring professional classes to prevent economic stagnation. An attempt to pull together some of the positions taken is provided by D Harvey, *The Condition of Postmodernity* (Oxford: Blackwell, 1989) especially ch 10. It should be noted however that Harvey's mission is to offer a theorisation of the transition that capitalism has undergone as a result of post-Fordism. He does not provide an engagement with the political discourse that Perkin in particular offers, see H Perkin "The Enterprise Culture in Historical Perspective: Birth, Life, Death and Resurrection?" in P Heelas and P Morris (eds), *The Values of the Enterprise Culture* (London: Routledge, 1992) at p 36.

[21] F Taylor , *The Principles of Scientific Management* (New York, NY: Harper & Row, 1947).

[22] G Paulucci, "The Changing Dynamics of Working Time" (1996) 5 *Time and Society* 145

[23] V Borooah, "Unemployment: The Role of Skills and Gender" in Lundy et al (eds), *In Search of the "Underclass"* (Queens University Belfast Law Faculty, 1997) and R Barnett, "A New Work-Life Model for the Twenty-First Century" (1999) 562 *ANNALS, AAPSS* 143 at 147–8.

[24] M Goyder, "Work, Worth and Wealth" (1997) May *RSA J* 13.

[25] R Bellamy and J Greenaway, "The New Right Conception of Citizenship and the Citizen's Charter" (1995) 30 *Govt and Opp* 469.

that had to be avoided. Thus contributions to the maintenance of both the public sector and the welfare state were to be kept as low as possible as the former was inefficient and the latter guilty of creating a dependency culture. The perceived values of the private sector were to be adopted by both sectors as a way of ending their respective ills.[26] The ascendancy of the New Right brought to a close the corporatist era of the 1970s[27] and marked the end of the post-war Keynesian welfare settlement.[28] Traditional "family values" were championed, rhetorically at least, by the New Right such as child care being provided by one, preferably non-working, parent with support from the working parent who worked a conventional 40 hour week. Care patterns which departed from this standard were blamed for all manner of social ills such as teenage crime and truancy. The reality of working life in this period was very different as the statistic above shows and there were no policy initiatives forthcoming to make this idealised picture of family life more achievable. The emphasis on this preferred pattern of family life unites the New Right position with that taken by responsive communitarians, such as Amitai Etzioni,[29] who also exhort a return to this type

[26] I Metcalfe, "Conviction Politics and Dynamic Conservatism: Mrs Thatcher's Managerial Revolution" (1993) 14 *International Political Science Review* 352 and R Chapman, "Concepts and Issues in Public Sector Reform: the Experience of the UK in the 1980s" (1991) 6 *Public Policy and Administration* 1. For a general account of the implementation of these policies see S Wheeler, "Contracting Out in the UK Insolvency Service: The Tale of Performance Indicators and the 'Last Cowboy'" (1997) 7 *Aust J of Corp Law* 227.

[27] For a review of this see N Fishman, "Reinventing Corporatism" (1997) 68 *Pol Quart* 31, especially pp 33–6.

[28] For some the New Right played a direct role in creating the conditions in the light of which welfare has to be radically re-examined, see for example P Taylor-Gooby, "In Defence of Second-Best Theory: State, Class and Capital in Social Policy" (1997) 26 *J of Soc Pol* 171. For others the case is not made out, see for example Colin Hay's response to Taylor-Gooby, "Globalisation, Welfare Retrenchment and 'the Logic of No Alternative': Why Second-Best Won't Do" (1998) 27 *J of Soc Pol* 525.

[29] A Etzioni, *The Spirit of Community* (London: Fontana, 1993) especially pp 55–7, 69–70. The policy difference between the two positions can be summarised as the emphasis of the individual's responsibility for children (the New Right position) and the idea that the community as a whole has an interest in the pattern of care that parents deliver (the communitarian position). See J Stacey, *In the Name of the Family: Rethinking Family Values in the Postmodern Age* (Boston, MA: Beacon Press, 1996) at pp 54–7 where she describes how the New Right has benefited from an "interlocking network of scholarly and policy institutes, Think tanks and commissions" which forged a consensus around *family values* (my emphasis) which influenced the ideology and politics of the Clinton administration. She specifically cites Etzioni as part of this network.

of traditional family life. Despite agreement on this point, as section 3 will show, the influence of responsive communitarianism has grown in political discourse while that of the New Right has fallen away.

This same time frame was also characterised by huge corporate collapses, for example BCCI and the Maxwell Empire, which often revealed instances of regulatory inadequacy or failure. The legitimacy of acquisitiveness and profit were further discredited by the demise of businessmen previously considered successful such as the Guinness executives and Asil Nader. Exposure of the lavish lifestyles of those who had enjoyed success and lost it brought about a groundswell of opinion that new right values had spiralled out of control. It was also the case that such life styles were beyond the reach of many; the policies of market freedom and economic self-regulation designed to create entrepreneurial and self-reliant individuals were failing to deliver sustained economic growth and a general increase in living standards. The large salary increases awarded by corporations, often those in the previously state-owned utilities sector, to their managing executives at a time when many of the population were facing job insecurity and/or the creation of new family strategies to deal with changing work patterns,[30] caused further cracks in the edifice of this model of capitalism. This was a model based upon profit accumulation and its subsequent redistribution on a highly selective basis to those who enjoyed particular financial or proprietary relationships with corporate actors. Perhaps ironically those actors (large corporations, their executives and their shareholders), around whom this particular brand of capitalism was constructed, attempted to reinforce it by using the tool of voluntary self-regulation to strengthen and further protect the positions of those who already occupied the position of most privilege; shareholders who received distributions of profit because of their proprietary relationships with corporations as shareholders. A succession of reports, recommendations and statements of best practice, compiled under the auspices of self-regulation, sought to improve standards of corporate governance generally and mechanisms for setting directors' remuneration specifically, for the benefit of shareholders.[31]

[30] For example changes in caring arrangements, see C Tilly, *Work Under Capitalism* (Boulder, CO: Westview Press, 1998) pp 128–31 and M Ruistin, "A Third Way With Teeth" (1999) *Soundings* 7 at 19.

[31] *The Financial Aspects of Corporate Governance* (the Cadbury Report) December 1992; *Directors' Remuneration*, (the Greenbury Report) July 1995; *Committee on*

In 1995 Fukuyama announced that the success of capitalism depended on the presence of "trust".[32] By trust he meant a more inclusive model of capitalism than that advocated by the New Right together with the development of underlying cultural values. His comparison was between Anglo-American capitalism, by 1995 seriously discredited, and the network capitalism of Japan with its greater degree of state involvement and high growth. There he saw the presence of the greater trust that could save capitalism. Japanese network capitalism was very different from the Anglo-American model. The use of the term "Anglo-American" capitalism is not without definitional problems. The casting of capitalism into models produces different paradigms based upon which factors are considered relevant.[33] Objections have been raised to the idea of an "Anglo-American" capitalism on the grounds that welfare provision in the UK is much more similar to European provision than it is to American provision.[34] That is undoubtedly the case. However I use the term "Anglo-American" to separate the UK and the US from "Alpine" or "Rhine" capitalism which I would generically term "European". My reasons for this are that internal and external corporate governance are more similar in the UK and the US compared with other jurisdictions and so are other factors such as the development of the legal form for the corporation and the relationship between the corporation and finance capital.

Like many of the Tiger economies of East Asia, Japanese network capitalism was characterised by different patterns of investment and loan finance, state support and a concentration on sunrise as opposed to sunset industries. However it proved to be just as fragile a model of capitalism; by the end of 1995 the Japanese economy was under

Corporate Governance, (the Hampel Committee) April 1998. The last two are published by Gee Publishing, London. The Cadbury report specifically articulates that its concern is only with shareholders and its recommendations deal with the provision of information to shareholders and such like. The other two reports follow from this one and so their preoccupation with the shareholder is pre-ordained as it were. See the comments of J Parkinson and G Kelly, "The Combined Code on Corporate Governance" (1999) 70 *Pol Quart* 101. The present administration has indicated that it is unlikely to remove the material covered by these codes from the arena of best practice and give them legislative force, see S Byers, Secretary of State for Trade and Industry, Speech to TUC/IPPR, 7 June 2000.

32 F Fukuyama, *Trust* (London: Penguin, 1995).

33 D Coates, "Models of Capitalism in the New UK World Order: the UK Case" (1999) XLVII *Political Studies* 643 at 648.

34 M Albert, *Capitalism against Capitalism* (London: Whurr, 1993).

pressure as a property boom came to an end and its growth rate fell dramatically.[35] By mid 1997 the same had occurred throughout East Asia.[36] These collapses[37] had a domino effect throughout Europe as demand slowed and component manufacture in sunrise industries such as semi-conductors fell away as there was a sudden excess of supply over demand. The switch from a Fordist system of production to a post-Fordist system had introduced manual workers to flexibility. The collapse of the Tiger economies and continued technology development have introduced the skilled – managers and professionals – to flexibility and its consequences of changing work patterns and job insecurity.[38] The effect of this is to proletise those groups that were normally spared the worst consequences of the cyclical nature of capitalism. What had become clear was that even this form of capitalism based upon high-tech sunrise industry, state involvement and less adversarial relationships between sectors was not immune from boom and bust cycles. My argument is that the consequence of the failure of both Anglo-American capitalism and network capitalism to deliver stability and security is the birth of a different kind of capitalism. This is a new model and within this new model there are social expectations that corporations will undertake a quest for re-legitimisation based upon responsible profit-taking and an acknowledgement that their responsibilities extend beyond those with whom they enjoy a proprietary relationship.

The birth of a new form of capitalism is also underlined by the lack of sustainability revealed in the planned Marxist economies of

[35] Fukuyama has an unfortunate habit it seems of championing structures that are about to collapse; in 1989 he declared the victory of "liberalism", in his terms "Anglo-American capitalism" and the free market. The cracks appeared in this form of capitalism shortly afterwards, see F Fukuyama, "The End of History" (1989) 18 *The National Interest* 3, later expanded upon in *The End of History and the Last Man* (London: Penguin, 1992).

[36] While there are strong similarities in the structure of these economies in comparison with the UK, American and European structures, when taken individually there are key differences between them, for an overview see J Henderson et al, "Deciphering the East Asian Crisis" (1998) 6 *Renewal* 73 and M Castells, *End of Millennium* (Oxford: Blackwell, 1998) 243–58 and 264–80.

[37] Reasons put forward for the collapses vary from a "crony capitalism" argument based upon the close, possibly in some instances corrupt, relationships between corporations, lenders and the state to a cocktail of poor governance mechanisms and globalisation. For a critical review of these arguments see R Higgott, "The Asian Economic Crisis and the Politics of Resentment" (1998) 3 *New Political Economy* 333.

[38] U Beck, "Capitalism Without Work" (1997) *Dissent* 51.

pre-1989 Central and Eastern Europe. Gibson-Graham[39] set out the strand of Marxian argument that predicts the periodic crises of capitalism followed by its fall and replacement with a form of socialism that can exist in the conditions that brought down capitalism. In fact events have turned this argument on its head. What has happened in those economies post the collapse of communism has proved to be neither the success of a form of market socialism nor the rise, as yet, of a satisfactory mode of capitalism in terms of economic growth and stability. This is a major generalisation. There are huge differences between the rate of change in individual countries. Many commentators separate Central Europe – Poland, Hungary and the Czech Republic from Eastern Europe – for example Russia and Bulgaria. However to one degree or another David MacGregor's comment that "the former communist republics have been baptised with blood and soaked in Pepsi-Cola" rings true.[40] The loosening of the structures imposed by Marxist governments has allowed differences of cultural social identity to come to the fore leading to, in some instances, armed conflict. These emerging economies have had to face two principal difficulties. One is the transition from collective public ownership to private ownership without the necessary structures in place to oversee such a transition.[41] The second not unrelated factor is the demands of institutions such as the International Monetary Fund that particular economic policies and goals must be in place before international assistance is forthcoming.[42] This does not mean that these economies had no cultural economic identity of their own. There is an assumption that in 1989 all of them were a total void and that there was no path dependency on which to build. That this was not the case is now becoming only painfully too obvious.[43] What is clear however is that these economies are limping

[39] J K Gibson-Graham, *The End of Capitalism (as we knew it)* (Oxford: Blackwell, 1996) at p 100.

[40] D MacGregor, *Hegel and Marx after the fall of communism* (Cardiff: University of Wales Press, 1998) p ix.

[41] A Sajo, "On Old and New Battles: Obstacles to the Rule of Law in Eastern Europe" (1995) 22 *JLS* 97 at 100 and K Ners, "Privatisation (from Above, Below, or Mass Privatisation) versus Generic Private Enterprise Building" (1995) 7 *Communist Economies and Economic Transformation* 105.

[42] W McBride, *Philosophical Reflections on the Changes in Eastern Europe* (Lanham, MD: Rowman and Littlefield, 1999) at pp 73–7.

[43] D Stark and L Bruszt, *Postsocialist Pathways* (Cambridge: Cambridge University Press, 1998) at pp 80–8. For the relevance of path dependency in the UK context see the text accompanying n 112.

towards capitalist market driven structures rather than more socialist orientated approaches. This has resulted in some cases in a form of voucher privitisation whereby state assets have been transferred not to individuals but to investment funds owned by the State Banks.[44] This leaves managers with managerial control but not ownership rights of disposition etc. Ownership rights are exercised by the state and what does not emerge in these circumstances is an entrepreneurial group,[45] class, call it what you will, operating within the parameters of the official economy[46] who deal with issues of inefficient management.

The Individual and the Collective Interest

The social response has been to look again at capitalism and its values. What the New Right defined as the risks to capitalism and continued prosperity – the Welfare State and public spending generally except in relation to defence – have now been redefined as necessary and even desirable because of the risks of capitalism. Unemployment and sickness are something that might strike any individual and what is required is a collective response. Acquisitiveness and personal self-advancement are now very much second place to quality of life issues such as personal happiness and the availability of a safety net should misfortune occur.

Many different interpretations can be attached to the mass, very public displays of grief following the death and funeral of Diana, Princess of Wales. The one that links most closely to my reading of the mid to late 1990s is that they were a collective demand for modernisation and change; a moving on and a collective mourning for past experiences. Mourning here is used in the sense of a ritual which marks the process of change and subsequent renewal.[47] We can contrast this event with the reading of the New Right offered by Tom Wolfe in *The Bonfire*

[44] For discussion of the possible methods that could have been used to achieve marketisation see P Bolton and G Roland, "Privitisation in Central and Eastern Europe" (1992) 15 *Economic Policy* 276.

[45] G Eyal et al, *Making Capitalism without Capitalists: Class Formation and Elite Struggles in Post-Communist Central Europe* (London: Verso, 1998).

[46] R Brady, *Kapitalism* (New Haven, CT: Yale University Press, 1999) at pp 44–62.

[47] See W Wheeler, "Together Again After All these Years: Science, Politics and Theology in the New Modernity" in A Coddington and M Perryman (eds), *The Moderniser's Dilemma* (London: Lawrence and Wishart, 1998) p 175 at p 178. Wheeler also includes the Dunblane shooting incident and the death of John Smith in her account as provoking similar public displays.

of the Vanities.[48] Wolfe's position is one of a moral nihilism in which the values of greed and self-advancement dominate over other potential values such as honesty, responsibility and care and over structures such as the legal system and local government.[49] The novel ends with the main protagonist, Sherman McCoy, abandoned by family and friends, fighting a lone rear-guard action against a manslaughter charge. The charge resulted from the duplicity of so-called witnesses and those within the legal system but also from McCoy's inability to grasp the opportunity to tell the truth when it would have served him better than prevarication.

While on the level of risk management there is this desire for a collective response, the structural changes to social and economic life that have followed on from post-Fordism have thrust the individual into the spotlight in a way that is different from the market individualism of the New Right. Access to information through the Internet and greater opportunities for travel have assisted in the breakdown of identity based upon geographical location and tradition.[50] In a globalised market events far from an individual's actual physical location can have an effect on economic and social existence. As Giddens describes it, these changes go to the root of the:

> "constitution of personal identities. The self becomes a reflexive project. . . . Individuals cannot rest content with an identity that is simply handed down, inherited, or built on a traditional status. A person's identity has in large part to be discovered, constructed, actively sustained".[51]

[48] (London: Jonathon Cape, 1988).

[49] B Sarachek, "Images of Corporate Executives in Recent Fiction" (1995) *J of Bus Ethics* 195 at 199.

[50] The destabilising of traditional identity is very much a Western phenomenon. In other places there has been a retreat into local identity based often on the restatement of religious or ethnic identities, for example the positions in Iran and Iraq. In other places the break-up of the Eastern Block has encouraged a rise of nationalistic feeling again founded on religious and ethnic identity. See M Jones "Blade Runner Capitalism, The Transnational Corporation and Commodification" (1998) 10 *Cultural Dynamics* 287 at 291 and the references contained therein. Globalisation is identified as the trigger for extremist political movements within the West as those who are excluded (segregated) from the benefits of the free market seek to establish for themselves an identity, see Z Bauman, *Globalization: The Human Consequences* (Cambridge: Polity, 1998) at p 3.

[51] A Giddens, *Beyond Right and Left* (Cambridge: Polity, 1995) p 82, see also U Beck, "The Reinvention of Politics: Towards a Theory of Reflexive Modernization" in U Beck, A Giddens, S Lash *Reflexive Modernization: Politics, Tradition and Aesthetics in the Modern Social Order* (Cambridge: Polity, 1994) p 1 at p 14.

While on one level this generates a certain amount of excitement for the individual, on another it causes a good deal of pain and consternation. It places the individual in a position of making choices and decisions in a world in which flexibility and uncertainty are rife. There are a number of ways of looking at the dilemma of the individual. As far as Sennett is concerned, it is a situation which leads to a corrosion of individual character. It prevents the transmission of ethical values between parent and child, for example.[52] For Bauman[53] the lacuna in which the individual finds her/himself positioned is both a threat and an opportunity. The individual has the opportunity to be moral in the sense of exercising the choice between good and evil but the difficulty is that the individual will struggle with both the enormity of the responsibility and the consequences of the choice made. It is important to note at this point that Bauman is using the idea of "morality" rather than the concept of ethical values favoured by Sennett. For Bauman ethics belongs to modernity, morality is the language of post modernity.[54] It is clear from the opening forays of *Postmodern Ethics* that Bauman does not mean the problems of social justice and human rights, to name but two of our current ethical issues, have gone away. Rather what he is seeking to do is to put out the limits of ethics as laws/truths which society/authority has created for the individual to follow and to substitute this for a life in which "the other" rather than "the self" is at the centre[55] and "the humanity of man [comes from] responsibility for the other."[56] Bauman's ideas of individual responsibility and morality

[52] R Sennett, *The Corrosion of Character* (New York, NY: Norton, 1998).

[53] Z Bauman, *Postmodern Ethics* (Cambridge: Polity, 1993) especially pp 1–13. Bauman is offering a continuation here from his earlier work, *Legislators and Interpreters: On Modernity, Post-Modernity and Intellectuals* (Cambridge: Polity, 1987). There, Bauman points to the idea of the declining importance of "legislators" or experts who set rules which individuals blindly perform in accordance with. They are to be replaced by "interpreters" who set out a range of explanations and values that may help the individual to come to their choice.

[54] H Letiche, "Business Ethics: (In-)Justice and (Anti-)Law – Reflections on Derrida, Bauman and Lipovetsky" in M Parker (ed), *Ethics and Organisations* (London: Sage, 1988) p 122 at p 135.

[55] Z Bauman, *Life in Fragments: Essays in Postmodern Morality* (Oxford: Blackwell, 1995).

[56] This is a quote from Levinas, which Bauman uses on p 85 of *Postmodern Ethics*, see *supra* n 53. A review of Bauman's recent work on Ethics, which is a model of clarity, is offered by A Latham, "An Ethics of the Ephemeral? The Possibilities and Impossibilities of Zygmunt Bauman's Ethics: a Review of Some Recent Books by Zygmunt Bauman (1999) 2 *Ethics, Place and Environment* 275

which centre not on rights but on recognition of the "other" have a resonance with the political discourse I describe below. They present a challenge for both individual and corporate behaviour.

These dilemmas are fictionalised by Douglas Coupland in *Girlfriend in a Coma*.[57] The difficulties of dealing with choice and hope, the individual and the collective run through his novel. Lois, a peripheral character, is the first to experience this explicitly. She feels afraid at imagining herself as "a citizen of a world containing hope".[58] The immediate hope for her is created by the awakening of her daughter, Karen, from a 17 year coma. However this is merely a metaphor for the possibility of hope for the world at large. On awakening, Karen's view is that the world has changed since she went to sleep and not for the better. In what sounds like a description of New Right values Karen observes that:

> "Husbands and wives both work. Kids are farmed out to . . . video games. Nobody seems to be able to endure simply being by themselves either – but at the same time they're isolated . . . . The whole world is only about work: *work work work get get get* . . . racing ahead. . . . People are frazzled and angry, desperate about money, and, at best, indifferent to the future".[59]

As Coupland moves his story along, the whole world falls asleep apart from Karen and her immediate circle of friends. They use this time to reflect upon what has happened to human existence and the choices that now face them in a world that is rapidly disintegrating. Their conclusion is that they "do not seem to have any values, any absolutes". They have "always manoeuvred . . . values to suit [the] immediate purposes".[60] However the way forward out of their dilemma is explained to them by a long dead school friend, Jared, who is also the narrator of the story. Jared points out:

> ". . . the futility of trying to change the world without the efforts of everybody else on Earth . . . the only thing that can keep the planet turning smoothly is human will forged into effort".[61]

[57] (London: Harper Collins (Flamingo), 1998). This is a truly excellent novel. I am very grateful to my friend, Tony Bradney of the Law Faculty, Leicester University for drawing it to my attention.

[58] *Ibid* at p 125

[59] *Ibid* at p 153 (original emphasis).

[60] *Ibid* at p 255

[61] *Ibid* at p 265.

He exhorts them to:

> "Go clear the land for a new culture – if you're not plotting every moment boiling the carcass of the old order – then you're wasting the day".[62]

There is a certain synergy between Jared's suggestion and Giddens's description of living in a "risk society". The fictional character Jared and Giddens may have slightly different starting points for their new beginnings[63] but the respective summations of the consequences of beginning again are similar. For Giddens risk society is one which lives "after nature" and after "tradition" where "life is no longer lived as a fate". It is a society "pre-occupied with the future" but not necessarily in a negative sense. The presence of risk allows the "taking of bold initiatives".[64] That is exactly what Jared is pushing his erstwhile high school friends to do. Coupland raises the question "*is there a difference between personal destiny and collective destiny*"[65] but inevitably leaves it unanswered. This is a question that Giddens also raises and to which he provides an answer. I examine his answer in due course. The apparent incongruence between the demands for collectivity and the question of individuality is also played through in the political response to the events of post post-Fordism to which I turn next.

A Political Response – Passage through the Symplegades[66]

The political response to the events and pressures described above is to outline a theory of political philosophy that its perpetrators describe as the "third way".[67] The description "third way" is intended to indicate that this a philosophy free from the previous constraints of the ideologies represented by the labels "right" and "left". For example Blair himself sets the third way position out in the following way:

[62] *Ibid* at pp 270–1

[63] The issue of the "starting point" is one which concerns the role of morality and values. Giddens, I think, sees the juxtaposition of particular values as a way forward without necessarily asserting that this is because we are moving from a value free or "immoral" world: A Giddens, "Risk and Responsibility" (1999) 62 *MLR* 1 at 5. For Coupland this is a more difficult call to make. I look at this in n 91 *infra*.

[64] A Giddens, *ibid* at 3–4.

[65] Coupland, *supra* n 57 at p 270 (original emphasis).

[66] As will became clear from the discussion in this section the clashing rocks are those of "right" and "left" political positions.

[67] S Driver and L Martell set out the path that Blair and New Labour have taken to reach the third way in *New Labour* (Cambridge: Polity, 1998). See also Coddington and Perryman (eds), *supra* n 47.

> "It is not the dogma of the old left, concentrating on means rather than ends. Nor is it the *laissez faire* of the New Right. Unlike the Old Left we want a market economy. But unlike the New Right we do not want a market society. Renewed Social Democracy (sic)".[68]

Blair is anxious for third way politics to be seen as a political position in its own right and not simply as attempting to chart the waters between the traditional positions of right and left. Rather "[i]t is about traditional values in a changed world".[69] Most recently Blair has cast these traditional values as an identity issue – that of "Britishness". This identity is represented by the "core" values of "fair play, creativity, tolerance and an outward looking approach to the world". [70] It is these values that the Third Way project of modernisation will be based upon.

The changes that Blair identifies include the ones discussed above: globalisation, advances in technology change and the move to skills based industry, the role of women and evolving political structures in both a national and international context. It is unlikely that any observer would disagree that these changes have indeed taken place. Disagreement occurs over the importance of each one and what if anything government should do. The politics, policies and values which are said, by the present administration, to be necessary have not met with universal acclaim. For example the third way is said to need (for which we can read "currently lacks") moral principles and priorities,[71] an ideology which can link the principles and priorities to current social and economic conditions and a more political element of how these policies will be packaged to make clear the principles and priorities.[72]

However this is not the forum in which to debate the merits of the third way as a political philosophy; there are critiques of it from right and left.[73] The fact is that the third way is a charismatic, accessible and

[68] Speech by Blair to the Civil Service Conference, Whitehall London, 13 October 1998.

[69] T Blair. *The Third Way*, (London: Fabian Society, 1998) p 1.

[70] Blair speech, 28 March 2000.

[71] Although in J K Galbraith's view the priorities of the Third Way have been identified as those that will appeal to the middle classes: "the increase in numbers and power of the middle income groups means that governments choose to meet their needs first", *The Guardian* 17 October 1998.

[72] S Szreter, "A New Political Economy for New Labour" (1999) 7 *Renewal* 30.

[73] *Marxism Today* devoted a special issue in October 1998 to a critique of Blairite policies, see in particular in that issue S Hall, "The Great Moving Nowhere Show". Hall's point, inter alia, is that the third way is a softening of the neo-liberalism of Thatcherism. Blair himself would appear sensitive to this charge, while asserting that the third way is

ultimately powerful rhetorical discourse. Indeed one of its popular attractions appears to be its crude characterisations of all previous political administrations as either New Right or Old Left. One nation conservatism and neo-liberal Thatcherism elide into the New Right and Tony Crosland's and Jim Callaghan's socialism become the Old Left. The comfort zone of sitting between two apparent extremes is attractive. The Third Way is accessible to the extent that it has been described as a "cultural studies version of [the economy]: an economics which is all signifiers and no exchange value".[74] The Third Way finds voice across Europe, South America and in the US.[75] In the UK it is expressed in terms which outline a vision to recast the relationships between government as provider/insurer, the corporate sector and the voluntary sector. The values of third way are set out as equal worth, opportunity for all, responsibility and community.[76] There is a sense in which events such as globalisation have taken away the need for national policies to be founded upon concerns like common security and thus there is a space to look at other issues such as disabled and gay rights.[77] When recast to take account of debates around the nature of the UK's involvement in Europe and the issue of constitutional change the values of the Third Way become the values of a "new modern patriotism". This idea of patriotism maps directly onto the concept of "Britishness" set out above in the following way; creativity will help to modernise and restructure the economy, fairness will assist in tackling child poverty, welfare reform, and the issue of matching rights to responsibilities. An outward looking approach to the world would place the UK as a key

neither left or right in outlook he ties the origins of its value structure to the "traditional left" and describes them as being recast "for the new world". See T Blair et al, "More on the Third Way" (1998) 15 *New Perspectives* 41 at 42 and M Kenny and M Smith, "(Mis)understanding Blair" (1997) *Pol Quart* 220.

[74] J Froud et al, "The Third Way and the Jammed Economy" (1999) 67 *Capital and Class* 155 at 160. Their point is that middle class consumption is dependent on confidence in the economy, that none of the economic policies of the Third Way can deal with a downturn in the domestic economy and that the only way to defend against this is to engage in a programme of government borrowing and spending. This would appear to be an attack on the third way's disciplinary base rather than its politics as their conclusion is that New Labour has learnt little from the mistakes in macro-economic management that Old Labour made.

[75] A Giddens, "Better than Warmed-over Porridge", *New Statesman* 12 February 1999, at 25.

[76] T Blair, *supra* n 69.

[77] Described as "cool politics" by Geoff Mulgan, *Politics in an Anti-Political Age* (Cambridge: Polity, 1994).

international actor mediating between the US and Europe and between East and West.[78]

In relation to the corporate sector the Third Way vision encourages the need for competitiveness and a realisation that competitiveness in a global market may require collaboration on a local level,[79] wealth creation to be shared with employees, job creation, responsible risk taking and the pursuit of entrepreneurial activity[80] and the need for partnership with local government and the voluntary sector to provide shared benefits.[81] "Family friendly" work place policies such as extended maternity leave, parental leave schemes to deal with family emergencies and child care facilities are all described as policies for improving "productivity . . . profitability . . . [and] the bottom line".[82] In the most recent expressions of the role of the corporate sector the key phrase has been "civic patriotism". This refers to the role of the corporate sector in not only funding partnerships between sectors in terms of finance but also in terms of time. This would equate to activism in civic life and help to endorse their membership of civic society.[83] Risk under the Third Way is a malleable concept. At one level it is seen as an inescapable evil which can only be combated by a collectivist response in terms of welfare. At another it is a desirable feature of business practice which is to be encouraged.

The Intellectualisation of Political Discourse

An intellectualisation of the Third Way philosophy is offered by Giddens in his two books, *The Third Way*[84] and *The Third Way and its*

[78] Blair, *supra* n 70.

[79] According to the former Secretary of State for Trade and Industry, Peter Mandelson, partnership with Regional Development Agencies and working on a common agenda of needs identified by Regional Development Agencies will result in more effective collaboration, speech to Business Link Annual Conference 7 October 1998.

[80] Speech by Tony Blair at the CBI Annual Dinner 27 May 1998, speech by Gordon Brown, Chancellor of the Exchequer, to the New International Conference 17 July 1998. These speeches summarise earlier exhortations made by Margaret Beckett, then President of the Board of Trade, see speech to PIRC Annual Conference 4 March 1998 and CBI Annual Conference 11 November 1997. See also her forward to the DTI Consultation Document, "Modern Company Law for a Competitive Economy" March 1998.

[81] Speech by Tony Blair at the NVCO Conference 21 October 1998.

[82] Speech by Stephen Byers, Secretary of State for Trade and Industry at New Ways to Work Conference, 9 May 2000.

[83] Speech by Gordon Brown to the NCVO Conference, 9 February 2000.

[84] A Giddens, *The Third Way* (Cambridge: Polity, 1998).

Critics.[85] The two expositions he offers follow broadly the same lines with the second offering not so much a direct response to critics, as its title might suggest, but a fleshing out of what the Third Way might mean in policy terms. Significantly in the *Critics* book he identifies the Third Way as a "left-of-centre politics" or as espousing the ideas of the "modernising left"[86] while still advocating the view expressed both by Blair and himself in his own previous book that the Third Way is not about debating the differences between the political positions of right and left.[87] Giddens, like Blair, sees the Third Way as a project which is mapping out the steps necessary for a renewal of social democracy.[88]

Just as Blair cites the Third Way as necessary to deal with various changes which have affected the structure of economic, social and political life, Giddens highlights a number of interrelated questions that have to be faced in any attempt to follow a social democratic agenda which ignores the ideological demands of left and right positions.[89] Giddens's questions, or dilemmas as he terms them, are how to deal with globalisation and individualisation, issues of environmental degradation and sustainable development, political engagement in a climate where polarisation between right and left has less political significance than before and political representation and annunciation in a world where NGO's and other pressure groups can transcend natural boundaries to set up global debates.

The aim of the third way in his view is to offer "citizens" a pathway through these dilemmas while keeping as a backdrop to the pathway a concern with social justice.[90] Significantly Giddens, in reiterating the message of his earlier work, Bauman and Coupland are all asserting that this is a time of change and transition, not the move from a period

[85] A Giddens, *The Third Way and its Critics* (Cambridge: Polity, 2000).

[86] *Ibid*. The phrase "left-of-centre" politics occurs on p 32, the term "modernising left" is used throughout.

[87] *Ibid* at p 38.

[88] This should not be taken as an assertion that there are no differences between the Blair third way and the Giddens third way and the steps necessary to realise them. An indication of some of their differences is provided by Froud et al, *supra* n 74 and S Driver and L Martell, "Left, Right and the Third Way" (2000) 28 *Policy and Politics* 147 at 156–7. However, these differences are not crucial to the discussion in this book.

[89] *Supra* n 84 at p 26.

[90] *Supra* n 84 p 65. There is a great deal of commentary on Giddens's Third Way position. The most balanced discussion in my view is provided by A Finlayson "Third Way Theory" (1999) 70 *Pol Quart* 271 at 274–8.

of moral decay to one that is underscored by morality.[91] The concern with social justice is mapped by Giddens onto a series of values which he presents as underpinning the Third Way project. As if to emphasise the abandonment of the polarity of right and left positions his values pull together what may otherwise be seen as contrary positions; equality and freedom as autonomy, for example, could be construed as pulling in opposite directions. The same melding together of opposite values can be seen in the Blairite discourse. An apposite example taken from policy statements in relation to the economy and the corporate sector would be the emphasis on the need for fairness and enterprise to operate in tandem.[92]

Stakeholding and the Third Way

Giddens believes that the summation of the Third Way mission to recast the relationships around which society is structured can be expressed as "no rights without responsibilities".[93] This statement is repeated by Blair in his expression of the Third Way in the Fabian pamphlet, "The Third Way". Dedicated followers of Blair outpourings will recognise this as the message of the Spectator Lecture of March 1995[94] which was Blair's first substantial public expression of the "New Britain" concept. The title of that speech, "The Rights We Enjoy Reflect the Duties We Owe" is repeated in the text of the Fabian pamphlet. However the Spectator Lecture was not the unveiling of the Third Way but the unveiling of the Stakeholder Society. Stakeholder Society was the idea that was used to underpin the reconfiguration of the relationships referred to above. It was supposed to herald,

> "a new social contract between society and the individual . . . in which [we] grant each citizen a stake in our society but demand from each clear responsibilities in turn".[95]

[91] *Supra* n 84 p 37. It may be that Coupland, and certainly Richard Sennett (see the text accompanying n 63), are more sympathetic towards the moral decay argument as in the US the intellectual backlash against the New Right has been more clearly articulated in these terms. See C Hoff Summers "Are We Living in a Moral Stone Age" (1998) *Imprimis* 1. Nevertheless in my view Coupland certainly can be read as offering "choice in the face of change". I have dealt with Bauman's rather different use of the term morality in the text accompanying nn 53–6.

[92] Speech by Gordon Brown, Chancellor of the Exchequer, at the Lord Mayor's Banquet, 11 June 1998.

[93] *Supra* n 84 at p 65.

[94] Spectator Lecture, 22 March 1995 at Queen Elizabeth Conference Centre.

[95] Tokyo Speech, January 1996.

Stakeholding is now conspicuous by its absence from the vocabulary of general political discourse. As the discussion below will show it is rather ironic that its last appearance in the context of a positive acclamation should be in the DTI Consultation Document, "Modern Company Law for a Competitive Economy" in March 1998.[96] In macro policy terms this absence does not signal a change of direction. Shorn of the stakeholder label, the text of the Spectator Lecture sets out what is now known as the Third Way; it points to the inability of current right and left ideologies to provide a way forward and advocates the need to modernise institutions to create the conditions for individuals to take opportunities, to reconstruct civil society and to embrace the idea of responsibility. Stakeholding was presumably being used to indicate that capitalism had triumphed and what was required was a bridge between traditional left ideas of a strong state and public ownership and new right ideas of the only relevant unit of human interest being the individual. Stakeholding would provide that bridge by offering a personalised incremental approach to the rebuilding of society.[97]

Fairclough, in his analysis of New Labour policies and rhetoric through the lens of language use, suggests a twofold rationale for the demise of stakeholding; the difficulty of ascertaining its meaning or the assumption that it must mean the model of corporatism previously advocated by old Labour.[98] In my view the reason for the demise of stakeholding was its lack of inclusion as a rhetorical and practical device. Stakeholding can be construed as an exclusionary discourse which focuses on labour market participants. Its only current application is in the field of pensions and this emphasises the link with the labour market. The primary target group for stakeholder pensions is seen as those in the "middle income groups" who are not already part of an employer occupational scheme.[99] They will be provided by private institutions in accordance with guidelines for governance structures laid down by delegated legislation.[100] Put simply they are a financial

[96] *Supra* n 80 and J Grieve Smith, "The Right to Manage or the Right to Work" (2000) 8 *Renewal* 33 at 40.

[97] B Burkitt and F Aston, "The Birth of the Stakeholder Society" (1996) 16 *Crit Soc Pol* 3.

[98] N Fairclough, *New Labour New Language* (London: Routledge, 2000) at p 84.

[99] This was set out in the Green Paper, *A New Contract for Welfare: Partnerships in Pensions* (Cm 4179) released in December 1998. Middle income groups were defined as those earning between £9,000 and £20,000.

[100] The enabling legislation exists in the form of the Welfare Reform and Pensions Act 1999. The supporting regulations are available only in draft form at the time of writing. The first stakeholder pensions will be available from April 2001.

product which will be provided by a cross sector partnership of Government and private sector financial institutions. Employers without an occupational scheme are under an obligation to identify a stakeholder scheme and to facilitate access to it for their employees.

The inappropriateness of stakeholding as a motif for rebuilding is clear from looking at the corporate sector. It is the case that stakeholding in that context has a particular intellectual background[101] which gives it a voice articulated in terms of Kantian style[102] imperatives such as "no stakeholder should be used as a means to an ends".[103] However, even without this inheritance, stakeholding translates into an approach based on an individual's private rights. It does not offer a negotiation structure for achieving these rights. It centres instead on the management of relationships.[104] Negotiation is not a possibility as it would mean attacking the very capitalist structures the continued existence of which it is trying to acknowledge,[105] hence the descent in design and delivery to notions and practices of social responsibility. Notions of social responsibility overcome the problem caused by the issue of rights within stakeholding but more importantly in my view social responsibility excludes a needs-based discussion.

Within academic discourse, stakeholding has begun to be used not as a way of carving rights out of existing structures by diluting the property rights held by others but as a way of creating additional primarily "opportunity" interests. The two most relevant to the corporation[106] are

[101] The principal exponent of this is R Edward Freeman. He supplies a history of the term and the concept in *Strategic Management: a Stakeholder Approach*, (Boston, MA: Pitman, 1984) pp 31–42. He claims an intellectual heritage for it derived from Adam Smith and Berle and Means.

[102] Philisophical purists would assert that Kant saw only humans, as rational moral actors, requiring to be treated as ends in themselves, hence my use of the term "style". See E Sternberg "Stakeholder Theory: The Defective State It's In" in W Hutton (ed) *Stakeholding and its Critics* (London: IEA, 1997) p 70.

[103] For a discussion of Kant's End-in-Itself expression of the Categorical Imperative, see M Slote "From Morality to Virtue"in D Stateman (ed) *Virtue Ethics* (Edinburgh: Edinburgh University Press, 1997) p 128 at pp 138–9.

[104] R Gray et al "Struggling with the Praxis of Social Accounting" (1997) 10 *Accounting, Auditing and Accountability J* 325 at 333f.

[105] Although on the possibility of achieving consensus within stakeholding as opposed to corporatism, see P Metcalf "Stakeholding versus Corporatism" (1996) 4 *Renewal* 75.

[106] I have excluded from this description the idea of fixed capital endowment on maturity as a citizenship right as being not sufficiently close to the actual possibilities of the moment, see B Ackerman and A Alstott, *The Stakeholder Society* (New Haven, CT: Yale University Press, 1999).

the idea of a community fund – the state holds a portfolio of shares in a variety of firms spread across the economy with the resulting dividends used for redistributive purposes perhaps into individual accounts. Another variation of this, relevant only to labour market participants, is that each employee should have an individual training account to which employers and the state also contribute.[107] The merit of this suggestion is that it may enable labour market re-entry through training acquisition. These ideas for opportunity created by corporate participation are ones that I return to in my final chapter. The one positive that can be taken from the stakeholding literature is the idea that interest groups in and around the corporation can be ranked as holding a primary or secondary interest. In chapter three I set out my alternative models for corporate behaviour and discursive practices. This notion of primary and secondary interests plays a role within those models.[108]

The idea of "no rights without responsibilities" used in conjunction with stakeholding conjures up images of the imposition of responsibilities in a private individualised sense, for example employees being made directors without any attempt to ascertain whether[109] the responsibilities that go with the rights are an acceptable package to their recipients. The responsibilities would include exposure to legal liability and ultimately personal financial liability in the event of insolvency through such actions as wrongful trading and fraudulent trading.[110] These responsibilities may result in a conflict of interest when the legal duty to the company owed by directors requires one decision and perceived moral responsibility to the workforce requires a different one for example.[111] A further critique is that stakeholding assumes

[107] D Soskice "Stakingholding Yes; The German Model No" in A Gamble and G Kelly (eds), *Stakeholder Capitalism* (London: Macmillan, 1997) p 219. Individual Learning Accounts became available in September 2000 for a range of primarily literacy, numeracy and IT skills courses. The accounts entitle the holder to discounted course fees and equipment grants. While the DfEE has conducted an extensive consultation exercise and recognises that it needs an interface with employers this link is not yet in place in terms of financial contribution from the corporate sector

[108] M Clarkson "A Stakeholder Framework for Analyzing and Evaluating Corporate Social Performance (1995) 20 *Acad Manag Rev* 92.

[109] S White "Social Liberalism, Stakeholder socialism and post-industrial social democracy" (1999) 7 *Renewal* 29 at 34.

[110] Insolvency Act 1986 ss. 213–214.

[111] A "live" example of this difficulty can be seen from the facts of *Cowan* v. *Scargill* (1984) 2 All ER 751. The judgment therein of Megarry VC demonstrates that the absence or perhaps rejection of a notion of moral or social responsibility in trustees (and for this we can read directors) is one that is engrained deep in doctrine. The National Union of

particular characteristics for industrial structures; non-adversarial industrial relations and a role for banks and other financiers which exceeds that of mere lenders. In other words it looks to mirror the political economy of countries such as Germany and Japan without considering the path dependency of the UK upon a different political and cultural inheritance.[112] The demise of the stakeholder/ing label is not to be mourned. In its absence Third Way politics can be seen as advocating public rather than private notions of rights and responsibilities. The interaction between "community" and the individual remains a problematic but open question; in Giddens' terms the search is on for a new relationship between the individual and the community.[113] Giddens explicitly rejects the idea that this search could be satisfied by the adoption of a communitarian solution.[114] My criticisms of communitarian politics come later in this chapter and they broadly endorse Giddens' position that communitarianism leads to a potentially unpleasant form of identity politics. His solution is and mine is to look to a civil society or to a polity which embraces all sectors of society – community, corporate, voluntary and so on and steers a middle course between individualism and collectivism. As the last part of this chapter shows our disagreement is more over process than substance.

3. CURRENT CORPORATE PRACTICES

The Beginning of Social Conscience

The idea of a corporate social conscience or corporate social responsibility is not a new one. It is a practice with a long history; definitions

Mineworkers (NUM) members appointed as trustees of the Mineworkers Pension Scheme Fund were unable to prevent investment in industries and markets that they as NUM members felt prejudiced the interests of present NUM workers. These workers were future beneficiaries of the scheme but the duty of trustees was to invest in the best return for all the beneficiaries (per Megarry VC at 760–1 and 764). This must mean present and future beneficiaries as Megarry VC goes on to make the point that many of the present beneficiaries have no interest in the continued prosperity of the mining industry (at 764h–j).

112 L Bebchuk and M Roe "A Theory of Path Dependence in Corporate Ownership and Governance" (1999) 52 *Stanford LR* 127 at 168 and J Ziegler "Corporate Governance and the Politics of Property Rights in Germany" (2000) 28 *Politics and Society* 195.

113 Giddens, *supra* n 84, at p 65.

114 Giddens, *supra* n 85, at pp 62–4.

and descriptions of what occurs have abounded since at least the 1920s.[115] There is a divergence in this area in the homogeneity of Anglo-American capitalism. In the US, corporate social responsibility as a practice developed very much earlier and as a general phenomenon[116] amongst large corporations. American corporations consciously cultivated the image of caring establishments, in which workers and customers were held in high esteem. The dominant image was of the pioneer[117] sending his new-found wealth back home to those less fortunate. Two ideas have been put forward as underlying the need for the creation of this image of self-advancement and caring. One is that through it the proponents of strict competition regulation[118] would be bought off as they would see "Big Business" as desirable.[119] The second is that it was a marketing device; products produced in an atmosphere of care and concern were apparently less likely to have defects and as this kept production costs low such products would be available to the consumer at a lower price.[120] The reality is probably a mixture of both of these explanations. The idea of linking the use of social responsibility policies to increased sales is one relevant to current corporate practice as the text below will show. This is not to say that American practice was, from the beginning of the development of large scale industry, characterised by massive generosity and underpinned by clear structures within corporations. In fact these did not begin to emerge until comparatively recently. [121]

In the UK, corporate social responsibility was, until comparatively recently, the realm of "otherness". It was presented during those years and also now, in retrospect, as being the province of non-conformists

[115] S Sheikh, *Corporate Social Responsibilities; Law and Practice* (London: Cavendish, 1996) pp 9–20.

[116] F Emerson Andrews ,*Corporation Giving* (New York, NY: Russell Sage, 1952).

[117] A Wicks et al, "A Feminist Reinterpretation of the Stakeholder Concept" (1996) 4 *Bus Ethics Quart* 475 at 479.

[118] See B Thomas, *American Literary Realism and the Failed Promise of Contract* (Berkeley, CA: University of California Press, 1998) at p 246 and in particular the material Thomas cites at n 32 in ch 8. References to specifically legal history as opposed to literary history can be found in H Hovenkamp *Enterprise and American Law* (Cambridge, MA: Harvard University Press, 1991).

[119] R Marchand, *Creating the Corporate Soul: The Rise of Public Relations and Corporate Imagery in American Big Business* (Berkeley, CA: University of California Press, 1998).

[120] A Tone, *The Business of Benevolence* (Ithaca, NY: Cornell University Press, 1997) pp 99–139, see in particular pp 130–5.

[121] *Supra*, n 115 at pp 72–3

such as Congregationalists and Quakers. It is certainly true that the leading examples of corporate social responsibility came, in the first instance, from employers who had these religious beliefs and displayed a paternalism towards their workforces which involved the provision of housing, leisure facilities and pension and savings schemes. Some even created financial participation schemes.[122] However this has become an easy and over-generalised model. These religious beliefs did not always result in this particular pattern of behaviour.[123] On occasions when they did, the corporations concerned were not necessarily behaving in this way out of a religiously-driven altruism only. They saw a link to the greater levels of productivity and employee loyalty that such behaviour might generate,[124] although unlike their American counterparts this was not used as an advertising feature.

It was the 1970s before there was any attempt at an "official" discourse of social responsibility in the UK. The events of the 1970s are a useful demonstration of the way in which political and social discourses can shape corporate behaviour. Three events stand out. In what was already a corporatist setting the CBI declared in the Watkinson Report in 1973 that:

> "there must be and seen to be an ethical dimension in corporate activity. Companies must in our view recognise that they have functions, duties and moral obligations that go beyond the immediate pursuit of profit and the requirements of the law."

This was to be achieved through the adoption of "a code of corporate behaviour in business" as "directors need not only guidance as to how to provide appropriately for such interests . . . but also encouragement to do".[125] As if foreshadowing the current debates about citizenship,

[122] See B Alford, *WD and HO Wills and the Development of the UK Tobacco Industry 1786–1965* (London: Methuen, 1973) pp 279–93 and T Corley, *Quaker Enterprise in Biscuits: Huntley and Palmers of Reading 1882–1972* (London: Hutchinson & Co, 1972) pp 103–11.

[123] C Dellheim, "The Creation of a Company Culture: *Cadburys* 1861–1931" (1987) 92 *Am Hist Rev* 13 at p 15 n 9 especially, but cf J Walvin, *The Quakers: Money and Morals* (London: John Murray, 1997) ch 11.

[124] J Baddon et al, *People's Capitalism* (London: Routledge, 1989) at p 152. Despite the current interest in corporate social conscience and the search that is being undertaken in various academic disciplines for a new approach to business enterprise there has been little critical examination of this movement. M Rowlinson, "Quaker Employers" (1998) 6 *Historical Studies in Industrial Relations* 163 is a welcome exception.

[125] *A New Look at the Responsibilities of the British Public Company* CBI, 25 January 1973. For contemporary comment see the *Times*, 30 January 1973, p 19.

good citizenship and the role of corporations in citizenship the report also said "mere compliance with the law does not necessarily make a good citizen or a good company". This was followed in 1975 by *The Corporate Report*, a discussion paper prepared by the Accountancy profession representative bodies. The paper suggested a methodology by which corporations could measure and publicise their community contributions of the previous financial year.[126] The sentiments of *The Corporate Report* were echoed by a subsequent Government Green Paper in 1977.[127] Contemporary accounts indicate that the practice was initially popular but its use declined rapidly as the political and social culture of the New Right took hold.[128]

Corporate Activity and the Third Way

There is a sense in which the Third Way agenda for the corporate sector is a corporatist one, in that it promotes partnership and bargain. It is advocating a climate in which corporations are encouraged to be dynamic and innovative and serial entrepreneurs are to be lauded and not penalised for risk taking. The bargain is that the state will, for its part, provide support through non-intervention in a regulatory sense except to foster competitiveness[129] and will allow markets a free reign. For Giddens corporate power is something that governments nationally and through international co-operation have to have the mechanisms to control but that as there is no alternative to the market, in his view, corporations should not be controlled simply for the sake of it.[130] The corporate sector, for its part, has to value its human capital and

[126] J Renshall, "Changing Perceptions Behind the Corporate Report" (1976) 1 *Accounting, Organisations and Society* 105.

[127] *The Future of Company Reports*, July 1977.

[128] M Jones, "Stakeholder Society: Measuring the Value" (1996) Dec *Accountancy* 65. This draws on the findings presented in contemporary surveys such as C Skerratt and D Tonkin, "Financial Reporting 1982–83: A Survey of UK Published Accounts" (1982) *ICAEW* and S Gray and K Maunders, "Values Added Reporting: Uses and Measurement" (1980) *ACCA*. For a detailed discussion of the economic, political and social background, see S Burchell et al, "Accounting in its Social Context: Towards a History of Value Added in the United Kingdom" (1985) 10 *Accounting, Organizations and Society* 381.

[129] Competition Act 2000.

[130] S Byers, Secretary of State for Trade and Industry, to Mansion House 2 February 1999. What Giddens perceives as fulfilling this "develop[ing] a wide ranging supply side policy, which seeks to reconcile economic growth mechanisms with structural reform of the welfare state", *supra* n 85 at p 52.

invest in it so that there is participation in the knowledge economy[131] and engage in partnerships with other sectors to provide services and benefits for all that the state working alone cannot. The key words for the corporate sector that survive the demise of stakeholding are "community" and "responsibility". To these the Third Way adds "partnership with government and between sectors" so that there can be a collaborative move towards the recreation of civil society.[132]

In concrete terms (although some would regard this as an inappropriate descriptive term for the Third Way) this means active corporate participation in initiatives that result from successful bids to the various programmes funded by the Single Regeneration Budget, participation in the New Deal job creation schemes for the young and long-term unemployed and involvement in the development of Regional Economies. Participation for the corporate sector often means the provision of matched funding or management ability alongside the financial input of the EU, central or local government or the third sector. All of these programmes, and successful initiatives run under their auspices, are linked in the sense that their object is the regeneration of particular pre-designated geographical areas and the reskilling of their inhabitants. Community rebuilding and regeneration is drawn then for these purposes along stereotypical geographical lines.[133] These ideas and policies for regeneration in particular areas are not the invention of Government post-May 1997. Urban regeneration and partnership financing of capital projects through the Private Finance Initiative (PFI) were all part of the policy agenda of the pre-May 1997 Conservative administration. There is a difference now

[131] "Knowledge Economy" has become a late 1990's buzzword. It is used to indicate that a combination of globalised markets and technology advancement require producers to manage innovation, skill and information to hold their market positions and that much of this can be done with reference to their own workforces, see C Leadbeater, "Welcome to the Knowledge Economy" in I Hargraves and I Christie, *Tomorrow's Politics* (London: Demos, 1998). A useful example is supplied by former Secretary of State for Trade and Industry Peter Mandelson: "[T]wo thirds of the value of a modern car is now to be found in the knowledge that went into designing, engineering and building it. Only one third can be attributed to the raw material. A team of a few people in another part of the world can now successfully compete with large household names in Britain and vice versa", Business Link Speech, 7 October 1998.

[132] For a more detailed outline of the expectations of business, see Tony Blair's speech to the CBI dinner, 17 May 2000.

[133] Department of the Environment, Transport and the Regions, "Regeneration Programmes–The Way Forward" (Discussion Paper) and "Involving Communities in Urban and Rural Regeneration. A Guide for Practitioners".

around the sort of discourse that accompanies some of these policies and initiatives. It is one of responsibility to community and partnership with community and other providers.[134] The neo-liberalism of the pre-May 1997 administration clothed regeneration policies with the rhetoric of the market and the general undesirability of welfare provision by central government.[135] In addition to these "outreach" ideas there are also expectations of corporations in relation to the on-going training of their own employees. Standing apart from the notions of partnership and responsibility is the Private Finance Initiative or, as these arrangements are also known, Public–Private Partnerships. This Initiative was introduced by the Conservative administration in 1992/3[136] and has been continued by the present Labour administration, albeit under slightly different accounting rules. It seems that the notion of "partnership" here denotes a meeting of capital sources only. These partnerships are not partnerships in the same way that the arrangements around training, job creation, urban regeneration and regional development are. These financial partnerships are designed to allow private sector funding of capital expenditure on infrastructure facilities such as new schools and hospitals that the public sector then rents. These arrangements are a device for increasing investment in public services without increasing public sector borrowing. There seems to be an emerging consensus among commentators that while these partnerships represent spending savings in some instances in the short term, in others the marriage of public and private sector cultures does not work either in terms of long-span cost-effectiveness or in terms of risk transfer to the private sector.[137] This does not mean that these partnerships cannot ever exist in any form. In chapters two and

[134] M Temple, "New Labour's Third Way: Pragmatism and Governance" (2000) 2 *Brit J of Pol and Int Rels* 302. This piece provides an interesting account of the evolution of the Third Way through the public/private joint initiatives that Labour run local governance structures began to grapple with from 1979 onwards.

[135] D Kerr, "The PFI Miracle" (1998) 64 *Capital and Class* 17. For a review of the progress of PFI since its inception in 1992 and its relaunching by the Blair administration see G Clark and A Root, "Infrastructure Shortfall in the UK: The Private Finance Initiative and Government Policy" (1999) 18 *Political Geography* 341.

[136] HM Treasury, *Private Finance: Guidance for Departments* (London: 1992) and *Breaking New Ground: Towards a New Partnership between the Public and Private Sectors* (London: 1993).

[137] J Hall, "Private Opportunity, Public Benefit" (1998) 19 *Fiscal Studies* 121 and R Ball et al, "Private Finance Initiative–A Good Deal for the Public Purse or a Drain on Future Generations" (2000) 29 *Policy and Politics* 95.

three I set out my ethical framework for corporate activity within the Third Way, which I believe will allow this type of partnership to be reconceptualised and revitalised.

Many corporations have been pursuing endeavours not that dissimilar to the programmes described above, under the labels of corporate social responsibility or corporate community involvement for some time. In the area of employee training it is estimated that the corporate sector spends £10 billion per annum.[138] British Telecom pumped £15 million into core community programmes in 1996/7. Grand Metropolitan spent £13 million on community investment in roughly the same period. That, as Grand Metropolitan proudly announces, is 1.5 per cent of its world-wide trading profit less interest.[139] British Petroleum's (BP) expenditure in the same period on community projects was £19.5 million, a figure that according to BP's Social Report for 1997 represents 0.5 per cent of its total pre-tax profit for 1997 and, as the Report points out, a figure that does not include their environmental operating costs. It is difficult to establish a precise figure for declared corporate contributions because, as is explained below, there is no single method of calculation but a figure of around £300 million is broadly correct for 1997.[140] When set against the income allocated to the Single Regeneration Budget of £1.4 billion, the £40 billion required to run the NHS in the same period, a figure of £300 million does not sound very substantial. However when looked at in the context of charity income it appears more substantial; £300 million is more than the fundraising of Cancer Research Campaign, British Red Cross, NSPCC and RNIB put together in the same period.

Competitive Social Conscience

These practices are occurring in a world that is globalised in the sense of markets, consumers and information. The availability of information through media such as the internet[141] and television makes social

[138] Source: "The Evaluation of Funding for the Development of Continuing Vocational Education" (University of Birmingham, HEFCE 98/44).

[139] Grand Metropolitan Report on Corporate Citizenship 1997.

[140] The sources for these figures are various but in the main they can be extrapolated from the Social Change publications; *The Major Companies Guide 1997–8* and *A Guide to Company Giving 1997–8*.

[141] D Crowther, "Corporate Reporting, Stakeholders and the Internet: Mapping the New Corporate Landscape" (2000) 37 *Urban Studies* 1837. Crowther makes a very interesting point here; the development of internet technology, while obviously empowering

dumping harder to hide. The same access to information makes it easier for representative consumer groups or less formal "activist" groupings to organise product and producer boycotts. Pressure groups, both single and multi-issue NGO's, act as informers and co-ordinators of consumer feeling using these methods for knowledge acquisition, information transmission and co-ordination of action.[142] The position of Nestlé is illustrative of this. From 1974 to 1984 consumers were urged by activists to boycott Nestle products as a demonstration of their feeling against Nestlé's practice of distributing Infant Milk Formula in the developing world. This boycott was re-introduced in 1988 due to Nestlé's alleged non-compliance with the World Health Organisation Code on the Advertising of Milk Substitute. Individuals can participate in the debate around the boycott or consult lists of Nestlé products using information posted on the Internet. Contributions to the formal policy process around consumer issues are also co-ordinated through bodies such as the Transatlantic Consumer Dialogue. This was launched in 1998 as a mechanism for US and EU consumer groups to make representations to the US Government and the EU Commission. The availability of global information, the ease of global communications and the decline in the importance of physical place and presence have made all of this very much easier.

Changes in values can also be monitored through looking at the growing popularity of ethical investment. In the US the total value of all assets consciously invested as "responsible investments" is $1.185 trillion.[143] In the UK the figure is put at in excess of £2.8 billion and can be compared with a figure of £500 million in 1995.[144] Obviously there are debates about what constitutes ethical investment; not every investor has the same view on issues such as tobacco production, road building and intensive farming. What is starting to emerge is a pyramid effect with individuals delegating ethical choices and assessments to fund managers who are promoting a range of ethical funds within a portfolio of "socially responsible investing". The oldest of these funds

individuals, is nevertheless subsumed at one level into the architecture of corporate reporting. Thus individuals still remain in a relationship of inequality with corporations.

[142] J Rosthorn, "Business Ethics Auditing – More than a Stakeholders' Toy" (2000) 27 *J of Bus Ethics* 9 and J Grolin, "Corporate Legitimacy in Risk Society: The Case of Brent Spar" (1998) 7 *Business Strat and Enviro* 213.

[143] This is the 1997 figure, *Report on Responsible Investing Trends* (1997) Social Investment Forum, Washington.

[144] EIRis Feb 2000.

are the Stewardship funds launched by Friends Provident in 1984. These particular funds account for about 50 per cent of the market share. About 20 other financial institutions have joined Friends Provident in the market for the money of the ethical investor.[145] It seems that an ethical profile is constructed from assessing positive corporate activity such as conservation and resource management against negative corporate activity such as the production of greenhouse gasses.

There are clear difficulties with this approach such as the lack of mechanisms to test the veracity of corporate statements and the inherent bias towards "clean hands" corporations such as those engaged in the telecoms industry. Ethical investing, while it is a potential curb on corporate power and activity, does not have the same popular appeal as consumer boycotts and lobbying which are open to all regardless of their ability or desire to become shareholders. Ethical investing does not necessarily involve moving corporate strategy away from Milton Friedman's assertion that all responsible corporations should do is care for shareholders.[146] Shareholders in this instance have demanded "ethical" policies be pursued to obtain return upon their investment. These demands can be satisfied without the corporations involved being forced to consider those outside the corporate property matrix.

The question of whether ethical profile, assertions of corporate social responsibility and the present popularity of ethical investing have a positive impact on corporate financial performance is a hotly debated issue. There are numerous studies, mainly based on US data, which give conflicting answers.[147] There are methodological difficulties in both conducting this type of research and comparing the results. The type of conduct studied varies, as does the approach to measuring financial performance. All the studies are firmly locked into the stakeholder paradigm which creates further difficulties as there is no standard to determine which groups are included and excluded.[148]

[145] A Lewis and C Mackenzie, "Morals, Money, Ethical Investing and Economic Psychology" (2000) 53 *Human Relations* 179.

[146] M Friedman, *Capitalism and Freedom* (Chicago, IL: University of Chicago Press, 1962) p 126.

[147] For a review of the literature and an indication of the answers provided by numerous different studies see C Verschoor, "A Study of the Link Between a Corporation's Financial Performance and Its Commitment to Ethics" (1998) 17 *J of Bus Ethics* 1509.

[148] For a detailed review of methodological problems see S Waddock and S Graves, "Quality of Management and Quality of Stakeholder Relations: Are They Synonymous?" (1997) 36 *Business and Society* 250.

The general view is that the worst that can be said about these activities is that they do not appear to depress financial performance.[149]

However whether financial performance is, in reality, improved or not in these circumstances is not really the issue. What is much more relevant is the fact that corporations clearly think that it is or at least that it has the potential to be. This explains the emergence of a competitive structure that encompasses social responsibility agendas.[150] In addition to competing in areas such as product development, production costs and ultimately price, corporations compete over their social awareness and responsiveness. Advertising of products is now not confined to the sponsorship of glamorous sporting events and advertising hoardings but takes place through links with charities. The idea is that consumers will have faith in the values of the charity and then, through the link with the charity, transfer that faith to the merits of the product or the producer depending on how narrowly the link is focused.[151] Cause-related marketing, as it is known as, has resulted in leading supermarket chains, for example, competing over the donations such as books and computers that they will make to schools as an incentive to would-be customers to patronise their establishments rather than those of their competitors.[152] Corporations have become increasingly interested in applying the label "citizen" to themselves. They see this as a way of developing market reputation, as identifying with the current debates in society and most importantly as labelling themselves as wishing to make a positive contribution to society.[153] Sklair sums up the idea as one which sees corporations as responsible for the "consequences of all their products and business practices, wherever they occur and whether intended or not".[154] It is possible to assert that

[149] R Roman et al, "The Relationship Between Social and Financial Performance: Repainting a Portrait" (1999) 38 *Business and Society* 109 at 121.

[150] C Smith, "The New Corporate Philanthropy" (1994) *Harv Bus Rev* 105.

[151] M Stork, "Brand Aid: Cause Effective" (1999) 40 *Brandweek* 20.

[152] S Wheeler, "Inclusive Communities and Dialogical Stakeholders: a Methodology for an Authentic Corporate Citizenship" (1998) 9 *Aust J of Corporate Law* 1 at pp 13ff and T Mescon and D Tilson, "Corporate Philanthropy: A Strategic Approach to the Bottom-Line" (1987) 29 *Calif Manag Review* 49.

[153] R Gray "Developing a Tight Fit is Crucial to CRM" (2000) *Marketing*, 4 May, 37. Gray's article cites Dean Sanders (founder of Good Brand Works, a social marketing consultancy as saying "I wonder how history will judge cause related marketing . . . My instinct is that it will be seen as a catalyst in the wider move to the socialisation of business".

[154] L Sklair, *The Transnational Capitalist Class* (Oxford: Blackwell, 2000) at p 149. Sklair's analysis of corporate citizenship is based upon an empirical study of corporate

corporate behaviour of this type can be described as a "crisis" response to attacks on the legitimacy of corporate existence and behaviour.[155] However against this assertion has to be set the opportunities afforded by forum shopping and globalisation generally. Rather, in my view, it is an attempt by corporations to capitalise on the concerns for others that we either possess or are being asked to possess by Third Way rhetoric. These attempts have to be turned into more than strategic corporate behaviour if the Third Way ideal is to be delivered upon.

Precise definitions for the notion of citizenship that corporations recognise are hard to come by.[156] It seems that in their terms anything from basic compliance with the legislative framework up the scale of altruism constitutes citizenship.[157] It is even possible to purchase, on a commercial basis, the wherewithal to be a corporate citizen from *The Corporate Citizenship Company*. This undertaking was established in 1997 as a commercial venture designed to assist corporate clients in achieving such goals as "identifying new opportunities and creative new ideas for corporate partnerships", "tracking emerging issues among key stakeholding groups to keep ahead of the game" and writing "wider social reports".[158] If corporate citizenship is to have any meaning at all as a descriptive term it needs to signify much more precise strategic interventions in society. As the next section demonstrates this is not an argument for general altruism in the field of corporate donations of money. This has the potential to be damaging both to the corporation and to the interests that it is trying to assist. It is in part because of the desire of corporations to be recognised as citizens that

reports, interviews with corporate executives on a global scale and discussions with NGOs, the focus of which is on global business. From this he has produced the best and most detailed account of corporate citizenship thus far.

155 N Brown and C Deegan, "The Public Disclosure of Environmental Performance Information – A Dual Test of Media Agenda Setting Theory and Legitimacy Theory" (1998) 29 *Accounting and Business Research* 21.

156 For a classic exposition of the corporate rationale for adopting the citizenship label see C Marsden and J Andriof, "Towards an Understanding of Corporate Citizenship and How to Influence It" (1998) 2 *Citizenship Studies* 329. The authors divorce themselves entirely from any theoretical perspective (moral, ethical or otherwise) on citizenship and advocate ad hoc action based upon "ethical values" and good business (eg at 337). The definitions of these terms and where they come from is not explained.

157 M McIntosh et al, *Corporate Citizenship* (London: Financial Times Pitman Publishing, 1998) pp xix–xxii. Sklair defines the concept of consisting of four elements: employee relations, philanthropy and community development, the health and safety of all those affected by the corporate activity and the environmental challenge.

158 <http://www.corporate-citizenship.co.uk>.

the theoretical (re)construction that this book looks for becomes both possible and necessary. This desire is tied in my next chapter to Aristotelian conceptions of citizenship, virtue and the governance of the polity. In my final chapter I take both of these ideas forward to look at ways in which a positive contribution to the Third Way agenda could be made by the corporate sector.

Should We be Grateful?

There is an argument that corporations are essentially private actors, albeit often large and powerful ones, and that as such any contribution they make to the wider society is a voluntary one and should be welcomed as a gift made over and above the requirements of the taxation regime. A rather different rationale, which ties together the idea of the corporation as a private actor with the idea of the corporation as a committed donor of money, is that it is essential for corporations to support the non-profit sector to prevent its absorption into a larger state. One way of controlling public spending and ensuring minimal government interference is for the corporate sector to bolster other organisations capable of providing some of these functions.[159] The idea of corporations as private actors is a contentious one. There are many arguments that can be marshalled to the effect that at the very least there is a strong public dimension[160] to their existence. Not least of course that corporations, that considered themselves the buffer between the retention of private interests and a growing state, were unelected and thus, unlike Government, outside the democratic process.[161] To accept the premise that society should be grateful for what it gets is to ignore all of the contrary arguments about the quest for corporate legitimacy in a time of crisis for the various modes of capitalism, the force of current social and political discourse and the desire that corporations themselves seem to have, rhetorically, at least, to be involved in a reconstruction of society.

159 R Eells, *Corporate Giving in a Free Society* (New York, NY. Harper and Row, 1956) at pp 104, 136.

160 Under the present political regime a public dimension to corporate existence is as likely to be achieved through 'moral regulation' as legislative intervention, see the discussion provided by G Wilson, "Business, State and Community: 'Responsible Risk Takers', New Labour and the Governance of Corporate Business" (2000) 27 *JLS* 151. At n 64 therein the author also references the conventional theoretical material that is usually put forward in the public/private debate on corporate status.

161 R Reich, "The New Meaning of Corporate Social Responsibility" (1998) 40 *Calif Manag Rev* 8 at 13.

As the failure of New Right regimes demonstrates that competition of itself does not create sustainable progress and development, hence the present stress on the need for competitiveness at a global level to embrace local co-operation and to pay attention to on-going skills training and adoption of new technology. The creation of a competitive structure out of social responsibility and involvement is not likely to result in successful and sustainable development. This is particularly important at a time when central government is looking to the corporate sector in partnership with others to provide services that were previously its domain and to embark upon new capital projects. It is undeniable that corporations through their current social responsibility activities are making a type of strategic intervention in society, the question is whether the strategic intervention is a desirable one or not.

The intervention is presently one that supports first and foremost profit-driven corporate aims. "Enlightened self-interest" is the best way to describe this type of intervention. The theory behind it is in part one of increasing the available "spend" of potential customers and in part about product marketing. Corporate donations to projects which improve living standards generate an immediate kickback to the corporation in terms of product demand. However this type of intervention may do nothing to deliver long-term benefit across a wider spectrum of society. Most large corporations now have a community affairs department or at least a community affairs officer. Ideas of competition and marketing are being pushed into the voluntary sector in the form of corporate demands for a "strong brand image".[162] This sort of pressure will create divisions of worthiness between voluntary sector concerns based on what causes corporations think will most appeal to potential customers.[163] This can be referred to colloquially as the appeal of fluffy animals and small children in competition with inner city concerns and perhaps the problems of some minority groups.[164] What is required is a strategic intervention that

[162] See the summary of the corporate positions on corporate community investment in *Corporate Citizen*, Autumn 1997, 5.

[163] The Report of the Commission on the Future of the Voluntary Sector, *Meeting the Challenge of Change: voluntary action into the 21st century*, (the Deakin Report) stresses the importance to the voluntary sector of corporate links and corporate involvement but also points out the need for voluntary sector to be able to maintain its own values. See also S Wheeler, "Common or self-interest? The relationship between corporate activity and voluntary action" in B Knight et al (eds), *Building Civil Society* (West Malling: CAF, 1998) p 127.

[164] The Deakin Report, *supra* n 163 at para 2.5.7.

is based less on corporate largess and views of what can be marketed most effectively, and more on the ideas of responsibility that are outlined above. In March 2000 the first government minister to be appointed with an express responsibility for corporate social responsibility rather unhelpfully linked it, without definition, to corporate reputation and greater enterprise without stressing the importance of partnership and interaction between sectors.[165] What I am arguing for is a corporate view of the public good that consists of considered and targeted interventions that impact on structures and groups that require assistance and require the type of assistance that is being offered. In this way corporate programmes will move the status quo forwards rather than backwards by negative impacts on infrastructure.[166] This type of input is crucial to the Third Way idea of a mixed economy with:

> "a synergy between public and private sectors, utilizing the dynamism of markets but with the public interest in mind. It involves a balance between . . . the economic and the non-economic in the life of society."[167]

Given the interest in ethical investing and the desire of consumers to purchase environmentally friendly products and enter buyer/seller relationships with socially responsible producers it is surprising that information mechanisms to enable these choices to be made are not better developed than they currently are. From 3 July 2000[168] occupational pension funds in the UK have been obliged to disclose in their statements of investment principles "the extent to which, if at all, social, environmental or ethical considerations are taken into account in the selection, retention and realisation of investments". This puts individual employees in the position of being able to lobby for change. However "exit" as a strategy is not likely to be a realistic option and shareholder activism, though on the increase, has never been a major part of the UK financial scene.[169] Trustees are still under an overriding

[165] Kim Howells, Minister for Corporate Social Responsibility, speech to Institute of Ethical Accountability and IPPR, 7 March 2000.

[166] U Haley, "Corporate Contributions as Management Masques. Reframing Corporate Contributions as Strategies to Influence Society" (1991) 28 *J of Manag Studies* 485 at 492f.

[167] Giddens, *supra* n 84 at p 100. See also U Beck, "The Democratization of Democracy–Third Way Policy Needs to Redefine Work" (2000) 5 *The European Legacy* 177.

[168] Occupational Pension Schemes (Investment) Regulations of 1996 as amended in 1998.

[169] For a view that these amended regulations will result in positive debate see R Taylor "How New is Socially Responsible Investment?" (2000) 9 *Business Ethics: A European Review* 174 at 178.

duty to provide the best financial return to the fund's beneficiaries. A growing number of corporations voluntarily produce annual social reports.[170] In 1999 the Institute of Social and Ethical Accountability and the Association of Chartered Certified Accountants set up an award scheme to recognise this voluntary reporting.[171] Somewhat ironically the joint recipient of this first award was Shell. However it is important to remember that the awards were set up to encourage reporting and transparency not to influence conduct.[172] The claims made in these voluntary social reports of positive community outputs are not tested against any particular standard. Corporations are making, for themselves, attempts to measure their outputs into the community in a uniform way. For example the London Benchmarking Group[173] made up of representatives from a number of leading corporations has developed a template which enables corporations to measure the level of their involvement against other corporations. It is a broad model measuring not only obvious items such as cash and product donations but also the less obvious such as the salary and overhead costs of employing personnel to effect these donations.

While this approach is clearly of competitive value to corporations[174] themselves, this instrument and the others like it are of little value to anyone outside the corporate sphere. There are no corresponding output templates so it is impossible to judge the effectiveness of the involvement from the standpoint of the broader social position; the workings of the model are far from transparent and it was itself designed without any dialogue with groups outside corporate management. The fact that competitive interest underlies the model mitigates against the possibility of the sector uniting behind a common set of principles. In addition to these self-generated models, corporations can also sign up to various

[170] A recent PIRC survey revealed that 79 of the top 350 corporations had a separate environmental report and 40 a separate social report.

[171] <http://www.accountability.org.uk>.

[172] A Dignam and M Galanis, "OECD Corporate Governance Principles" (2000) *Euro Bus Law Rev* 396 and R Hooghiemstra, "Corporate Communication and Impression Management – New Perspectives Why Companies Engage in Corporate Social Reporting (2000) 27 *J of Bus Ethics* 55 at 61f. These pieces gives details of some of the social dumping that Shell and other multi-nationals have engaged in.

[173] The group was formed in 1995. Its template and a summary report can be found in *Companies in Communities: Getting the Measure* (1997).

[174] Para 4.4 of the summary report refers to the fact that adoption of the template has enabled one corporation to report a 29% increase in the value of its community involvement and another a 70% increase.

"kitemarks" provided by third party organisations.[175] The purpose of these kitemarks is usually to evidence a corporation's adoption of a particular stance on specific issues such as environmental degradation or employee working conditions. While this type of intervention is a step forward, there are still a considerable number of negatives. Not least of these is that what each mark signifies is not particularly transparent, their proliferation destroys their impact and at most they designate basic compliance with static codes.

Companies legislation requires that certain information, primarily about employees, has to be included in the Annual Report. There is no specified format and the information is often to be found scattered throughout the document.[176] The Annual Report is at least a publicly available resource as are the vast majority of social reports. However the problematic nature of the sort of information that is disclosed can be illustrated by looking at an example from literature produced by British Telecom. BT claim to have spent £770,000 on twenty business projects. These projects are reported to have attracted £6.5 million in partnership funding and resulted in 90 start-up businesses and job training to 6,800 people. While this is a very laudable achievement there is no information in the public domain about the survival rate of these start-up business or indeed the profiles of those who started them. Was this a venture that allowed some individuals to realise their potential through self-employment or did it serve to siphon additional support funding to those who were already experienced at self-employment? There is no way of finding out the nature of the job training that was given and how many of those who received it found long-term employment as a result.

As part of its review of company law, the Company Law Review Steering Group has raised, as a question for consultation, the issue of whether corporations should have additional accounting requirements imposed upon them that would create a type of social report. The information required would report on their relations with employees, suppliers, customers, community and their philanthropic activity and/or environmental performance.[177] However the Steering Group

[175] For example SA8000 underwritten by the Council on Economic Priorities Accreditation Agency and launched in October 1997.

[176] R Gray, "The Practice of Silent Accounting" in S Zadek et al, *Building Corporate Accountability* (London: Earthscan, 1997) p 201.

[177] "Modern Company Law for a Competitive Economy: The Strategic Framework". This Steering Group was set up in the light of the document released in March 1998 (see the discussion accompanying note 96 above). For the stance it offers on reporting issues see paras 5.1.44–5.1.47, 6.4–6.30.

makes its own view of additional regulation clear in the statement "there is a . . . danger, . . . that reporting duties without real content will lead to perfunctory, 'boilerplate' compliance – costs without benefit".[178] While the market orientation of the Steering Group is rather repugnant, its observations on the likely effectiveness of regulation is apposite. Empirical studies of business compliance with regulation support the position that regulation is unlikely to achieve the regulator's objective.[179] It is also the case that the Third Way position rejects the regulatory option.[180] Its idea is that a resettlement of society is achievable through voluntary participation and a harnessing of energy and resources on a voluntary basis. For corporations to fulfil these goals, an ethical starting position and an operational culture which reflects this starting point is required, not mandatory compliance with additional regulation.[181]

However ethical positions are unlikely to be of interest to the Steering Group whose orientation towards market solutions is also clear from their treatment of issues of corporate "philanthropy". Philanthropy is not given any definition but it appears to be used to donate the use of corporate resources in situations where there is no immediate benefit to shareholders.[182] Previously this type of situation might have been dealt

[178] *Supra* n 96 at para 5.1.46. This position on reporting is maintained in the Steering Group's March 2000 proposals for consultation: "Modern Company Law for a Competitive Economy: Developing the Framework", Executive Summary, para 13.

[179] The empirical literature reveals two different types of behaviour; compliance and non-compliance. An example of the non-compliance literature would be K Hawkins, *Environment and Enforcement* (Oxford: Oxford University Press, 1984). An example of the creative compliance literature is D McBarnet and C Whelan, "The Elusive Spirit of the Law: Formalism and the Struggle for Legal Control" (1991) 54 *MLR* 848.

[180] Demos has suggested that liability for corporation tax should be linked to the amount of community involvement undertaken with the best performers receiving an exemption from taxation. The difficulty with this suggestion is twofold; it destroys the voluntary nature of involvement and that it ignores the fact community involvement by corporations will never result in the sort of resource redistribution that the taxation regime achieves. Communities geographically isolated from a large locally based corporation may suffer for example. See (1998) 24 *Corporate Citizen* 32.

[181] See S Driver and L Martell, who cite both Blair and Darling, in opposition when the later was Shadow Chief Secretary to the Treasury, as asserting that regulation would not change corporate culture, only persausion and voluntary agreement: "New Labour's Communitarianisms" (1997) 17 *Crit Soc Pol* 27 at 43. This position is reinforced by Stephen Byers in his speech to the UK–US Enterprise Conference on 5 July 2000 where he states that Government had a responsibility not to intervene and dictate how "businesses must conduct themselves".

[182] *Supra* n 177, para 5.1.43.

with by the ultra vires rules.[183] Successive reforms and the present proposals for reform by this Steering Group limit the scope of the rule to, at best, a matter of internal discipline.[184] As far as the Steering Group is concerned "regard to the need to sustain and enhance the company's reputation" will probably be sufficient to prevent directors using corporate generosity to enhance their own personal reputations and desires without considering shareholder wishes.[185]

It remains the case that shareholders have little formal[186] opportunity to input suggestions for effective corporate community involvement. Their only opportunity would appear to be Annual General Meetings. At one level we could ask whether it matters what shareholders want and why they should be given additional privileges above the ones that they already enjoy. However the rise in ethical investment may mean that shareholders and potential shareholders whose position is not one of "short term profit before all else" are being denied a platform on which to make useful and constructive inputs. The Steering Group's concentration on directors' duties and shareholder protection in a context of increasing competitiveness displays a worrying emphasis on the importance of the market as an institution divorced from wider concerns such as inclusion and shared advancement. The Steering Group's most recent proposals in March 2000 try to overcome this by talking the language of inclusion alongside the language of wealth generation and competitiveness. The two are an uneasy fit to say the least. The question "in whose interests should the company be run" appears to have several different answers. Directors are to have an objective of "wealth generation and competitiveness for the benefit of all". The "benefit of all" however then becomes a phrase which means the pursuit of success "for the benefit of shareholders as a whole". Success is to be achieved with regard to all the relationships on which a company depends.[187] The Steering Group describe this approach as

[183] For the history and development of the ultra vires doctrine see B Pettet, "The Stirring of Corporate Social Conscience: From 'Cakes and Ale' to Community Programmes" in M Freeman (ed) (1997) 50 *Current Legal Problems* 279 at 280–286, 301.

[184] *Supra* n 177, para 5.3.18.

[185] *Supra* n 177, para 5.1.43.

[186] There are of course informal mechanisms of intervention available to institutional investors, see B Black and J Coffee, "Hail Britannia? Institutional Investor Behaviour under Limited Regulation" (1994) 92 *Mich LR* 1997.

[187] The phrase "the company depends" is a problematic one. It feeds into an existing debate within stakeholder theory about exactly which groups the corporation does depend upon. The idea of corporate dependency is known as the "survival thesis". Opposite ends

"shareholder orientated but inclusive of a duty of loyalty".[188] It is hard to see the value in real terms of this duty of loyalty. It is easier to see the Steering Group presenting the corporation here as a closed and hierarchical structure based upon proprietary rights. This type of approach typifies the difficulties that the legal academy has had in constructing paradigms for corporate behaviour. A more constructive way forward would be the creation of a forum for inclusive communications based around a discourse not of rights or protection but of needs – who needs what as a share of corporate profits. In chapter three I try to explain how this idea of a discourse of needs can be translated into a template for corporate behaviour.

Such a communication strategy is unlikely to be adopted by the Department of Trade and Industry in response to the suggestions of the Steering Group. The Steering Group is independent of Government and the Department of Trade and Industry has not missed the opportunity[189] to indicate that its horizons are very much narrower even than those of the Steering Group. It has stressed that the only issues it sees as relevant are disclosure and allied to this a change in the nature of directors' duties. Directors' duties are thought to need to change in much the same way as the Steering Group sets out. Disclosure relates to directors disclosing to shareholders "what the company is doing in a whole host of areas that relate to their stakeholders" and within this is included "relations with suppliers, customer complaints . . . environmental and social and ethical policies . . . material to the business". The idea of this disclosure is apparently so that "shareholders, customers and other stakeholders can make informed decisions". What these informed decisions will be about and how this second idea of interest groups making decisions relates to the first of disclosure to shareholders which implies at best a paternalistic relationship between shareholders and stakeholders and at worst little coherence, is not clear.

of the spectrum of argument are represented by Sternberg and Freeman. For Sternberg the corporation depends for its survival upon shareholders, state and customers, see E Sternberg, "Stakeholder Theory Exposed" (1996) 2 *Corporate Governance Quart* 4 at 6. For Freeman the corporation depends upon a much wider range of groups for survival including its employees, see W Evan and R E Freeman, "Stakeholder Theory of the Modern Corporation: Kantian Capitalism" in T Beauchamp and N Bowie (eds), *Ethical Theory and Business*, 3rd edn (Englewood Cliffs, NJ: Prentice Hall, 1988) 75 at pp 100–2.

188 "Modern Company Law for a Competitive Economy: Developing the Framework" at paragraph 3.39, see *supra* n 177.

189 Speech by Stephen Byers to TUC/IPPR Seminar on Corporate Governance 7 June 2000.

A recent example of the conflicting interests of constituency groups and how the type of suggestion set out above merely fuels controversy is supplied by BMW's decision to cease production at its plant in Longbridge, West Midlands. This was a decision made on economic/profit grounds without, it seems, shareholder consultation or discussion with other groups. Even if the Department of Trade and Industry's vision of communication had occurred it is difficult to see that *ex post facto* reporting, which, as now, would still be the case, would have made any difference.[190] Stakeholders would have expressed their dismay but what decisions they could have made are not clear. However the adoption of corporate governance structures imported from Rhineish capitalism such as works councils are unlikely to provide the answer either. As I have argued previously, many works council agreements provide for only annual meetings. In the context of a corporate group structure these meetings are likely to result only in the provision of knowledge that some redundancy or closure will occur somewhere in the group and they do not, as interaction settings, lend themselves to fulsome and inclusive discussion.[191] What is much more likely to assist in the resolution of these sorts of conflicts is the readiness of government to intervene on an *ad hoc* facilitative basis,[192] the continued drawing in of the corporate sector as partners to government and third sector initiatives and the encouragement of discursive practices in and around the corporation at a more localised level. It is these ideas that I take forward to my third chapter.

4. AN ETHICAL POSITION FOR CORPORATIONS

The Need for a New Cultural Personality

Competitive corporate social conscience will not solve the legitimacy crisis that corporations have been plunged into following post-Fordism and the demise of the New Right response nor will it plug corporate

[190] For a view to the contrary see M Allen "Stakeholding by any other name: A Third Way Business Strategy" (2000) 8 *Renewal* 51.

[191] S Wheeler "Works Councils: Towards Stakeholding" (1997) 24 *JLS* 44 at pp 57–8. The precise example I use there of these sorts of problems is the Coates Viyella agreement. It seems from recent reports that this same situation which is not dissimilar to the BMW/Longbridge situation has occurred again, see M Steel, *Guardian*, 16 May 2000.

[192] For a positive indication on this front see Tony Blair, Speech to the CBI Dinner, 7 May 2000.

activities into the third way programme. As Giddens recognises, the acceptance of market structures as inevitable does not of itself create or sustain ethical frameworks.[193] These frameworks come rather from broader society. Thus what is needed is an ethical underpinning to corporate activity which on the one hand recognises the need for profit-making as essential to a redistribution capacity but on the other integrates the corporation into a larger goal structure. Corporations need a new cultural persona, for want of a better term, which sees their involvement in social programmes in the wider society not as driven by the need for profit with ad hoc useful outcomes but as an activity in its own right. Corporations need to put themselves in a position, through dialogue with other sectors, whereby the label "citizen" that they have flirted[194] with becomes not part of a competitive discourse but part of a directed and targeted campaign of service to wider society.[195]

Meanings of Community

The difficulties that the corporate sector faces in adopting a new cultural persona is illustrated by its use of the term "community" as a signifying label for executives and resources devoted to socially orientated programmes. Corporate "community" affairs and liaison departments select recipients for corporate social conscience benefits on the basis of their marketability either directly or as part of a cause related marketing venture. The idea of "community" as a problematic has escaped the corporate sector. It is seen as the obvious nomenclature with which to cloak all those who do not fit within a specific category under a typical stakeholder analysis. In fact "community" cannot bear this weight of significance. It is far too crude and simplistic a generalisation about identity. In an era of individual identity, post-traditional values, and multi-culturalism, "community" does not have a ready meaning. Within any geographical area or group selected to receive corporate assistance, there are likely to be different communities cutting across each other drawn on lines such as race, religion, gender, age, waged or

[193] *Supra* n 85 at pp 36 and 164.

[194] For example the Financial Times organised a conference on Corporate Citizenship in November 1997.

[195] An apposite description of the current position of corporations is provided by Charles Leadbeater in *Civic Spirit: The Big Idea for a New Political Era* as "a crisis of belonging" (p 12). *Civic Spirit* is a Demos distribution pamphlet with no publication details.

unwaged and sexuality where individuals self-identify as belonging to more than one group. The corporate sector is facing exactly the same difficulty about collective and individual identity as we have already identified as existing in social and political discourse. Figure 1 below is a representation of the way in which community is traditionally presented as a discrete entity. As this discrete entity it holds all those persons and identities which are not placed in a category elsewhere. Figure 2 below demonstrates in a very crude fashion the inaccuracy of the model in Figure 1. Not only are suppliers to a corporation, customers of a corporation and those involved in national and local regulation of a corporation, members of a community or communities but so also are employees, shareholders and directors of a corporation, those living close to a corporation's physical activity, those dependent for their livelihoods on the corporations continued presence and so on.

The more complex mapping in Figure 2 above points to the inappropriateness of corporate participation in "community" rebuilding based on anything other than an ethical position which itself rests on a broadly based teleological idea, accepts difference and addresses the position of difference through a dialogue about needs. A way through the problem of "community" as an entity built upon flexible and multiple individual identities is provided by both Giddens and Bauman. The solution offered by Giddens is that policy and practice can recognise individuality and collectivity by seeking to build a cosmopolitan society that ignores petty feuds based on nationalism.[196] This is, in fact, more of a stalking horse than a positive solution. It draws attention to the sweeping assumptions that current political discourse makes about the concept of community[197] – the reliance for example upon geographical tradition as a fixed point, the idea that racial tensions, discrimination and even hatred are issues of the past[198] and the idea that there are shared problems and solutions.[199] Community has become the talisman of New Labour thinking and integral to the Third Way. Blair speaks of "community" as standing "at the heart of his beliefs". He presents community as the "answer to the challenges of a changing world" and as an

[196] Giddens, *supra* n 84 at 129–31.

[197] For a discussion of the different ways in which community has been applied see R Levitas, "Community, Utopia and New Labour" (2000) 15 *Local Economy* 188.

[198] For ideas on what is wrong with the rather cosy world that Giddens seems to think exists, see A McRobbie, "Feminism and the Third Way" (2000) 64 *Feminist Rev* 97 at 104–5.

[199] S MacKian, "The Citizen's New Clothes: care in a Welsh community" (1998) 18 *Crit Soc Pol* 27 at 31.

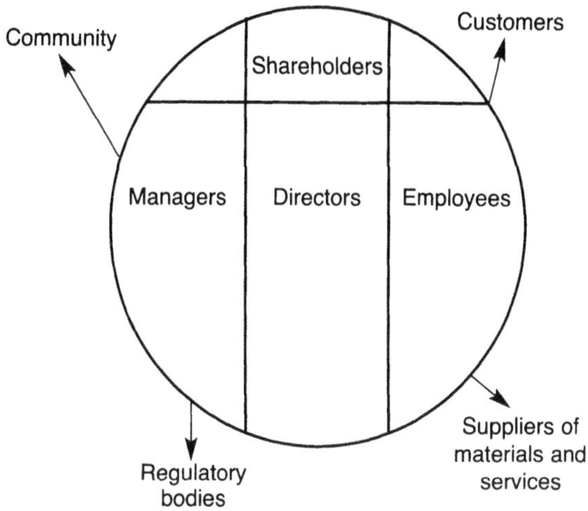

Figure 1.1

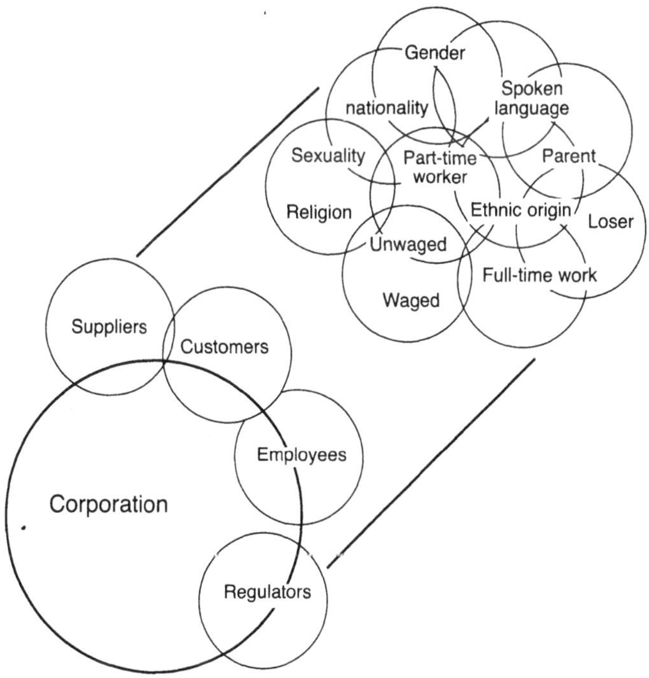

Figure 1.2

active body that can prevent others feeling lonely and helpless.[200] Community is in this sense the micro-narrative to the meta-narrative of the Third Way; it is being used to describe the alternative to both market individualism and state ownership. At this level it is being used to denote a collective recognition of the importance of both responsibility and opportunity,[201] although as I make clear in my introductory notes responsibility and opportunity do not stand in a reciprocal relationship to each other.

At times the concept of community applied in this way runs into communitarian political strategies.[202] There appear to be two significant influences. One is the traditional Christian Socialist tradition in the form of the ideas of Halsey and Tawney.[203] Some commentators have pointed to the role of Blair's own admitted Christian faith at this point.[204] However this is a connection that Blair himself rejects.[205] The question of the influence of religion and its various teachings over the Blairite vision is revisited in the next chapter. The second influence is that of the American responsive communitarians personified by Etzioni.[206] I have many difficulties with the thinking that underpins responsive communitarianism not least the idea that a "good society is . . . dependent on its moral infrastructure" when that moral infrastructure is defined so as to advocate traditional marriage as a key component for example.[207] Indeed more recently Etzioni has produced a Third Way outline of his own in the form of a Demos pamphlet.[208] His vision turns on the notion

[200] Speech to Women's Institute, London, 7 June 2000.

[201] S White, "Interpreting the Third Way: Not One Road But Many" (1998) 6 *Renewal* 17 at 20.

[202] H Tam, "Rediscovering British Communitarianism" (1998) 9 *Responsive Community* 79. For the ways in which it has become important to New Labour in this context see L Driver and L Martell, "New Labour: Culture and Economy" in L Ray and A Sayer (eds), *Culture and Economy After the Cultural Turn* (London: Sage, 1999) p 246 at p 254.

[203] C Bryant, *Reclaiming the Ground* (London: Spire, Hodder and Stoughton, 1993) and The After Socialism Group, *Beyond Fear* (Edinburgh: St Andrews Press, 1998).

[204] M Freeden, "The Ideology of New Labour" (1999) *Pol Quart* 42 at 48.

[205] T Blair, *New Britain* (London: Fourth Estate, 1996) p 59.

[206] S Wheeler and G Wilson, "Corporate Law Firms and the Spirit of Community" (1998) 49 *NILQ* 239.

[207] See *supra* n 29 and A Etzioni, *The New Golden Rule* (London: Profile Books, 1997) at pp 176–88. For some commonality between this brand of communitarianism and Christian Socialism see A Deacon and K Mann, "Agency, Modernity and Social Policy" (1999) 28 *Jnl Soc Pol* 413 at 429.

[208] A Etzioni, *The Third Way to a Good Society* (London: Demos, 2000).

of social justice, in a way similar to Giddens.[209] Although Etzioni styles himself as giving a clearer picture of the Third Way[210] it is in reality a reiteration of his earlier work – that construction of a moral culture through discussion about values rather than interests or wants will provide a new set of behaviours.[211] While it is obvious that there has to be a new settlement of society that is based on balancing rights against reciprocal behaviour, it is also obvious that this balance cannot entirely exclude an examination of interests or wants. There is a raft of current political policies that reflect the "authoritarian side of communitarianism",[212] for example the positions taken on the treatment of asylum seekers, the attempts to abolish jury trials and the restrictions on welfare benefits. There is a danger that unless there is continuing debate and dialogue within appropriate frameworks around notions of responsibility, opportunity and rights then those already on the fringes of any particular community may find themselves further marginalised or excluded as their rights became increasingly conditional.[213]

My misgivings around responsive communitarianism extend to its processes as well as its substance. Etzioni advocates respect for difference rather than simply tolerance.[214] However this is far from the positive it sounds. The whole methodology that Etzioni offers for building "community", and his suggestions that identity politics stand in the way of this, suggest that cosmopolitan society[215] is in fact going to be built on the dominant values of the majority and differences in culture, identity and belief at best ignored and at worst labelled as "abnormal".[216]

209 It should be noted however that there seems to be a misunderstanding on Etzioni's part about what is meant in the Blair/Giddens world by "rights and responsibilities". Etzioni indicates on p 29 that evading responsibilities should take away basic citizenship rights such as the right to vote and the right to free speech. Blair/Giddens are advocating a much closer link between rights and responsibilities for example welfare rights are conditional on participating in schemes around training etc. Etzioni's concerns possibly come from participation in democratic system where certain rights are expressly confered by constitution.

210 *Supra* n 208 at p 14.

211 *Supra* n 207 at pp 34–35.

212 S White, "Which Way? The Third Way and the Puzzle of New Labour" (1999) 21 *Harv Int Rev* 54 at 58.

213 M Powell, "New Labour and the Third Way in the British Welfare State: A New and Distinctive Approach?" (2000) 20 *Crit Soc Pol* 39.

214 A Etzioni, *supra* n 207 at p 204.

215 H Tam, *Communitarianism* (Basingstoke: Macmillan, 1998) pp 189–216, in particular pp 205–8.

216 A Crawford, "The Spirit of Community: Rights, Responsibilities, and the Communitarian Agenda" (1996) 23 *JLS* 247 at pp 252–6.

Despite Giddens' express rejection of the authoritarian form of communitarianism his idea of how to build cosmopolitan society does have a certain resonance with Etzioni's position. The solution offered by Bauman is much more in tune with the reality of the difficulties created by the breakdown of traditional identities. Bauman is offering neither a glib easy "fix" nor the possibility of the exclusion of minorities. As such his position becomes more of a challenge; it is achievable and so it can be looked upon as a goal. Bauman's position is that it is not possible to give any guarantee that a community will be/can be built but if it is accepted that what is needed is citizen engagement with the running of common affairs and then from that position, accepted that there is a link between autonomous individuals and a self-reflexive and self-correcting political community, then the achievement of community is a possibility.[217] In my next chapter I take Bauman's ideas of citizen engagement and examine them through the lens of Aristotelian notions of engagement and pursuit of life through the virtues.

[217] Z Bauman, "Alone Again: Ethics after Certainty" in G Mulgan (ed), *Life After Politics* (London: Fontana Press, 1997) p 1 at pp 9–12.

2

Aristotle, Virtue Ethics and the Corporate World

1. AN INTRODUCTION TO ARISTOTELIAN PHILOSOPHY

The previous chapter concluded by looking at Bauman's linkage of the ideas of citizen engagement with issues of running common affairs and caring generally which might lead, in his view, to a community of responsible citizens. Bauman refers in this context to the *polis*, a term which resonates with the philosophy of Aristotle. It is my view that the use of this word is extremely apposite in the situation in which we find ourselves. Bauman and Aristotle both occupy the ground between liberalism and communitarianism. My focus in this chapter is on the ethics of Aristotle and his thinking on political systems to the extent that I engage with his view of the relationship of the individual to the collective and to a lesser extent with his position on governance of the collective. In this chapter I want to explore the possibilities offered by Aristotelian ethics as a way of offering a system of behaviour for corporations that is based not upon ideas of duty but upon ideas of values or virtues in Aristotelian terms. Aristotelian philosophy has made a return to fashion in recent years but not so much so that I do not spend a considerable amount of time in this chapter explaining why this is and why it is one of my chosen frames of reference.

There are some elements of Aristotelian philosophy that may seem unacceptable within the moral and political mores of the twentieth century.[1] For example Aristotle credits active reason – the faculty that

[1] Indeed Aristotle's moral and political views did not enjoy majority support within his own contemporary society, C Farrar, *Inventing Politics: The Origins of Democratic Thinking* (Cambridge: Cambridge University Press, 1988). James Davidson makes the point that philosophers, historians and dramatists of this period, and presumably of any other, did not write to leave a record for readers engaging with them years later. They wrote to challenge beliefs, assumptions and stereotypes of their time. See J Davidson, *Courtesans and Fishcakes* (London: Fontana, 1998).

allows human individuals to make sense of the order of the world around them and contemplate rational positions – as being connected with a power external to the body. It comes from a force, in a sense a divine and ethereal force, present in the world. The idea of the existence of a divine or superior presence is not one that would now attract universal approval from a theoretical or a more social and cultural perspective. Aristotle's views on slavery, on which I comment in more detail later, do not reflect twentieth century thinking either. In his specifically political writing Aristotle actively supports a restricted franchise embracing only adult male Athenians, something which all current liberal constitutions would find unacceptable, with their claims to recognise the principle of equality. However there is a considerable linguistic communality between the discourse around current concerns of the place of the individual with the collective and the relationship of the individual to the collective and the discourse of Aristotelian philosophy. Both speak in terms of the ideas of civic responsibility created through individual participation and commitment. The synergy between the two is further strengthened by looking at the similarity of their projects. Aristotle, in a way that Bauman echoes in a considerably less optimistic tone, appeals to the creation of a common good through the civic engagement of citizens with each other and the collective. Aristotle, unlike Bauman, offers a series of structures through which this may occur.

Aristotle was concerned with promoting and supporting the idea of what was then enlightened and democratic government through the ideal of the *agathos polites*, the model of the good citizen that he shared with Plato, over an emerging trading economy and a sophisticated city state for which wars against the Persians and other Greek states were no longer the most pressing concern. The heroes of Homer's Illiad and Odyssey were likely to be no more than mythical and barbaric figures to the Greeks that formed Aristotle's intended audience.[2] Indeed one reading[3] of Aeschylus' trilogy *Oresteia*, first

[2] R Solomon, *Ethics and Excellence* (New York, NY: Oxford University Press, 1992) at p 196 and E Hall, "The Sociology of Athenian Tragedy" in P Easterling (ed), *Greek Tragedy* (Cambridge: Cambridge University Press, 1997) p 93 at p 100f.

[3] C Rocco, *Tragedy and Enlightment* (Berkeley, CA: University of California Press, 1997) ch 5 especially pp 146-56 and 159-64. At the same time Rocco offers an analysis of the use of gender in *Oresteia*. Given the tension that has existed at times between feminist scholarship and that of classical studies, see for example S Okin, *Women in Western Political Thought* (Princeton, NJ: Princeton University Press, 1997), his is a fascinating intervention.

performed around 458 BC, is that the author's changes to the narrative found in the Odyssey were made to support and secure the emerging civic discourse. In particular he sees a desire to boost the ideas of political participation free from the constraints of hereditary privilege and the determination of justice by courts of law. The significance of these ideas are seen in the action of Athena who convenes a court of law and calls upon the "best citizens" to judge the innocence or guilt of Orestes. This ends the cycle of violence based upon the primeval need for personal vengeance in favour of the judgement of the collective. The interests of the divine within the democratic city are maintained by Athena's actions in providing the casting vote in favour of innocence and the city. Bauman's attention is focussed on the project that is set out in the current political and social discourse which my previous chapter explained. This is how to remarshall contemporary society towards an inclusivity that both recognises resurgent nationalisms and prevents oppression of minorities, how a minimum standard of living irrespective of employment can be achieved, and how the partnerships between sectors that are a necessary adjunct to achieving this can be created. In short both Aristotle and Bauman are advocating an ethical and spiritual rebirth of the individual. To the extent that their projects are similar Aristotle has valuable insights to offer on the position of the individual as a simple and complete entity. The choices that confront us as individuals now are very much more complex than Aristotle could ever have envisaged. Bauman draws attention to exactly this issue in his discussions around postmodernity. While not losing sight of this lacuna between Aristotle and Bauman my intention in this chapter is to concentrate on what Aristotle can offer as a way forward towards inclusivity and re-engagement. The pessimism of Bauman is something that I return to at the beginning of my final chapter.

The idea of an intellectual return to the paradigms of political thought, social interaction and the like of classical Greece is not one novel to Bauman or to me. Disciplinary boundaries within the academy have become stretched in recent years due, in large part, I think, to the sense of intellectual freedom that the rise of postmodernism has engendered. This intellectual freedom has also allowed the work of Roman and Greek scholars to be studied as texts that exist only in translation, thus opening up their study to a whole range of scholars from different sections of the academy whose lack of classical language training would previously have excluded them from passing any respected comment on the canon of Classical Studies. Classical thought in terms of philosophy and literature has been interpreted through the lens of more modern interventions, such as poststructuralism,[4] semiotics and psychoanalysis.[5] It has been used to supply the interpretative framework for new, as in contemporary, political and philosophical positions.[6] Engagement with the issues presented in classical thought offers an opportunity to stand back from contemporary problems and examine them from an angle untainted by current concerns.[7] Later in this chapter I look at the work of Anscombe on the intellectual renaissance of virtue ethics and within my discussion of that, the work of T H Green and the British Idealists. Their work illustrates my point that engagement with classical Greek philosophy can provide the bedrock for explanation of the contemporary.

Outside the academy the encouragement of postmodernity towards a more reflexive existence and a broader input into life space has given classical thought a resurgence in popular appeal that is not dependent on having received a particular type and style of education. For example Tom Wolfe's recent novel *A Man in Full*[8] features the philosophy of Epictetus.[9] The novel is written in Wolfe's usual style of a series of character vignettes with the linkages between them developing throughout the work. The sayings of Epictetus are used as the main strand which ties together the novel's two most opposing characters;[10]

[4] For a review of the impact of this form of criticism in particular see J Perudotto, *Man in the Middle Voice: Name and Narrative in the Odyssey* (Princeton, NJ: Princeton University Press, 1990) ch 1.

[5] For a discussion of both a semiotic and a psychoanalytical approach see C Segal, *Interpreting Greek Tragedy* (Ithaca, NY: Cornell University Press, 1986).

[6] P Euben, J Ober and J Wallach (eds), *Athenian Political Thought and the Reconstruction of American Democracy* (Ithaca, NY: Cornell University Press, 1994) and B Williams, *Shame and Necessity* (Berkeley, CA: University of California Press, 1993) are but two examples.

[7] See M Nussbaum's discussion of her journey into Aristotelian philosophy and why she has "grounded" her work there, M Nussbaum "Aristotle, Politics and Human Capabilities: A Response to Antony, Arneson, Charlesworth and Mulgan" (2000) 111 *Ethics* 102 at 103-4.

[8] (London: Jonathan Cape, 1998)

[9] Epictetus is generally classified as a later Stoic philosopher. In common with Aristotle he left behind no tracts of his own authorship in the sense that what we have are his lectures put together by one Arrian. The writings are in places repetitious to put it mildly. For an over of his teaching see R Ryle, "Epictetus" (1894) 2 (OS) *Proceedings of the Aristotelian Society* 123 and E Zeller, *Outlines of the History of Greek Philosophy* (London: Routledge and Kegan Paul, 1931).

[10] Their opposite positions are perhaps emphasised by Wolfe in the geographical locations he gives them; Oakland California for Hensley and Atlanta Georgia for Coker.

Charlie Coker, Atlanta-born white man made good by his own not-so-honest endeavour and favourable market conditions and Conrad Hensley who seemingly enjoys no luck in life and appears destined to struggle to survive, never mind reach the summit of his ambitions. Epictetus's philosophy empowers Hensley to make the most of his qualities of endeavour and honesty and Croker to face up to his debts. He rejects his lavish possessions and the struggle to keep them in favour of preserving his character.[11] Epictetus is used to present answers of almost bullet point simplicity to the big questions and dilemmas of life; possessions, friends and families, even our own bodies, are temporary, all that an individual has power over is that individual's own character. This individual imbued with the background influence of a divine being, has few choices and accepts destiny.[12] Wolfe in my view is not the only person to seek refuge in the apparent clear and uncomplicated dictates of classical philosophy,as we shall see.

The Framework of Virtue Ethics

Virtue ethics, often but not always identified with Aristotelian philosophy, has also become the predominant theory in modern moral philosophy in a time-frame of less than an intellectual generation overcoming Kantian and utilitarian positions.[13] In 1978 Philippa Foot was writing of the omission of "virtues and vices from moral philosophy";[14] by 1994 both Cottingham and Cordner were describing it as "prominent" and "promising".[15] This development has continued with the appearance of a number of texts and readings books, which give a quantity of space to, if not focus on, virtue ethics.[16] Under their broadest definition virtue ethics are a set of ethical principles which concentrate

[11] See *A Man in Full* (New York, NY: Farrar, Straus & Giroux, 1998) p 722.

[12] *Ibid*, p 683.

[13] See for example Robert Louden's assertion that "[t]oday one finds fewer and fewer theorists engaging in efforts to construct viable utilitarian or deontological systems; Aristotle has replaced Mill and Kant as the classical moral philospher most likely to inspire allegiance", R Louden, "Virtue Ethics and Anti-Theory" (1990) 20 *Philosophia* 93 at 94.

[14] P Foot, *Virtues and Vices* (Oxford: Blackwell, 1978) p 1.

[15] Coincidently both these views appear in the same volume of *Philosophy*; J Cottingham, "Religion, Virtue and Ethical Culture" (1994) 69 *Philosophy* 177 and C Cordner, "Aristotelian Virtue and Its Limitations" (1994) 69 *Philosophy* 291.

[16] See, for example, M Baron, P Petit, and M Slote, *Three Methods of Ethics* (Oxford: Blackwell, 1999) and D Statman (ed), *Virtue Ethics* (Edinburgh: Edinburgh University Press, 1997).

on establishing moral positions from which ethical decisions can be made. These are not moral positions which give rise to a single answer to an ethical dilemma either as a result of a moral law or as a result of an *a fortiori* application of fixed principles. Rather virtue ethics encourages contemplation of the options that confront the individual who has developed moral positions. Key to virtue ethics is the development over time of the moral character.[17] A number of significant modern philosophers style themselves as neo-Aristotelians, these include figures such as MacIntyre, Slote and Nussbaum.[18] Some of the modifications offered to the Aristotelian paradigm by this field of scholarship, particularly those of Nussbaum and MacIntyre, are discussed in my third and final chapter.

There are numerous recent expositions of applied ethics in fields such as education,[19] health care and, pertinently for this chapter, business ethics[20] which claim an intellectual association with Aristotle. Discussion of some of the business ethics literature appears below. Here it is worth making the point that the appearance of applied ethics with an Aristotelian flavour in health care and education is, in philosophical terms, not particularly surprising. Both are well within the remit of Aristotle's general philosophical position. Its application to business issues is of more interest since at first the connection between business and ethics is hard to see. The parts of Aristotelian philosophy that would seem to engage directly with business ethics, rather than issues of economic principle such as value and exchange, make a case for slavery, and condemn profit-making activity, indulged in for its own sake, and

[17] J Barton, "Virtue in the Bible"(1999)12 *Christian Ethics* 12.

[18] Neo-Aristotelian scholarship has become a field of study in its own right. Wallach, for example, who is hostile to the whole enterprise of neo-Aristotelianism, divides the field into three categories; analytical Aristotelianism in which he includes scholars such as Broadie, fundamental Aristotelianism into which he places Nussbaum, and traditional Aristotelianism which includes MacIntrye. Something of his definition of neo-Aristotelianism can be gathered from the fact that he rejects the idea that Hannah Ardent might be within the field. She is excluded because her work is influenced by Aristotle but not defined by Aristotle, see J Wallach, "Contemporary Aristotelianism" (1992) 20 *Political Theory* 613 at 618.

[19] D Carr and J Steutal (eds), *Virtue Ethics and Moral Education* (London: Routledge, 1999). J Steutel, "The Virtue Approach to Moral Education: Some Conceptual Clarifications" (1997) 31 *J of Phil of Ed* 395.

[20] Denis Collins asserts a claim to be the first such proponent by virtue of a literature search of the Business Periodicals Index, see D Collins, "Aristotle and Business" (1987) 6 *J Bus Ethics* 567 at 571.

usury.[21] It is important once again to look at the context in which Aristotle was expounding this philosophy and so admit a certain degree of relativity, both temporal and cultural, into the dissemination. Cultural relativity is an issue that I address in chapter three. Slavery was universally practised and accepted as a hereditary status.[22] Aristotle was not opposed to economic activity as such; shoemakers, carpenters and builders receive mention without condemnation for example. His concern was with justice in exchange evidenced by an attempt to achieve proportional equality of goods and reciprocal action.[23] Usury was not necessary to stimulate this type of activity. Its goal then was seen as being an anti-social one of exploitation driven by greed.[24] The economy that concerned Aristotle was a stagnant one in which material goods were in fixed supply thus capping total wealth. A collective or common good could only be reached if each individual citizen set out to acquire no more than he actually required for life. Economic activity could not be an end in its own right. This is not dissimilar to the message that corporations are receiving at the moment. Obviously the economy of post post-Fordism is one of growth and there is no need to advocate restrictions on wealth accumulation per se. What is advocated is that with profit acquisition comes responsibility to ensure wide participation and the conferral of benefits. Usury continued to be condemned by the

[21] There are a number of texts devoted to Aristotelian economic thought. Several of these are referenced below. Useful overviews are provided in S Fleetwood, "Aristotle in the 21st Century" (1997) 21 *Cambridge J of Economics* 729 and J O'Neill, "Essences and Markets" (1995) 78 *The Monist* 258.

[22] Aristotle considered slaves an "animate form of property" and slavery as a necessary ingredient for conducting tasks. He refers to the impossibility of shuttles weaving themselves for example (*Politics* 1254al. One interpretation of this is to assert that in an industrialised and technocratic economy slavery would be unnecessary as shuttles could indeed weave themselves. However against this has to be set the text which follows on from the passage referred to above. It leaves little doubt that Aristotle subscribed to the view that some individuals were naturally destined to be slaves; those born into slavery and those captured in war, *Politics* (hereinafter "*P*") 1254a17-1255b4.

[23] See *Nicomachean Ethics* (hereinafter "*NE*") 1132b21-1134a11. The passages that deal with fair exchange/justice in exchange can be seen not as Aristotle's interest in economics but as Aristotle putting forward an ethical position or question. Judson puts this as "What is the basis of fairness in the exchange of goods" and then suggests the answer "it is the strength of the needs which exchangers have when they satisfy these conditions which in central cases determines the equivilence of return of goods", L Judson, "Aristotle on Fair Exchange" (1997) XV *Oxford Studies in Ancient Philosophy* 148 at 148 and 172.

[24] See *Nicomachean Ethics*. Aristotle heaps invective upon those who lend small sums at high rates of interest, they do this he feels for an improper desire for or love of gain.

medieval church. However it later became an acceptable and very necessary part of economic life in the rise of the industrial economy, where it was considered facilitative as opposed to exploitative.[25] Much more assistance for developing a model for contemporary business ethics comes from the wider Aristotelian perspective on ethical behaviour, the relationship of the individual to the community and the governance of that community.

In this chapter I want to develop my conception of Aristotelian virtue ethics and begin to explain the link between this and the contemporary concerns of Bauman. I see this link as being much stronger than a mere happenstance use of a common vocabulary, and indeed one strong enough to overcome the obvious differences between Athens in 350BC and a world in the post post-Fordist twenty-first century. Central to demonstrating this link is an examination of the broad trajectories of philosophical thought which over a period of some 500 years has first spurned and then re-embraced an idea of Aristotelian virtue ethics. I attempt to trace the fate of Aristotelian ethics through its association with Aquinas and then Catholicism. In my view this has become a positive association in very recent times as Catholicism has risen to a position from which it could be regarded as the religion of the establishment if not the Established Church. Alongside this, ideas of individual spirituality and sacrifice have developed as a counterpoint to the truisms of the Enlightenment. What should emerge from this discussion is that it is no longer definitive of virtue ethics to describe it as "what Aristotle did"[26] or to put this in the more familiar negative construction "what Kant did not suggest"[27] or what is wrong with Kantian[28] and utilitarian

[25] J Noonan, *The Scholastic Analysis of Usury* (Cambridge, MA: Harvard University Press, 1957) and A Jonsen and S Toulmin, *The Abuse of Casuistry* (Berkeley, CA: University of California Press, 1988) at pp 181-94

[26] R Putnam, "Reciprocity and Virtue Ethics" (1988) 98 *Ethics* 379.

[27] What I mean by this is that there is, in my view, a modern school of virtue ethics, that does not see virtue ethics as purely Arisotelian and thus standing in direct opposition to Kantian ethics, which is traditionally cast as an ethics of duty. For example Bobbio is much more conservative in his discussion of the difference between virtue ethics as traditionally conceived and ethics of duty or obligation. He sees them both as requiring a good action. Virtue ethics achieves this by "describ[ing], . . . and propos[ing] [the action] as an example [ethics of duty] prescribes the action as behaviour that must be followed or regarded as a duty: N Bobbio, *In Praise of Meekness* (Cambridge: Polity, 2000) at p 22.

[28] For a discussion of the place of virtue within Kantian ethics see A Wood, *Kant's Ethical Thought* (Cambridge: Cambridge University Press, 1999) at pp 331-6.

ethical theories.[29] My end point is that virtue ethics offer much to help balance the crisis of conscience between the individual and the collective. Aristotelian thought is attractive in offering a route through the competing but discredited narratives of free market capitalism and planned economies.

Aristotelian Structures and Institutions and the Corporation

Aristotle's *Politics* (hereinafter *P*) and *Nicomachean Ethics* (hereinafter *NE*), taken together, as it is thought Aristotle intended,[30] offer a model for construction and maintenance of a society beginning with the individual. Hence *NE* is an account of what the individual citizen has to be and to do in order to live a good and successful life. *P* concentrates on what is, for Aristotle, the natural outcome of living a good life. This is participation in the *polis*. The inter-relationship that Aristotle constructs between the individual and the larger community is best explained by looking at the opening passages of *P*. These build on the position taken in *NE* that for every individual, *eudaimonia* is the ultimate goal and highest good and that it is achieved through practice of the virtues. Every association is formed for some good and the *polis* aims at the highest good. Through participation within the *polis* individuals can practice the virtues that bring about *eudaimonia*. Aristotle regards the *polis* as a natural phenomenon;[31] it exists to promote the happiness of all as identified by individuals through pursuit of the virtues.[32]

Whether participation in the *polis* in terms of political participation is the only form of participation that Aristotle envisages to satisfy this idea of *eudaimonia* is a matter of some debate. If the *polis* is viewed purely as a political entity then obviously participation and so fulfillment of *eudaimonia* can only be through political participation. There

[29] J Oakley, "Varieties of Virtue Ethics" (1996) IX *Ratio* 128

[30] S Cashdollar, "Aristotle's Politics of Morals" (1973) 11 *J of Hist of Philosophy* 145.

[31] *P* 1252a1-7

[32] *P* 1253a18. This is the passage in which Aristotle refers to the *polis* as prior to the individual by using a bodily analogy with the *polis* as body and the citizen as hand or foot. As Taylor points out there is a danger that this passage could be construed as advocating that the good of the individual is always subject to the superior good of the state. However Aristotle's meaning is quite the opposite; political participation is required to promote the well-being of citizens and the good of the *polis* is an aggregate of the good of individual citizens. See C Taylor, "Politics" in J Barnes (ed), *Cambridge Companion to Aristotle* (Cambridge: Cambridge University Press, 1995) p 233 at pp 239-40.

is considerable support for this interpretation.[33] However a far more constructive interpretation which would allow the individual to reach *eudaimonia* even in conditions where political participation is impossible, is to view the *polis* as a social as well as a political community.[34] The idea of a political forum and a social phenomenon combined sits well with the idea that *NE* and *P* are intended to offer a holistic view of the human condition. *Eudaimonia* is usually translated as "happiness" or "flourishing"[35] which indicates a condition, for the majority of us, of a purely transitory nature. As Duvall and Dotson point out this is difficult to square with the assertion in *NE* that *eudaimonia* is an activity of the soul.[36] Their suggestion is that a better conception of *eudaimonia* is as an activity whereby individuals "[get] their act together" to be "completely moral and intellectual beings".[37]

The next issue to deal with is where, within the structure that Aristotle gives to society, would the corporation be situated. There are several possibilities from the corporation as a *polis* or as a smaller community like the village or household, to the corporation as an individual. A vital precursor to labelling the corporation as an individual is the location of the corporation's soul. For Aristotle a condition precedent for all living beings was the possession of a soul. Without a soul a corporation cannot engage in *eudaimonia*. If the corporation has a soul then the next question might logically be whether other bodies,

33 See for example T Irwin, "The Good of Political Activity" in G Patzig (ed), *XI Symposium Aristotelicum: Studien zur Politik des Aristoteles* (Gottingen: Vandenhoeck & Ruprecht, 1989) p 73 and D Keyt, "Three Basic Theorums in Aristotle's *Politics* in D Keyt and F Miller (ed), *A Companion to Aristotle's Politics* (Oxford: Blackwell, 1991) p 118.

34 R Mulgan, "Aristotle and the Value of Political Participation" (1990) 18 *Political Theory* 195. Mulgan posits the view that Aristotle means "political" in the sense that "tribal" or "post-industrial" is likely to be used, ie, as an all encompassing term which includes every area of life. He dislikes the use of a "public/private" divide (*koinon/idion*) in translation as it attracts a Western liberal idea of privacy that Aristotle did not have. The whole point of Aristotle's analysis was to facilitate and encourage interaction with the community. See also J Ober, *The Athenian Revolution* (Princeton, NJ: Princeton University Press, 1996) p 166. Ober's view is that the passages from *P* 1274b32 to *P* 1283b40 show that Aristotle saw *polis* also as a geographical term which would necessarily include those living within it including non-citizens. The cohabitation of citizens and non-citizens is taken by Ober to be crucial to the nature of the *polis* as a community. On this basis *polis* has to be seen as a concept wider than the merely political.

35 R Kraut, "Two Conceptions of Happiness" (1979) 88 *Philosophical Review* 167

36 *NE* 1098a17.

37 T Duvall and P Dotson, "Political Participation and *Eudaimonia* in Aristotle's *Politics*" (1998) XIX *History of Political Thought* 21 at 26.

often unincorporated, such as Charities or Trade Unions have a soul. As my argument in relation to this point develops below it will, I think, become clear that the case for these bodies possessing a soul has to be considered on an individual basis against a general template of inquiry.

The stance of some business ethicists is to ignore the Aristotelian distinction between the *polis* as a political and social community and the individual and therefore offer no firm positioning of the corporation while still purporting to rely upon Aristotelian philosophy.[38] This approach has a certain superficial attraction in the sense that it overcomes the problem of fitting into Aristotle's structure a form of association that has no parallel in Fourth Century BC Greece. However I have several difficulties with using Aristotelian ethics in this way. It involves placing the emphasis within the application of Aristotelian philosophy to the corporation on the virtues themselves rather than on the conceptual structure of which the virtues are a part. This means not addressing issues such as the teleological nature of the pursuit of the virtues and the question of motive. As I point out in my discussion of the virtues below, this is the most significant part of Aristotle's philosophy for corporate behaviour. There is also a tendency to present Aristotle's virtues as "hard and fast" rules and principles. This of course is contrary to the Aristotelian position.[39] Some, at least, of the virtues that Aristotle identifies have no more application to modern living and the corporation than the corporation has a place within Aristotle's original thinking. So it is not as though this position deflects criticism that Aristotle did not write with a corporate structure in mind. The most important point to be made about this approach is that it involves no attempt to inquire how even base line positions might be identified, never mind virtues, for application. I have already identified this problem of dialogue and value construction in relation to the modern communitarians, most obviously the work of Amatai Etzioni, in my first chapter. It is a problem to which I return in the third and final chapter.

[38] B Shaw, "Sources of Virtue: The Market and the Community" (1997) 7 *Bus Eth Quart* 33; R Duska, "Aristotle: A Pre-Modern Post-Modern? Implications for Business Ethics" (1993) 3 *Bus Eth Quart* 227; B Shaw and J McCraken, "Virtue Ethics and Contractarianism: Towards a Reconciliation" (1995) 5 *Bus Ethics Quart* 297 and K Schudt, "Taming the Corporate Monster: An Aristotelian Approach to Corporate Virtue" (2000) 10 *Bus Eth Quart* 711. Schudt also rejects the idea that corporations can have souls (at 712 and 721). His solution is to create corporate virtues as an adjunct to profit-making and ignore all other aspects of Aristotelian philosophy.

[39] I Maitland, "Virtues Markets: The Market as School of the Virtues" (1996) 6 *Bus Ethics Quart* 1.

Notwithstanding my conclusions immediately above, if we take the application of the virtues to the next stage ie to the corporation itself, then we have to confront the following problems. The application of the virtues themselves concentrates on creating a new blueprint for the performance of individual corporate executives[40] in relation, principally, to the internal governance of the corporation. By internal governance here I mean the treatment of each other, existing and potential employees, in relation to issues that are concerned with the day to day running of the corporation such as discrimination and equality issues. It may be the case that within this narrow agenda individual business executives have developed effective ethical policies. There are two difficulties with advocating the adoption of the virtues by individual business executives, rather than the corporation as a whole. One is that what is ignored or denied is the ability of the corporation to outlive these particular executives. The corporation has the potential to continue in existence long after the departure of particular individuals to another corporate world or just another world. The second is, in Bauman's terms,[41] the adiaphorisation of individual business executives; their moral neutrality. This is caused by their distance from the consequences of their actions through the way in which the corporation is organised and the way in which they perceive their role in it. Even physical closeness as sometimes occurs between executive and employee is not sufficient to prevent this ethical distance from arising. The face of the employee (the other) becomes clouded by the totality of the organisation and its processes. Once this occurs then individual executives, freed from the moral demands of the other, are able to concentrate on purposive or procedural issues, technical events as Bauman describes them. Structures of ethical behaviour have to be inculcated into the corporation as a holistic and potentially perpetual[42] structure if they are to have any significant impact.

40 B Shaw, "Virtues for a Postmodern World" (1995) 5 *Bus Ethics Quart* 863 at 874.

41 Bauman's ideas such as moral neutrality and ethical distance began in *Modernity and the Holocaust* (Cambridge: Polity, 1989). There he seeks to explain why the Holocaust occurred and why it was not prevented. He does this in terms of the supression of human desire to be moral, the existence of ultra-efficient bureaucracies and the imposition of rules by those bureaucracies.

42 See P French, "Responsibility and the Moral Role of Corporate Entities" in T Donaldson and R E Freeman (eds), *Business as a Humanity* (New York, NY: Oxford University Press, 1994) p 88 at p 97. French is positively eulogistic about the role that corporations can play in sustaining "[t]he protection of civilization and the environment for future generations. It is certainly the case that corporations are in a position of infinite

This last point sets out a case for the corporation to be given a specific place within the Aristotelian structure but it does not necessarily mean that the place that the corporation should occupy is that of *polis*. This is inappropriate from both the perspectives of the corporation and wider society. As I alluded to earlier, corporations are currently engaged in presenting themselves as "citizens". To give effect to this desire would mean incorporating them not as the receiver of the good works of other citizens but as individuals within the structure. It may well be that the corporate perspective of what it is to be a citizen or a participating individual is not the same as that envisaged in current social and political discourse. However the corporate desire to be included at this level is an opportunity for corporate education to take place and so one not to be missed.

From a more general viewpoint the corporation that was seen as a *polis* would not be in a reciprocal relationship with its component parts such as employees, customers and providers of services. In Aristotelian terms the *polis* is constructed by what individuals put in and nothing is attached to what the *polis* puts out. The same points militate against the corporation being classed as a micro community in the way that Aristotle deals with villages and households. Aristotle holds out the idea of all associations being formed for some good purpose.[43] This has a certain resonance with the concession theory of incorporation;[44] corporations owe their existence to a concession of the state in allowing their formation. In the nineteenth century and earlier this was a way of viewing the idea of incorporated associations. It also had considerable factual accuracy; in the UK incorporation was allowed only by Royal Charter until 1844.[45] Adam Smith saw incorporated structures as being

lifespan and this point has a rhetorical and symbolic importance about it because it plays into one of the advantages of the corporate form over other forms of business association that law as a discipline emphasises. However the reality of fluctuating markets and business fortunes dictates that corporations may have an existence considerably shorter than a human lifetime. See on this point for a snapshot view of the first business associations to incorporate; L Shannon, "The First Five Thousand Limited Companies and their Duration" (1932) 3 *Economic History* 396, and G Robb, *White Collar Crime in Modern England* (Cambridge: Cambridge University Press, 1992) pp 24-30.

[43] This is the sentiment which forms the opening passage of Book 1of *P*, para 1252a1.

[44] See M Stokes, "Company Law and Legal Theory" in S Wheeler (ed), *The Law of the Business Enterprise* (Oxford: Oxford University Press, 1994) p 81 at p 88 for an explanation of this. For differences in the constitutionality of the concession being made by the State between the US and the UK, see W Goedecke, "Corporations and the Philosophy of Law" (1976) 10 *J of Value Inquiry* 81 at 84f.

[45] Companies Registration and Regulation Act 1844.

desirable only in circumstances where what was to be carried out by the corporation was a project with the greatest public utility requiring large-scale investment unlikely to be available from private venturers. Smith's examples of such industries were water supply, banking, insurance, and canal construction.[46] Since the availability of incorporated status as a mainly administrative process it is hard to assert that all corporations are formed for some good purpose. The Registrar of Companies would be unlikely to register a company which declared as its purpose the sale of an illegal drug or promotion of bare knuckle boxing but this aside the legality of a corporate purpose does not necessarily make it good in an Aristotelian sense.[47]

Corporations as Individuals

It would appear then that the only place for corporations within the Aristotelian structure is at the level of the individual. It is only this designation which places the corporation in a position where its desire to be a citizen can be realised. It would place corporations in the position to address the expectations of it formed by both the social and political discourses that are outlined in chapter one and where it can re-establish

[46] Ekelund and Tollison, "Mercantilist Origins of the Corporation" (1980) *Bell Journal of Economics* 715. The picture painted there is that Smith was afraid of the self-interested behaviour that incorporators would indulge in. A simpler picture which synchronises Smith's view on educational institutions and religious institutions with that on joint stock corporations is offered by A Ortmann, "The Nature and Causes of Corporate Negligence, Sham Lectures, and *Ecclesiastical* Indolence: Adam Smith on Joint-Stock Companies, Teachers, and Preachers" (1999) 31 *History of Political Economy* 297.

[47] Andrew Fraser sees the activities of the nineteenth century judiciary in relation to *ultra vires* actions as a guarantee that the corporation would be held to the terms of its charter and thus to some good public purpose. See A Fraser, "The Corporation as a Body Politic" (1983) 57 *Telos* 5 at 13. While that may have been true before incorporation was freely available, once it was ultra vires judgements concentrated on balancing creditor and investor protection. There is a considerable history of both judicial activism and commercial creativity to lessen the impact of ultra vires. See B Pettet, "The Stirring of Corporate Social Conscience" in M Freeman (ed), *Current Legal Problems* (Oxford: Oxford University Press, 1997) p 279 for an outline of these events. Since the Companies Act 1989s. 3A corporations have no longer been required to list all possible business activities in the Objects clause of their memorandum but to register instead as a General Commercial Company. In this case the object of the corporation is to carry on any trade or purpose whatsoever. The Company Law Review Steering Group in *Modern Company Law, The Strategic Framework* are of the view (see para 5.3.17) that the sec 3A reform has been little used because corporations fear that "it might not cover everything that directors might . . . wish . . . to do – eg participate in community initiatives or give a guarantee to another company ". The empirical source of this information is not given.

its legitimacy. To keep faith with the Aristotelian structure the corporation is required to have a soul and the capacity for rational thought. The issue of corporate "personhood" – whether it exists and what it means if it does exist – is one that the disciplines of both philosophy and law address. The 1844 legislation mentioned above conferred the status of "separate *legal* identity" on corporations which satisfied the administrative formalities for registration that it set out. The emphasis on *legal* here is mine, to draw attention to the fact that what is conferred on corporations by this intervention is a fairly narrow part of individuality. The separate legal individual nature of the corporation is played out in arenas such as taxation policy and law where the corporation is taxed on its profits just as corporate executives are taxed on their wages and shareholders on their dividends.

The conceptual nature of separate legal personality is often clouded by practical concerns which relate not to the separate nature of the corporation but to the idea of limited recourse or limited liability.[48] The two are linked in the sense that what attracts investors to the corporation is invariably the risk-limiting nature of limited recourse. It is this limited liability which is directly under attack in instances such as creditor actions for debt recovery in insolvency and liability for statements of financial support and credit worthiness between separate corporations within the same corporate group.[49] Essentially what is happening here is that the challenges that are made are ones couched in the specific that are then pulling against a more general economic rationale for limited liability. The separate nature of the corporation, distinct from those investing in it, frames the action but it is the limited liability afforded to the members that is under attack.[50]

[48] After much debate limited liability was made available to corporations in the Companies Act 1862. For a summary of these debates see S Wheeler (ed), *The Law of the Business Enterprise* (Oxford: Oxford University Press, 1994) pp 8-10.

[49] In my view the recent collection of essays edited by Ross Grantham and Charles Rickett illustrates the elision of the conceptual issue of corporate individuality with practical issues around the scope of limited recourse. In this very interesting collection entitled *Corporate Personality in the Twentieth Century* (Oxford: Hart Publishing, 1998) there are essays on the position of creditors *vis-a-vis* a limited liability structure and on corporate regulation but the actual issue of personality and individuality for the corporation merits barely a mention.

[50] The separate nature of personality on the one hand and limited recourse on the other is most clearly presented within legal scholarship by the Law and Economics movement. This does not engage at all with idea of separate personality as it is not relevant to its view of corporate structure, see the introductory notes to this book, but it does comment extensively on the limited recourse doctrine, see for example Easterbrook and

Where the disciplines of law and philosophy come together is in the consideration of the issue of responsibility and the corporation. The debate on this point within the legal academy stems primarily from the legal definitional requirements of some criminal offences. Most criminal offences require, in addition to an act which causes harm to another, a mental element; *mens rea*.[51] The criminal law is naturally individualistic in outlook[52] but its obsession with individualism encompasses only that of a human kind. This leads it to declare that in the case of a corporate perpetrator separate legal personality is not sufficient to allow *mens rea* to be fixed upon the corporation. The corporation for the purposes of *mens rea* becomes an aggregation[53] of its human components and there is then a search for a directing mind[54] – a human individual of sufficient seniority[55] to be the personification of the company. This is known as the identification theory. The perpetrator of a particular act or omission is not the object of the search. While

Fischel, "Limited Liability and the Corporation" (1985) *52 U Chi L Rev* 89 which is probably the most well known piece on this topic from this perspective.

51 The literal meaning of this is "guilty mind". According to Smith and Hogan, *Criminal Law*, 8th edn (London: Butterworths, 1996) p 56 "all serious and most minor offences require proof of a fault element . . . The traditional term for the state of mind which must be proved [is] "*mens* rea" (original emphasis).

52 C Clarkson, "Kicking Corporate Bodies and Damning Their Souls" (1996) 59 *MLR* 557 at 560.

53 The idea of the corporation as an aggregation of its parts, with parts conventionally taken to mean directors and shareholders only, forms another strand of the legal analysis of corporate existence along with the concession theory. For discussion of these positions in general terms see D Millon, "Theories of the Corporation" (1990) *Duke LJ* 201and M Hager, "Bodies Politic: The Progressive History of Organizational 'Real Entity' Theory" (1989) *Univ of Pittsburgh Law Rev* 575. It is not my intention to engage with the questions raised by this literature. My inquiry has a different starting point, namely can a corporation be considered an individual in a holistic sense, whereas the starting point from this perspective is what underscores the corporation's legal personality.

54 Denning LJ in *HL Bolton (Engineering) Co Ltd* v. *T J Graham & Sons Ltd* [1957] 1 QB 159 at 172; "[a] company may . . . be likened to a human body. It has a brain and a nerve centre which controls what it does. It also has hands which hold the tools and act in accordance with directions from the centre." This is interesting for its use of analogy but also because it clearly envisages those who bear the tools are not responsible for corporate acts.

55 *Tesco* v. *Nattrass* [1971] 2 WLR 1166 is an illustration of this point. The House of Lords decided by reference to a very simple model of company structure that the acts of a branch manager of a store could not be considered as acts of the company. See C Wells, *Corporations and Criminal Responsibility* (Oxford: Oxford University Press, 1993) at pp 109-10.

individual figures within particular corporations may not be without some influence over collective corporate strategy, the idea of a directing mind militates against a finding of liability except in the smallest of companies.[56] For example despite the finding of the Department of Transport inquiry into the sinking of the *Herald of Free Enterprise* that "from top to bottom the body corporate was infected with the disease of sloppiness" and that "[t]he failure on the part of the shore management to give proper and clear directions was a contributory cause of the disaster",[57] Turner J in a subsequent prosecution of the company for corporate manslaughter[58] was able to form the view that there was insufficient evidence of a directing mind for the charge to be put to the jury. Recent attempts to improve corporate responsibility have all centred around board level responsibility. The offence of corporate killing proposed by the Law Commission follows the structure of director responsibility by focussing on corporate conduct and whether it had fallen below what could have been expected.[59] This offence, as conceived by the Law Commission, has never found its way to the statute book[60] and it has now been overtaken by a Home Office paper.[61]

In short then, at the point where the recognition of corporate legal personhood should have the most impact on the existence of a

56 See for example *Kite and Others, Independent*, 9 Dec 1994.

57 Department of Transport, *The Merchant Shipping Act 1894, mv Herald of Free Enterprise*, Report of Court No 8074, (London: HMSO 1987) para 14.1.

58 *P&O European Ferries (Dover) Ltd* (1991) 93 Cr App R 73.

59 Legislating the Criminal Code: Involuntary Manslaughter, Law Commission Report No 237, 5 March 1996.

60 The offence was endorsed by the Home Secretary at the Labour Party Conference in October 1997, but as Mr Justice Scott Baker, the trial judge in the failed attempted prosecution of Great Western Trains for corporate manslaughter for their involvement in the Southall Rail Disaster of September 1997, pointed out this recommendation has still to progress to the statute book, see *The Times*, 3 July 1999. Interest in opening up the possibility of convicting corporations of this offence rose following the Paddington Rail Disaster in October 1999, see *Guardian*, 7 October 1999 for comments in support of this position attributed to Deputy Prime Minister John Prescott and Home Secretary Jack Straw. In *AG's Ref 2/99* the Court of Appeal confirmed that the identification theory was still the correct way to approach the issue of corporate responsibility for manslaughter in the absence of legislative intervention.

61 *Reforming the Law on Involuntary Manslaughter: The Government's Proposals*, May 2000. The Home Office paper accepts the broad outline of liability suggested by the Law Commission. In addition to pinning liability on the failure of management systems, the Home Office invited comments on whether any individual who could be shown to have had some influence on or responsibility for events should be subject to potential unlimited disqualification and in extreme cases criminal sanction.

corporate soul and the corporations's capacity for rational thought, law currently rejects these possibilities[62] in search of another individual – a senior figure within the corporation who possesses the directing mind. As will become clear, my own argument takes the opposite trajectory from conventional legal analysis on the point of intention and individuality. It is precisely because large corporations are large that I advocate their status as individual and responsible actors.

The most detailed discussion within philosophy of corporate responsibility is provided in the work of Peter French.[63] As a result, the position taken by other commentators coalesces around agreement or not with French's position. The common strand between the parallel debates in law and philosophy is their methodology. Both look at the internal decision-making structure of the company. For legal analysis this inquiry results in the vast majority of cases of individual action not being attributable to the company. For philosophical analysis the question is framed rather differently and there is a wider range of answers. For French the internal decision-making structure makes it not only possible to recognise the individuality of corporations as distinct from decision-making individuals but also to assert that corporations are moral actors in their own right capable of intentionality. He illustrates his position thus:

> "[a]lthough X voted to support the joining of the cartel because he was bribed to do so, X did not join the cartel, Gulf Oil Corporation joined the cartel. Consequently, we may say that X did something for which he should be held morally responsible, yet whether or not Gulf Oil Corporation should be held morally responsible for joining the cartel is a question that turns on issues that may be unrelated to X's having accepted a bribe".[64]

[62] The interpretative possibilities that law could adopt and the struggle that it in fact embarks upon are set out in L Moran, "Corporate Criminal Capacity: Nostalgia for Representation" (1992) 1 *Socio-Legal Studies* 371. There is a dearth of legally grounded scholarship which comments directly upon law's position on the corporate form. Wells is one such attempt, see n 55 *supra*. Moran, in a later piece than that already cited above, offers the most original comment to date on judicial and juristic attitudes towards the corporate form, see L Moran, "Eloquence and Imagery: Corporate Criminal Capacity and Law's Anthropomorphic Imagination" in P Rush, S McVeigh and A Young (eds), *Criminal Legal Doctrine* (Aldershot: Dartmouth, 1997) p 156.

[63] P French, *Collective and Corporate Responsibility* (New York, NY: Columbia University Press, 1984), "The Corporation as a Moral Person" (1979) 16 *Am Phil Quart* 207, "Responsibility and the Moral Role of Corporate Entities" in T Donaldson and R E Freeman (eds), *Business as a Humanity* (New York, NY: Oxford University Press, 1994) 88 .

[64] P French, "The Corporation as a Moral Person" (1979) 16 *Am Phil Quart* 207 at p 214.

While this example would not command universal approval[65] for the idea of a corporation having sufficient metaphysical standing to be considered an individual, there is one point on which I think French makes an unassailable case. It is one he shares with Robert Solomon: that "business is a social practice".[66] By this both Solomon and French are drawing attention to the cultural imbeddedness that corporations, particularly large ones, enjoy within current societal structures. As I explained in the first chapter, work practices and structures dictate to those in work and their families the shape of their lives.[67] To those out of work, corporations dictate quality of life through product pricing and the location of sales outlets and contribution to community infrastructure. It is this description of business activity which allows us to (re)personalise the corporation. This is fundamental to pinning on corporations an ethical position rooted in character and conduct. In chapter three I look at how corporations in some cases do deliver and in other cases might deliver on this type of agenda.[68]

I would add to this, in support of both French's and Solomon's position, the way in which our mental picture of corporate activity is drawn. We refer to corporations as forming and pursuing policies, as taking positions on issues and as having the ability to sponsor events for example. The larger corporations enjoy almost iconoclastic status, becoming synonymous with particular phrases such as "Never Knowingly Undersold", particular products and particular logos and colour arrangements. We know that corporations are vulnerable to adverse publicity in some circumstances and that past events can colour

[65] There are a range of criticisms to which the following references provide a fairly comprehensive overview: J Ladd, "Corporate Mythology and Individual Responsibility" (1984) 2 *Int J of Applied Philosophy*; R Manning, "Corporate Responsibility and Corporate Personhood" (1984) 3 *J of Bus Ethics* 77 and E Wolgast, *Ethics of an Artificial Person* (Stanford, CA: Stanford University Press, 1992) at pp 79-95.

[66] R Solomon, "Business and the Humanities: An Aristotelian Approach to Business Ethics" in T Donaldson and R E Freeman (eds), *Business as a Humanity* (New York, NY: Oxford University Press, 1994) p 45 at p 64. Solomon is one of the most well known proponents of the appropriateness of Aristotelian philosophy for business ethics. Solomon in the context referred to here considers the corporation to be an individual. However he also views the corporation itself as a *polis* like entity made up of individuals. This dual view is most clearly expressed in R Solomon, *Ethics and Excellence* (New York, NY: Oxford University Press, 1992)at p 57.

[67] D Smith, "Women, the Family and Corporate Capitalism" in F Stephenson (ed), *Women in Canada* (Toronto: General Publishing Company, 1977) p 1 at p 17.

[68] A Shah, "Corporate Governance and Business Ethics" (1996) 5 *Bus Ethics, A European Rev* 225.

corporate policy for years to come.[69] It may be individual corporate executives who are recognising the legitimacy crisis that is facing the corporate sector, but it is individual corporations that are seeking citizenship for example. As the corporate investment base becomes ever wider through the growth of institutional investment and, with the exception of family-held corporations and small incorporated partnerships, shareholders and directors are separate individuals, corporations have a case that they should be seen in a political sense[70] as individual actors.[71] This must be the next stage in the analysis begun by Berle and Means.[72] They identified a separation between ownership and control and as a result charged corporate managers with creating responsible corporations. In an era of flexibility, technological advancement and job mobility, corporations themselves bear this responsibility[73] as individuals.

Aristotelian Governance and Corporate Governance

Aristotle confronts a similar dilemma to that addressed in current social and political thinking – what is the role for the individual? The answer for Aristotle is that the individual has, as the ultimate goal, participation in the *polis.* The individual obtains entry to the *polis* through a series of layered communities such as households (*oikia*) and then villages (*kome*). This idea of building a community in this way has much in common with Etzioni's position, to which I referred in the

[69] Almost exactly the contrary view is expressed by Thomas Donaldson in *Corporations and Morality* (Englewood Cliffs, NJ: Prentice Hall, 1982) at p 20. For Donaldson the fact that corporations share some characteristics with human beings "is inadequate to establish moral agency". My point is that irrespective of this corporations are too large and significant not to be in some sense moral actors.

[70] This view should be compared to that of Fraser (see the text accompanying n 82 below for a detailed account) who has quite a different method of creating corporate political involvement and accountability within an Aristotelian structure.

[71] M Bovens, "The Corporate Republic: Complex Organisations and Citizenship" in E Christodoulidis (ed), *Communitarianism and Citizenship* (Aldershot: Ashgate, 1998) p 158 at pp 160-2.

[72] A Berle and G Means, *The Modern Corporation and Private Property* (New York, NY: Macmillan, 1932).

[73] The question of corporations bearing responsibility as individuals has provoked some interesting discussions of what sanctions could accompany a failure to take responsibility. An interesting discussion of this and a review of the literature can be found in L Dunford and A Ridley, "'Soul to be Damned, No Body to be Kicked': Responsibility, Blame and Corporate Punishment" (1996) 24 *Int J of Soc of Law* 1 at 8f.

previous chapter. The difficulty with Etzioni's idea is that whereas Aristotle is looking at a homogeneous society and common interests, Etzioni is not. Aristotle is of value in this context because he provides a way of persuading individuals to look beyond their own position to that of others. The position that Aristotle requires individuals to take in this layering-up exercise of pursuing life through the virtues is very different from Etzioni's. Etzioni is using layering-up as a way of arriving at common values. *Eudaimonia* can not be found in any of these communities as they lack complete *autarkeia*. This can only be found within the *polis*. The term *autarkeia* is usually translated as "self-sufficiency".[74] This conjurs up images of Felicity Kendall and *The Good Life*.[75] There is a sense in which this is what Aristotle means. He uses *autarkeia* in the context of a "territory" being able to produce a variety of crops and being large enough to allow the people living there to enjoy a comfortable life.[76] However he uses the same word in a rather different and more profound sense to describe the need for individuals to embrace community life. In Aristotle's view an individual who asserts *autarkeia* without embracing community life must be either a "beast" or a "god".[77] *Autarkeia* is a community good not an individual virtue. My translation of *autarkeia* is, in an attempt to link the corporate world of the twenty-first century with that of fifth century BC Athens, "sufficient". "Sufficient" to me sums up the Aristotelian position of distributing the goods necessary for the good life and is also a moniker for twenty-first century corporate existence – there is room for a greater populace to participate in corporate life both financially and discursively.[78] In sum then I place corporations at the level of the individual citizen and would seek to encourage them on the level of individual actors to participate, along with the voluntary sector and government, in a *polis* type community. The idea of participation being

[74] *Autarkes* is usually translated throughout *P* in this way. However as Meikle points out a better translation at times may be independence as a first order meaning. See S Meikle, *Aristotle's Economic Thought* (Oxford: Oxford University Press, 1995) at pp 44-5.

[75] A BBC Television situation comedy from the 1970's the central theme of which was a household run on self-suficiency in terms of the material concerns of life: food, power and clothes etc.

[76] *P*1326b26.

[77] *P*1253a25.

[78] In *P*1256b31-2 Aristotle draws attention to household management issues and goes on in *P*1256b40-1259a37 to describe how money became a medium of exchange and the dangers and undesirability of continuous accumulation of wealth.

the pinnacle to which the best citizens aspire, is ideal for encouraging corporations to undertake the role of participation that the Third Way maps out for them. It would effectively ensure that corporations saw themselves as contributing to the accumulated good of all other individuals and not as in some way hosted by a wider society and yet separate from it.[79]

Aristotle discusses the forms of government which he deems most appropriate to the *polis* and the ones which he sees as inappropriate. My use of Aristotle centres more on his moral philosophy than his political philosophy. However a brief exposition of his political philosophy is relevant for two reasons. First as already indicated, for Aristotle, moral and political philosophy were part of an integral presentation. In the realm of moral philosophy an individual pursues the virtues, and successful pursuit of the virtues results in *eudaimonia*. There is then a seamless transfer to the realm of political philosophy where ultimate *eudaimonia* is political and social participation in the *polis*. Political participation must necessarily be on the basis of interaction with one of Aristotle's favoured forms of government. This structuring of personal moral development leading into political philosophy can be seen in the opening paragraphs of *P* book VII[80] for example. Second, Aristotle's ideal forms of government for the *polis* have occasioned difficulties for neo-Aristotelians. Aristotle favoured three forms of government; government by an aristocracy, by monarchy and by the polity.[81] In opposition to these three favoured forms of government he sets up three corresponding forms of which he disapproves; oligarchy, tyranny and democracy.

Of the most favoured forms Aristotle's preference was for government by an aristocracy. An illustration of aristocratic government in the Aristotelian sense is provided by the scholarship of Andrew Fraser, who, coincidentally, has developed his model in the field of corporate governance and accountability.[82] Fraser's idea for corporate governance

[79] J Morse, "The Missing Link between Virtue Theory and Business Ethics" (1999) 16 *J of Applied Phil* 47.

[80] *P* 1323a14-1323b36, see the discussion in M Nichols, *Citizens and Statesmen* (Totowa, NJ: Rowman and Littlefield, 1992) pp 125-51.

[81] By polity Aristotle means constitutional government but not democracy. His idea of constitutional government is government by the masses for the common interest. He is of the view that in practice the masses will be represented by one or a few individuals of particular character, often with a military connection, see *P* 1279a40.

[82] A Fraser, *Reinventing Aristocracy: The Constitutional Reformation of Corporate Governance* (Aldershot: Dartmouth, 1998).

is that it should be undertaken by active and committed shareholders. These active and committed shareholders will constitute an aristocracy, a civic elite. In order to encourage participation and debate in shareholder senates, voting should be distributed not as part of the rights attached to shares but as a personal right of each investor. Fraser, in true Aristotelian spirit, has no interest in constructing an aristocracy from the largest or wealthiest shareholders[83] but from those that are committed to the governance project he outlines; the re-creation within corporations of a sense of political responsibility and accountability. Thus an aristocracy is constructed from those who come forward and present themselves as committed citizens. The values that this aristocracy will pursue will be those that a free people would expect from leaders in business, politics and intellectual life.[84] Fraser's ideas may not accord with those who perceive the reform of corporate governance as only being a worthwhile enterprise if it were part of a wider dismantling of capitalism but they are significantly more radical than those which suggest greater involvement for institutional investors.[85] Aristocracy in the sense in which the word is used in current parlance equates to Aristotle's oligarchy.

Aristotle's precise reasoning in favour of or in condemnation of a particular form of government is beyond my immediate interests. Aristotle's ideas for governance were/are considered suitable by commentators for third century BC city state Athens. The difficulty for neo-Aristotelians has been the criticism levelled at them for failing to develop a model of democratic positions and liberal values suitable for a twentieth century AD world within their moral philosophy.[86] The restrictive nature of Aristotelian governance models is used as the basis of a Marxist critique that equates neo-Aristotelianism to neo-conservatism. This neo-conservatism is considered to be an abuse of

[83] Fraser, *ibid*, (at p 85) does see the opportunity to participate being triggered by a minimum property holding in the corporation. However he does not give details and this does not appear to be a major component of his position

[84] There are difficulties with Fraser's approach at both the micro level of corporate law and at the macro-level of value selection and accommodation of different cultural traditions. For a discussion of these problems and the identification of others see S Wheeler, "Fraser and the Politics of Corporate Governance" (1999) 26 *JLS* 240.

[85] In chapter 1 I referred at length to the various reports into corporate governance both from the corporate sector itself and from bodies such as the DTI.

[86] See for example the criticisms directed at MacIntyre's *After Virtue* and Galston's *Justice and the Human Good* by Slote in M Slote, "Virtue Ethics and Democratic Values" (1993) 24 *J of Social Philosophy* 5 at 6.

Aristotelian thought and responsible for models of political thought which reduce political ethics of institutional practice to the realm of private morality.[87] As the description of Fraser's model for corporate governance demonstrates it does not necessarily follow that reliance upon Aristotle's preferred models of governance will result in a system that eschews radicalism. However the connection between perceived narrow and elitist forms of governance and individual ethics of character certainly did not assist in trying to ensure that Aristotelian thought was maintained as a primary reference point in moral philosophy prior to its recent resurgence.

2. HISTORY: CHARACTER, DUTY AND CATHOLICISM

Virtue and Character in Aristotle

Aristotelian philosophy advocates that an individual should live life according to the virtues and Aristotle duly provides a list of the virtues: courage, temperance, generosity, style, pride, ambition, gentleness, truthfulness, wittiness, friendliness, modesty, good nature, righteous anger. There are at least several individual virtues in this list that contemporary society, in so far as it is possible to point to a generalised shared position, would not consider merited the title of virtue, for example, pride. In the same way there are also others that would probably figure as virtues in any age, for example, truthfulness. Absent from Aristotle's list are any of the virtues that we would traditionally associate with the Judeo-Christian world and other religions as well – repentance, remorse, forgiveness to name but a few. Given the stress that Aristotle laid upon battlefield courage it is unlikely that he would have regarded moral courage ending perhaps in humility rather than physical victory as a virtue. However the key point here is not the virtues themselves but the structure for life of which they are part. Of greater significance to my mind at this point is the "agent-centred" teleological situation of the virtues. In chapter three I put forward a list of what might be considered the virtues for our age – the era of post post-Fordism – taken from the various positions identified in chapter one. There I use the work of Alisdair MacIntyre as the methodology for identifying contemporary virtues.

87 H Schaedelbach, "What is Neo-Aristotelianism" (1987/8) 7 *Praxis International* 225 at 235 and G Giorgini, "Crick, Hampshire and MacIntyre, or does an English Speaking Neo-Aristotelianism Exist?" (1989/9) 9 *Praxis International* 249.

I use "agent-centred" here as the counter-point to "act-centred" ethics. By this I mean that what is important is not a particular individual act but the character of the doer of the act. The virtues are qualities of character[88] that can be learned and practiced.[89] They are not ethical principles of themselves nor can actions done in their name possess an ethical character. Virtues can be taught and inculcated, and indeed must be, which is not the case with compliance with pre-ordained principles or "best-off" solutions. This position is essentially anti-Kantian[90] and anti-utilitarian,[91] both of which are philosophies that are traditionally classed as act-centred approaches to ethics. The apparent simplicity of these propositions makes a neat, if basic ideological point, and, as one would expect, ignores a huge range of debate in between. One of the major questions for contemporary ethics is the extent to which both Kantian[92] and utilitarian ethics are capable of addressing the issue of character while maintaining a strong foothold in their traditional places.[93] Richard Hare,[94] for example, engages with moral virtues such as courage and perseverance while drawing heavily upon Kantian and utilitarian ideas for his framework. Rawls[95] uses components of character such as tolerance and respect within a basically Kantian structure.

A common complaint amongst those who are not supporters of virtue ethics is that the basic approach of virtue ethics is not certain enough to enable anyone to identify anybody else as virtuous nor does it

[88] *NE* 1105b28.

[89] *NE* 1103a33. According to this passage which appears at the beginning of book 2, virtue is of two types: intellectual and moral. Intellectual virtue is possessed as a result of birth and honed by teaching, moral virtue can be acquired through habit.

[90] The definition of this position I would give as obeying the moral law which itself is founded on a universal and impartial law of rationality.

[91] I take as my definition for this acts that are done if they are ones that give the best outcome for as many people as possible.

[92] For an account of how character can be interpreted, to an extent, within the Kantian position, see B Herman, "Making Room for Character" in S Engstrom and J Whiting (eds), *Aristotle, Kant and the Stoics* (Cambridge: Cambridge University Press, 1996) p 36 especially at pp 51-3 and G F Munzel, *Kant's Conception of Moral Character: The "Critical" Link of Morality, Anthropology and Reflexive Judgment* (Chicago: University of Chicago Press, 1999) especially chs 2 and 3.

[93] For a brilliantly clear overview of these debates see the introductory essay in R Crisp and M Slote (eds), *Virtue Ethics* (Oxford: Oxford University Press, 1997) p 1.

[94] R Hare, *Moral Thinking: Its Levels, Method and Point* (Oxford: Oxford University Press, 1981).

[95] J Rawls, *Political Liberalism* (New York, NY: Columbia University Press, 1993).

assist in answering the question "What is the right thing to do?" in particular hard cases. In other words this is an attempt to push towards act-centred rather than agent-centred approaches to ethics. In many ways this is an accurate summary of virtue ethics but rather than undermine the concept, it instead demonstrates its potential as an approach to many of the dilemmas that confront us. The work of Rosalind Hursthouse[96] is pertinent here. Hursthouse takes as one of her examples the debates around abortion surrounding the position of the foetus and the position of the carrier. In her view by considering the different motives and thinking behind decision-making virtue ethics can be used to examine particular actions and to form moral rules for guidance. Abortion is a classic hard case in which there are likely to be sharply conflicting views. By setting out the approach virtue ethics would take in such a situation Hursthouse is answering Bauman's question posed in chapter one about how the individual can be moral when exercising the very difficult choice between good and evil.[97] Virtue ethics requires individuals to inquire into the sort of people they need to have become or the type of characters they must develop in order to be able examine the spectrum of choices available. The moral voice will come not from a system that provides right answers but from one which allows the construction of and the playing out of a series of different propositions. This assistance in the process of value construction and the exercise of choice would help Jared's school friends, whose dilemmas and difficulties were explained in chapter one, to rebuild their world.[98]

For corporations a character-based approach has the advantageous effect of distancing rights-based dialogues but the disadvantage of insisting upon consideration of the various possible outcomes of particular acts for example.[99] The teleological nature of the Aristotelian position comes from the stress laid upon the importance of the end result/goal of an activity and of the motive that underlies the doing of particular acts. The doing of a virtuous act does not make the doer virtuous unless the doer did the act for its own sake and not resentfully or as part of an exercise to enhance reputation.[100] At this point

[96] R Hursthouse, "Virtue Theory and Abortion" in R Crisp and M Slote, *supra* n 93 at p 217 and "Applying Virtue Ethics" in R Hursthouse, G Lawrence and W Quinn (eds), *Virtues and Reasons* (Oxford: Oxford University Press, 1995) at p 57.

[97] See ch 1, n 53 and the text *infra*.

[98] See ch 1, nn 57-62 and the text *infra*.

[99] T White, *Business Ethics* (New York, NY: Macmillan, 1993) 14.

[100] *NE* 1105b5, see also R Audi, "Acting from Virtue" (1995) 104 *Mind* 449 at 455.

Aristotelian philosophy enters an on-going debate within business ethics scholarship: whether the intention behind an act of corporate social conscience should matter as long as the outcome of the act was broadly acceptable. Adoption of Aristotelian principles would end this debate. A stance such as this would be very useful for moving corporations away from the "feel good" factor obtained from an act of social responsiveness structured by competition and into a position where there was more effective participation in the political and social project identified earlier. The whole point is that there is no underlying principle about what ought to be done[101] only the question about what individual actors should become. This would allow corporations to assert that profit was merely one objective that was held along with others.

Part of living life through the virtues is contained in making a well-judged choice between two extremes. This is often expressed as the choice between virtue and vice, or realising the mean. Each virtue is a mean in the sense that it occupies the middle ground between two vices. For example courage is the mean between cowardice and ill-considered rashness. But over and above the mean that each virtue represents, the individual pursuing the virtues is required to follow the mean ground between excess performance and falling short.[102] Over-zealous performance in relation to a virtue is no more meritorious than under performance or non-performance. The mean is a relative standard for each individual to determine in relation to each virtue, for example what might be cowardice for a professional trained soldier might be quite appropriate behaviour for an ordinary citizen. As a relative standard it would permit corporations to weigh community contributions against the need for long term investment in plant for example. It would permit the resources committed to the wider society to reflect the level of commercial success over any given period. Most importantly it would allow the corporate entity to set its own standards for contribution to society against the backdrop of the accumulated choices of individuals collected together in the *polis*.

[101] The issue of the importance of motive to Aristotle is often used to emphasis the difference with the Kantian principled approach to actions which asserts that the doer acts out of a sense of duty. However there is a school of thought which advocates that this is an inaccurate reading of both of them and that they are far closer to each other in putting forward an idea of moral motivation, see R Louden, *Morality and Moral Theory* (New York, NY: Oxford University Press, 1992) p 295 and C Korsgaard, "From Duty and for the Sake of the Noble in S Engstrom and J Whiting (eds), *Rethinking Happiness and Duty* (Cambridge: Cambridge University Press, 1997) p 152.

[102] *NE* 1006b36.

Aristotle gives no account of the process of practical reasoning by which an individual might construct a system of thinking in order to determine what it might be desirable to do in any given situation.[103] In book six of *NE* he underscores this absence by asserting that intuition, deliberation and experience are what result in an ability to deal with situations.[104] Aristotle's emphasis on the character-based individual nature of ethics, his idea of an individual searching out and finding virtue, and then within that a personal mean, could have been constructed with the current corporate legitimacy crisis in mind. The role that Aristotle gives to personal development and choice[105] takes us back to one of the core issues raised by life in an era of post post-Fordism – the need to accommodate and balance both the individual interest and the collective interest. Aristotle's approach to human existence through ethics can take us towards the Third Way vision by preserving ideas of hope and individual destiny. The demise of both right and left political positions has left the individual in the position of facing up to individual responsibility and the idea of making a wider social commitment.[106] Aristotle's scheme offers a way forward which embraces both these positions.

The Rebirth of Virtue Ethics

The intellectual renaissance of virtue ethics, with the assistance of a generous amount of hindsight, is generally attributed to an article by Elizabeth Anscombe in 1958.[107] The article has become something of a *cause célèbre* and is widely cited and extracted. I am going to examine the arguments that Anscombe put forward in 1958 to promote virtue ethics and I also wish to tie the rise of populist interest in ancient philosophy and the works of Aristotle in particular to this. My suggestions are that the demise of religiously derived duty-based positions and the

[103] See G Striker, *Essays on Hellenistic Epistemology and Ethics* (Cambridge: Cambridge University Press, 1996) at 170-176. The particular chapter in which these pages are contained was first published as "Greek Ethics and Moral Theory" in *The Tanner Lectures on Human Values* (1988) IX p 181.

[104] See *NE* 1141a33-1143a13

[105] On the importance of choice within the structure of virtue ethics, see D Cates, *Choosing to Feel: virtue, friendship and compassion for friends* (Notre Dame, IN: University of Notre Dame Press, 1997).

[106] R Aronson, "Hope After Hope?" (1999) 66 *Social Research* 471 at 487f.

[107] G E Anscombe, "Modern Moral Philosophy" (1958) XXXIII *Philosophy* 1 and the comments of D Leal, "The Bearer of Virtue" (1999) 12 *Studies in Christian Ethics* 1.

apparent security that the ancients offer in times of political and social change are also key to the rebirth of interest in virtue ethics. Anscombe makes three points. I will deal with her final point first so as not to disrupt the lineality of my own argument. Anscombe's opening salvo is that she disagrees with the arguments of modern moral philosophy and the position that it takes. In 1958 this meant that her disagreement was with the Oxbridge version of Kantian rule and principle-dominated moral philosophy from G E Moore and Henry Sidgwick[108] onwards. Indeed Sidgwick is the object of specific criticism by her.[109]

Anscombe's trenchant criticism of Sidgwick ignores the work of T H Green and his disciples.[110] They conducted a lengthy flirtation with ideas that were diametrically opposed to Sidgwick and in fact much closer to those of Anscombe herself. Green, by all accounts, was a popular and influential[111] figure in terms of his intellectual positioning to the extent that much of his work was published posthumously in 1882. Green's intellectual stance was not unlike that taken by modern virtue ethicists. He was clearly influenced by Hegel and Kant, but, in a pure Aristotelian[112] sense, he also saw individual character as a building block towards the idea of a broader collective social responsibility

[108] For an account of the work of Sidgwick see M Walker, *Moral Understandings* (London: Routledge, 1998) pp 30-46.

[109] Anscombe is supported in her view by Jenks. Jenks' account of the Oxford philosophical school is that up to 1940 there was no philosophy of ethics other than versions of Kantianism at the level of research and as personal belief systems. The matter of what was taught as student texts was very different, see C Jenks, "T H Green, The Oxford Philosophy of Duty and the English Middle Class" (1977) 28 *Brit J of Soc* 481 at 485.

[110] Anscombe does not reference Green in her 1958 piece.

[111] R Jenkyns, *The Victorians and the Ancient Greeks* (Oxford: Blackwells, 1980) at p 247 describes Green as the "most influential philosophical voice in Oxford during his short life"

[112] This is not an uncontroversial statement. Thomas indicates that in his view Green was little interested in or engaged by Greek philosophy. He cites Nettleship's *Memoir* of Green as evidence for this, see G Thomas, *The Moral Philosophy of T H Green* (Oxford: Oxford Universitiy Press, 1987) p 39. However almost exactly the contrary position is put forward by Turner, *The Greek Heritage in Victorian Britain* (New Haven, CN: Yale University Press, 1981) at p 365. Perhaps this controversy can be diluted somewhat by accepting the influence of Hegel over Green (although Thomas also downplays the significance of Hegel to Green at pp 45-54 in comparison to the view of Robert Murray for example, see *Studies in the English Social and Political Thinkers of the Nineteenth Century vol II* (Cambridge: Heffer & Son, 1929) at pp 280-304) and the influence of Aristotle over Hegel, see A Wood, *Hegel's Ethical Thought* (Cambridge: Cambridge University Press, 1990) at p 214.

expressed through community. Green's reference points are to social institutions such as marriage and the family which do not enjoy the same privileged status in contemporary society as they did in Victorian Britain. However Green also advocated that education and so the possibility of living Aristotle's good life should be extended to a much wider class of people than Aristotle's aristocracy. Green recognised that the broader life experience of more than a city state would create loyalties and desires above immediate physical or geographical community.[113] Green's engagement was with Aristotle's ideas and structures rather than his specific institutions. This, in my view, places Aristotle and Green on a continuum that ends in the world of choice and uncertainty that Giddens and Bauman explore.

Turner[114] credits Green with giving intellectual shape to the ideas of a growing number of intellectuals who wanted "social reform without socialism".[115] Their reasons for wanting social reform were rooted in the economic changes that were taking place and the social unrest and political discourse that accompanied these changes.[116] This is a situation, in fact, not unlike the one that we are currently facing. In very general terms, by the time of Green's death, economic growth in Victorian Britain was declining or at least stagnating after a period of rapid industrialisation.[117] The move from rural and aristocratic capital

[113] T H Green, *Prolegomena to Ethics* ed A C Bradley (Oxford: Clarendon Press, 1894) see in particular paras 253-9.

[114] *Supra* n 112.

[115] The conventional view of Green's followers has always been that they divided into right and left positions depending on the level of state involvement they saw as necessary for social reform, see A Vincent and R Plant, *Philosophy, Politics and Citizenship: The Life and Thought of the British Idealists* (Oxford: Oxford University Press, 1984). However the similarities of the so-called right and left poles of Green disciples; the need to change the social environment, a desire for neither non-interventionist laissez-faire politics nor collectivism are pointed out by Carter, see M Carter, "Ball, Bosanquet and the Legacy of T H Green" (1999) XX *History of Political Thought* 674 at 676.

[116] A typical example of this movement would be *Fabian Essays* published in 1889 by Bernard Shaw, Sidney Webb et al. This proved popular among middle class socialists for some years.

[117] It is a contentious issue whether the late Victorian economy was actually in decline or whether it performed as well as it could given the boundaries within which it operated. For a review of the principal arguments in the field and a spirited assertion that there is more to the concepts of industrialisation and economic decline than the discipline of economics can tell us, a view with which I concur wholeheartedly, see M Wiener, *English Culture and the Decline of the Industrial Spirit 1850-1980* (Cambridge: Cambridge University Press, 1981) 159-70.

to industrial capital was continuing, accelerated by the ravages of death duties[118] and the rejection of absentee landlordism in Ireland, a traditional source of income for the landed aristocracy.[119] By the time Edwardian Britain had succeeded Victorian Britain this change in capital bases was expressed in the reform of the House of Lords and increased spending on defence. At the same time the effects of laissez-faire capitalist enterprise created pressure to combat the associated effects of an unstable labour market and consequent poverty. The connection between poverty and capitalism was not one recognised by Green. Instead he saw poverty as the result of poor education and character deficiency. However he also saw the need for a softened moralised capitalism which did not prevent industrial development.[120] This is an observation similar to that made throughout the responsive political rhetoric of the Third Way that I set out earlier. The response to the uncertainties of employment and poverty in Edwardian Britain came in the social reforms of the liberal governments of this era.[121] In the context of what had previously been a very limited state this was a response every bit as ideologically different from what had gone before as the present promotion of corporate, voluntary and state partnerships and the reinvigoration of ideas of community. Thus my point is that in a time of previous similar change and upheaval the intellectual resort had been to the philosophy of Aristotle and in particular to the configuration of the relationship between the individual and the collective. As A C Bradley the editor of Green's posthumously published *Prolegomena to Ethics*[122] noted "[w]ith every step in the moralising of politics and the socialising of morals, something of Greek excellence is won back."[123]

[118] Death Duties were first introduced by the Finance Act 1894, ss. 1-15, ch 30, 57 and 58 Vict.

[119] The work of David Cannadine is the most obvious reference point here, see *The Decline and Fall of the British Aristocracy* (London: Pan Macmillan, 1992).

[120] See A Vincent, "A Moralised Capitalism and an Ethical State" in A Vincent (ed), *The Philosophy of T H Green* (Aldershot: Gower, 1986) p 1 at pp 13-20. The most pertinent passages of Green's original work can be found in R Nettleship (ed), *Works of Thomas Hill Green Vol II Philosophical Works* R Nettleship (London: Longmans, Green & Co, 1906) paras 227-32 and 531-2.

[121] For example the Insurance Act of 1911 and the Old Age Pensions legislation of 1908.

[122] (Oxford: Clarendon Press, 1884).

[123] A C Bradley, "Aristotle's Conception of the State" in E Abbot (ed), *Hellenica* (London: Rivingtons, 1880) p 181 at p 241.

The Triumph of Virtue Ethics

One of Anscombe's other points is relatively easily dealt with. She took objection to the idea that modern moral philosophy felt able to provide an answer to the question, "how an unjust man is a bad man?"[124] without first developing a philosophy of psychology in order to determine the intersection between virtue and character. Her plea for the development of a psychological element to ethics has gone largely unheeded.[125] Her final point was that the concepts of obligation and duty of themselves carried no moral sense but that the way in which the "*law*" (her emphasis and for this read legal and by this she means a moral, natural law) conception of ethics had developed them and imposed particular meanings meant that an ethics structured in this way should be discouraged.[126]

This last point encapsulates the position that modern moral philosophy finds itself in but more than that it raises the question that many intellectuals trying to theorise the social and political changes that have taken place in recent years are faced with. For some the answer will lie in a more overtly political arena than the one in which I situate my answers. Their answers will lie within the spectrum of right and left politics rather than outside as my acceptance of the end of "right and left" political positions places me. Anscombe's demand that concepts of obligation and duty based upon "law" pass out of moral philosophy has largely occurred in my view. I offer two explanations for my position on this. I use both of them to explain why it is that I consider virtue ethics to be not only currently fashionable but also the key philosophical tool for moving towards an inculcation of Third Way policies into corporate behaviour. My understanding of Anscombe's complaint is that what she was advocating was the end of a conception of ethics that was based upon a rationalist natural law. This natural law is derived not from faith but from a position situated squarely within the Enlightenment tradition of conceiving separately of the divine on the one hand and the secular on the other with a meeting arranged only through pure reason. This did not exclude the existence of God. For Kant, for example, although morality could be shown to be objectively

[124] Anscombe, *supra* n. 107, at pp 3-4.

[125] Even those who have looked at developing a psychological perspective have questioned its appropriateness to character based virtue ethics, placing it instead within a more Kantian act-centred philosophy, see J Doris, "Persons, Situations and Virtue Ethics" (1998) 32 *Nous* 504.

[126] Anscombe, *supra* n. 107 at pp 6-9.

ascertained through reason, God was necessary to make it possible for human existence to know the highest good and to adjudicate between "virtue and experienced happiness".[127] It is this that has led to Kant being hailed as one of the greatest "Christian moralists".[128] There is a sense in which the medievalists had already made this separation[129] but the difference is the type of worlds that each approach was confronting. This is particularly clear from the work of Aquinas, which I touch on in more detail below. Aquinas' concern was the world of the self, the Enlightenment project was to relate the self to the wider world in which science and rationality had a large part to play.[130]

Kant is the very embodiment of the Enlightenment tradition and in this criticism Anscombe must be seen as attacking Kantian moral philosophy and in particular its rejection of character and virtue and its replacement of this with a concept of duty instead.[131] Expressed in this way the impression created is that the use of science and the search for rationality as an underpinning for everything including faith[132] was the death knell for virtue ethics. Indeed any consultation with the works of Joseph Butler,[133] a contemporaneous critic of the Enlightenment

[127] M Moore, "Good without God" in R George (ed), *Natural Law, Liberalism and Morality* (Oxford: Oxford University Press, 1996) p 221at p 222 and in particular the references contained therein at n 8 and at p 247.

[128] A Geary, "Faith, Love and a Christianity to Come" in P Oliver, S Douglas Scott and V Tadros (eds), *Faith in Law* (Oxford: Hart Publishing, 2000) p 53 at p 59.

[129] M D'Arcy, "St Thomas Aquinas" in J Macmurray (ed), *Some Makers of the Modern Spirit* (New York, NY: BLP, 1933) p 45 at p 55

[130] J Macmurray in *supra* n 129 at p 179.

[131] For a further explanation of the rejection of the Enlightenment project see S Salkever, *Finding the Mean* (Princeton, NJ: Princeton University Press, 1994) at p 106f. For an account of how postmodern and communitarian critics deal with the Enlightment see R Wokler, "The Enlightenment Project and its Critics" (1997) 58 *Poznan Studies in the Philosophy of the Sciences and the Humanities* 13 at 13-24. The remainder of Wokler's piece (24-30) deals with what he considers to be an inadequate expression of the Enlightenment by these critics.

[132] Kant was a committed Lutherean. However Christian philosophers and theologians often see his work as difficult to accommodate within Christian theology because of the way in which he constructs human knowledge, see for example N Wolterstorff, "Is it Possible and Desirable for Theologians to Recover from Kant" (1998) 14 *Moral Philosophy* 8. For spirited responses see J Privette, "Must Theology Re-Kant" (1999) XL *Hey J* 166 and C Firestone, "Kant and Religion: Conflict or Compromise" (1999) 35 *Rel Studies* 151.

[133] T Roberts (ed), *Butler's Fifteen Sermons Preached at the Rolls Chapel and a Dissertation on the Nature of Virtue* (London: SPCK, 1970).

project, or Alasdair MacIntyre,[134] its leading present critic, would confirm this.[135] However as Schneewind[136] points out, of as much if not more, significance was the emergence of Christianity and its philosophy of duty to God.[137] In Christian thinking duty to God is expressed in terms of obedience to a divine law. Ironically it is the decline of the cultural importance of both Christianity in this form and rationality as pre-eminent which forms, in my view, one reason for Anscombe's plea being rendered into actuality. Science and its relentless march towards the solving of the insoluble, the curing of the incurable, the creation of the completely new to order through genetic modification, and the reproduction of the old through cloning has led to a backlash against the rational. Earlier I offered a reading of consumer groups in which I constructed them as informed by the information structures offered by globalisation and technology, and thus able to select products on the basis of environmental and human rights concerns. To this I would add a general public concern to reclaim and ultimately to control the power of science by rejecting things such as genetically modified food for example.[138]

[134] A MacIntyre, *After Virtue: A Study in Moral Theory*, 2nd edn (London: Duckworth, 1985).

[135] This is not suggest that because Butler and MacIntyre identify a common enemy that their conclusions are the same, on this point see J Worthen, "Joseph Butler on the Enemies of Virtue" (1999) 12 *Studies in Christian Ethics* 48.

[136] J Schneewind, "The Misfortunes of Virtue" (1990) 101 *Ethics* 42 at 44. Natural lawyers from Grotius onwards have tended to take the existence of God and obligation to God, if not as a given, then certainly as an end point, see J Finnis, *Natural Law and Natural Rights* (Oxford: Oxford University Press, 1980) at p 44 and then at p 407. The idea of a natural law free from religious conviction is the province in the main of political liberals outside the philosophical and jurisprudential natural law tradition. Moore's essay cited above is a dynamic and very interesting exception to this.

[137] Slote and Crisp in their introduction to *Virtue Ethics*, *supra* n 93 at p 18, raise the position of love in relation to Schneewind's reading of Christianity. Christian love, I would argue, is the duty to love God which Christianity insists is displayed through love of friends, strangers and good works, ie love is the subordinate of duty. My position is expressed with much greater clarity than I have managed in A Martin (ed), *Beyond Fear* (Edinburgh: St Andrews Press, 1998) pp 96-102. The sentiments there are what I was trying to express here. Any inconsistencies should be resolved in favour of Andrew Martin and the "After Socialism?" Group.

[138] The present Government has recently agreed to a three year moratorium on the growing of genetically modified crops. The Ministry of Agriculture Food and Fisheries has put out a fact sheet to deal with common questions and areas of concern, such as who can place genetically modified food in the food chain and the protective measures that are in place for consumers to warn them of its presence. See also K Walley et al, "UK Consumer Attitudes Concerning Environmental Issues Impacting the Agrifood Industry" (2000) *Bus Strat Enviro* 355.

There is now a growing movement in which emotions are placed outside the rational in a positive sense.

The response to the death of Princess Diana is a very good example of this. To the people who put flowers outside Kensington Palace and who lined the roads from London to Northampton on the day of her funeral she was a stranger even if her image was an icon. The death of Diana marked the opening of an empty space with no pre-determined pattern. Diana was not a "front-line" Royal in protocol terms – she no longer enjoyed the status of HRH – nor was she a heroic figure of wars past such as Mountbatten or Churchill. Both of them were honoured with state funerals and all the trappings that go with them. However as the mother of the likely future monarch she could not be classified as a purely private figure either. This vacuum created by the ambiguity of her identity was filled by popular displays of emotion and grief.[139] These displays were irrational in the extreme on their own terms but they, nevertheless, by the end of the week between her death and funeral, had assumed a pattern of their own. For example the initial refusal of the Scottish Football Association to rearrange a football match in that period was condemned as inappropriate, disrespectful and insensitive, by the standards of behaviour that had emerged during that week.[140] What is significant about this event for the major themes I explore in this text is that much of the loss that many mourners felt was not so much for the person that they "knew" only from afar but for her support of a particular type of behaviour and value set that transcended political debate. She typified the importance of contribution to the good of others, of not being afraid to care, to listen and to participate. It is these values that I wish to return to in my final chapter.

The idea of Christianity as an all-embracing meta-narrative in a multi-cultural and post-modern society is a problematic one.[141] We

[139] There are of course other less generous interpretations of what was and was not pre-ordained. On one view the extensive media coverage and the opportunity for public relations that it afforded to Tony Blair as Prime Minister – his first statement post the announcement of her death described her as the "People's Princess" and Britain as a "nation in a state of shock, in mourning" – set the stage for what followed. See for example the editorial of *Living Marxism*, 2 September 1997. However this says little for the power of individual thought and character! If followed to its logical conclusion there would be no need for anyone to rail against the ravages of individualism.

[140] A series of discussions themed around particular signifiers such as "story" and "image" so as to put the events of that week into a broader cultural frame can be found in the Special Debate section of (1998) 39 *Screen* 67-84.

[141] Within Theology Studies there is a debate about the extent to which Christianity

have only to look at the importance to communities of participation in festivals such as Diwali and the structure derived for collective worship in schools to see that this is the case.[142] Christian observance has also been replaced by an air of individual reflexivity and the project of self-development.[143] Individual spiritual fulfilment is more likely to be provided by new age religion or through commitment to non-traditional single issue politics such as a branch of the peace movement or the ecological movement for example. The image of Princess Diana as a Madonna figure, which appeared in the Liverpool Tate Exhibition *Heaven* in early 2000 is central to the idea of the secularisation and individualisation of religion. Princess Diana is an iconoclastic figure not because of her piety or religious observance particularly but because of her embrace of the socially excluded.[144] A broad notion of sacrifice now figures more prominently in our lives than before. By sacrifice I mean not sacrifice as love of or duty to the God or a God perhaps mediated through some state level concept of nation or people, but sacrifice for love of each other. My point is that the nature of sacrifice has changed

can and has addressed the postmodern challenge. In many ways it seems that the issues that confront Theology are no different from those which confront the sociology of Richard Sennett or the socio-politico views of Giddens: how to present a narrative which deals with the problems presented by the global order and yet still resonates with the concerns of those at local level. See N Boyle, *Who Are We Now?: Christian Humanism and the Global Market from Hegel to Heaney* (Notre Dame, IN: University of Notre Dame Press, 1998) at pp 91-2. Boyle suggests that while the Church will have a universal presence for the narratives of the grand process the "little narratives . . . of what the big new world is squeezing out or ignoring . . . will be told at diocesan, parochial, or base-community level. While I find Boyle's work on this level of great interest I do not endorse his view of postmodernity: "the pessimism of an obsolescent class – the salaried official intelligentsia – whose fate is closely bound up with that of the declining nation-state" at p 318.

[142] School Standards and Framework Act 1998 requires that a daily collective act of worship take place (ss 69-71) and that collective worship be wholly or mainly Christian in content (sch 20). However under section 394 of the Act the Head Teacher of a school covered by ss. 69-71 can apply to the Standing Advisory Council for exemption from sch 20. The Council will determine the content of collective worship based upon the pupils' family backgrounds.

[143] This is a comment based upon anecdotal press comment. It is a view which receives academic support from S Bruce, *Religion in Modern Britain* (Oxford: Oxford University Press, 1995) see in particular ch 2. However this is not an uncontentious text, see T Jenkins, "Two Sociological Approaches to Religion in Modern Britain" (1996) 26 *Religion* 331.

[144] D Levitte Harten, *Heaven* (Stuttgart: Hatje Cantz, 1999) at p 239. My reference here is to the portrayal of Princess Diana as a Madonna like figure.

and progressed. Just as Aeschylus' *Oresteia* marks the move from ritual sacrifice to judicial decision for the appeasement of wrongs[145] so the idea of sacrifice for Christian or nationalistic reasons has been replaced by other themes. In Western Europe and the US, pacifists and ecological activists are not being asked to fight for their country as part of a mass movement as on previous occasions and thus they are free to frame their sacrifice as one for "saving" and "protecting the planet for future generations".[146]

Demonstration of the individuality of sacrifice can be seen in Mark Wallinger's sculpture *Ecce Homo*. This piece was commissioned to fill, on a temporary basis, the empty plinth in Trafalgar Square. It depicts the lifesize figure of a man, bound and wearing only a loincloth and a crown of barbed wire. When in position it stood on the very edge of the plinth looking down on the square but itself dwarfed by much larger figures of generals, former monarchs and ultimately Admiral Lord Nelson. Much of Wallinger's work has centered on religious texts and imagery and an ongoing theme for him has been the language, both spoken and visual, of the universal and the local.[147] While Wallinger's title for his sculpture comes from the version of the crucifixion narrative found in John's Gospel it is possible to take the figure out of its obviously, at one level, Christian context. Britain has very few public representations of Christ dated after the Reformation[148] and the very ordinariness of Wallinger's figure speaks to the suffering and sacrifice of ordinary man. This is not a depiction of a heroic figure in the terms that the other sculptures in Trafalgar Square represent heroic achievement. Its place on the edge of the plinth, itself dwarfed by other figures, standing alone, encourages us to empathise with its loneliness and at the same time embrace it for the significance of its representative force.

The rhetoric of remembrance for wars past has also changed. It has become a mourning of a sacrifice made for known or at least identifiable individuals within the collective. Much was made in the early part

[145] G Newton, "Vengeance is His: Justice in the Oresteia (1994) 4 *Angelaki* 135 at 137.

[146] S Hunt and R Benford, "Identity Talk in the Peace and Justice Movement" (1994) 22 *J of Contemp Ethnog* 488 at p496.

[147] K Davey (ed), *English Imaginaries* (London: Lawrence & Wishart, 1998) and D Burrows, "Beyond Public Belief: Mark Wallinger's *Ecce Homo*" in *Public Art Journal* (London: Tate Gallery Publishing, 2000).

[148] The lack of religious sculpture and art post the reformation is due to the strictures imposed on the creation of imagery, thought to have overtones of Catholicism, during the establishment of the Protestant Church and before the restrictions on Catholic worship were relaxed. I deal with some of this material below.

of the last century of the idea that an individual, usually male, was under a Christian duty to make an offer of himself as a sacrifice.[149] It became a frame for much of the contemporary poetical[150] and journalistic[151] comment upon the First World War in particular. The construction of many First World War monuments both at Government level under the auspices of what was then called the Imperial War Graves Commission and at local civic level emphasised,[152] through the use of images such as the bronze sword on the vertical strut of the crucifix, the link between Christianity, duty and sacrifice. [153] Now this idea of duty

[149] The role given to sacrifice within Christianity is not a settled one by any means. For a broad overview which offers comment upon a number of leading passages from the Pauline epistles, see R Daly, "Is Christianity Sacrificial or Antisacrificial?" (1997) 27 *Religion* 231.

[150] An example of this would be the work of Geoffrey Dearmer. Dearmer's poetry was typical of the heavy religious overtones of the sacrifice that was being made by those who fought and in particular those who died. Dearmer described the death of his brother at Gallipoli in *Killed Sulva Bay October 6th 1915* as "help[ing] to purify the world". Similarly in *A Prayer* he refers to "[w]hen all the world is free, And, cleansed and purified by floods of pain We turn, and see the light in human eyes;". Dearmer's work was published in 1918 and 1923 to critical acclaim. However he features little now in collections of First World War verse which prefer the work of poets such as Sassoon, Owen and Graves whose heavily anti-war sentiments were atypical of those expressed at the time.

[151] See the examples from this period provided by T Bogacz, '"A Tyranny of Words': Language, Poetry and Antimodernism in the First World War" (1986) 58 *J of Mod Hist* 643.

[152] For the process of establishing the Imperial War Graves Commission and description of the work that it undertook in the commissioning of memorials and the composition of inscriptions see T and V Holt, *My Boy Jack* (Barnsley: Leo Cooper, 1998) 139-54 and S Hines, *A War Imagined* (London: Bodley Head, 1990) pp 270-9. For an analysis that devotes more attention to civic commemoration and mourning see J Winter, *Sites of Memory Sites of Mourning* (Cambridge: Cambridge University Press, 1995) at pp 78-99.

[153] The most obvious New Testament reference which engages with the issue of the love of man for his fellow man rather than the love of Christ is found in John's Gospel Ch 15 v12-13 "This is my commandment: that ye love one another, as I have loved you. Greater love hath no man than this, that a man lay down his life for his friends" (Authorised King James Version). A clear link is made here between love and divine command. Winter *supra* n 146 at pp 219-21 points to a distinction in the literature contemporary with the First World War between Old Testament motifs of sacrifice in the form of the father's sacrifice of his son (Abraham and Issac) and the New Testament idea of the sacrifice of Christ for humanity. While this distinction clearly exists as a matter of theology I am not convinced that it comes through in the way that Winter suggests. I do not see the majority of the poetry produced at that time displaying this level of sophistication. I am much more open to the idea that *ex post facto* reflective literature on that period embraces that level of subtelty, see C Lanone, "Scattering the Seed of Abraham: The Motif of Sacrifice in Pat Barker's *Regeneration* and *The Ghost Road*" (1999) 13 *Lit & Theology* 259.

has been replaced by one of secular sacrifice made so that others can enjoy "their tomorrow".[154] The move towards viewing sacrifice as secular is also significant for its challenge to exclusivity. There is the aforementioned breaking of the link to the Christian meta-narrative. This then extends on to break the link between duty, sacrifice and maleness. There appears to be a growing understanding of the proposition that feminist scholarship has made for many years that women and children are also part of sacrifice. One of the earlier references I made to the funeral of Princess Diana in September 1997 commented that the occasion could be read as a mourning for the past and a demand for moving on. The past that was being mourned was on one level oppression by tradition and custom but on another it was oppression by the mode of capitalism advocated and perpetrated by the New Right.[155] The intermingling of the secular and the religious can be seen, for me at least, in Stanley Spencer's *The Resurrection, Cookham*.[156] This depiction of the resurrection includes a representation of the last judgement. Christ appears in the graveyard at Cookham seated on a throne but not garlanded in celestial splendour. Instead of the expected fear and accountability of Judgement Day, what Spencer offers for those whose graves are opened is a continuation of earthly life; the smelling of flowers, reading and conversing – a celestial renewal of what each individual enjoyed/performed on earth. The activities of War remembrance in the 1990s show a not dissimilar pattern.[157] Each year seems to be the anniversary for mourning a long ago event. 1999, for example, was hailed as the "last act of remembrance" of the century. The two minute silence on Armistice Day itself, abandoned much earlier in the century, was reintroduced in 1995 and has been continued since then by popular

[154] These words paraphrase those found on the memorial at Kohima: "When you go home, tell them of us and say: for your tomorrow we gave our today". They also appear on the memorial in Newcastle to the dead of the war in Burma, dedicated in 1991.

[155] C Harris, "Secular Religion and the Public Response to Diana's Death" in T Walter (ed), *The Mourning for Diana* (Oxford: Berg, 1999).

[156] 1926, Oil on Canvas, Tate Gallery London.

[157] A comparison can be drawn between the public pressure that was brought to bear to get the Whitehall Cenotaph, originally planned as a temporary wooden structure, made permanent and the public pressure for recognition of Princess Diana and participation in mourning for her. The literature on the Cenotaph is headed by David Cannadine's "War, Death, Grief and Mourning in Modern Britain" in J Whaley (ed), *Mirrors of Mortality* (London: Europa, 1981) 187. For a contribution which draws these two events together see R Richardson, "Disposing with Diana: Diana's Death and the British Funerary Culture" in D Gilbert et al (eds), *Diana and Democracy* (London: Lawrence & Wishart, 1999) p 21.

demand; a space in which individuals can contemplate the sacrifice made by other individuals for them as a collective.

Virtue and Catholicism

My second reason for viewing Anscombe's plea for a restructuring of moral philosophy as having been answered also lies in the relationship of religious faith to philosophy. However on this occasion it is faith specifically in the form of Catholicism and philosophy in the *persona* of Aristotle rather than the link between virtue ethics, individualism and the collective. As with my previous point my reasoning rests upon a reading of modern cultural and social life which views traditional boundaries as broken down or breaking down and so previously forbidden territories as capable of exploration and even embraced. In crudely simple terms the traditional position is that Aristotle was absorbed into Christian thinking by Aquinas and through Aquinas into Catholicism.[158] Aquinas engaged with Aristotle in a variety of ways; by writing a commentary on *NE*, by devoting the second half of *Summa Theologiae* to integrating Aristotelian theories of substance and matter into Christian thinking and by incorporating Aristotle's political structures based upon the *polis* and its governance into his ideas on God as creator and ruler.[159] Until that point Aristotle's place in the intellectual tradition had been more narrowly confined to his contribution to logic.

In terms of ethics the conventional narrative is that Aquinas took Aristotelian virtue-based thinking[160] and adapted what he found there that he considered pagan to Christian thinking and embraced the remainder into his synthesis.[161] For example both Aristotle and Aquinas saw happiness as the ultimate goal of existence. For Aquinas

[158] For an account which embellishes considerable the traditional narrative on this point see B Kent, *Virtues of the Will: The Transformation of Ethics in the Late Thirteenth Century* (Washington DC: Catholic University Press, 1995) especially ch 2.

[159] H Hamilton Bleakley, "The Art of Ruling in Aquinas' *De Regimine Principum*" (1999) XX *History of Political Thought* 575 at 592f

[160] The extent to which Aquinas was a follower of Aristotle for his thinking on moral issues and the extent to which he was influenced in this by natural law is a matter of some debate see J Porter "What the Wise Person Knows: Natural Law and Virtue in Aquinas' *Summa Theologiae*" (1999) 12 *Studies in Christian Ethics* 57 and the references contained therein.

[161] T O'Meara, "Virtues in the Theology of Thomas Aquinas" (1997) 58 *Theological Studies* 254.

happiness could only be found in the contemplation of God, this was only achievable by those who reached heaven. In the *Summa contra Gentiles* Aquinas engages in detailed discussion of Aristotelian positions on issues such as the soul, truth and proofs for the existence of God. His position once again is that he endorses much Aristotelian thought, appropriately adapted by him for Christianity. Aquinas was public in his recognition of Aristotle as a philosopher not simply through the commentaries he wrote on Aristotle's works but also in his commissioning of accurate translations of Aristotelian texts from their original Greek into medieval Latin. Aquinas was canonised in 1323 and became in effect the most revered theologian in the Roman Catholic church as a result of Pope Leo XIII's encyclical *Aeterni Patris*.[162]

Through Aquinas, Aristotle was tied inescapably into Roman Catholic thinking. The figures that are set up as the philosophical opponents of Aristotle, Aquinas and virtue ethics are the Protestant intellectuals of the Enlightenment. From the start of the seventeenth century onwards Catholicism was the victim of a "master discourse" which denigrated it as backward and medieval while promoting Protestantism as allied to "science and reason"[163] and therefore legitimate.[164] England was gripped by a sectarianism that was designed to keep Catholics out of public life and at least the majority of

[162] The encyclical letter was issued on August 4th 1879. In it Leo XIII described Thomas Aquinas as the prince of Scholastic theologians whose work in the Middle Ages had united the work of the early Fathers of the Church into one philosophical system. Leo X111 later instructed that the philosophy of Aquinas be taught in all Roman schools. Kenny in the Introduction to his edited collection of essays on Aquinas comments that this association with Catholicism has harmed the reputation of Aquinas as a philosopher for three reasons. First it means that non-Catholics are often not prepared to study Aquinas for fear that it is akin to a manifesto statement for a religion which is not theirs, second Aquinas is often presented in a very simplistic manner for the religious tract market and third he is considered to take at the outset of inquiry his conclusion that the question he is exploring is answered by the doctrine of Catholicism. See A Kenny (ed), *Aquinas: A Collection of Critical Essays* (London: Macmillan, 1969) p 2.

[163] For an account of the Catholic Church's relationship to science see J Brooke and G Cantor, *Reconstructing Nature* (Edinburgh: T&T Clark, 1998). The authors make the point that truly objective history in this area is difficult if not impossible and that there is considerable evidence that the Church's objections to "science" were based around the provision of proof rather its outright supression even though this was at the time and after the event the impression given, see p24 and 107-37 esp. I am grateful to my former Leeds colleague Professor Tom McLeish for drawing this account to my attention.

[164] R Tumbleson, *Catholicism in the English Protestant Imagination: Nationalism, Religion and Literature !600-1745* (Cambridge: Cambridge University Press, 1998) p 98f.

institutions. For example the Oxbridge colleges were constitutionally prevented from allowing those who would not take the "Protestant Oath" from graduating with a degree. This situation remained unchanged until the later half of the nineteenth century[165] and the Act of Settlement 1701 still prevents a member of the royal family from becoming or marrying a Catholic and retaining rights of succession. Law was one of the few professional careers that was open to a non-graduates. An academic career was of course unlikely to be available to those who had not been permitted to read for a degree.

Moves to relax this sectarian stance began from the end of the eighteenth century onwards with a series of legislative interventions[166] designed to ease the position of Catholics. The activities of Newman and the Oxford Movement allowed Anglo-Catholicism to grow and flourish.[167] The increased profile of Catholicism resulted not only in recruitment to it[168] of a series of high profile British and American intellectual and cultural figures but also in the bringing closer together of ritual and interpretative practices between the Church of England and the Church of Rome. Pope Pius IX re-established the Catholic Hierarchy into the life of the Catholic Church in England which had been absent since the reign of Elizabeth I. This saw the establishment of thirteen sees and the archdiocese of Westminster. The effect of this was to restore to Catholics in England, their numbers swelled by immigrants escaping from the Irish potato famine, the religious governance and leadership that their counterparts in other European states enjoyed. Nevertheless the Catholic Church and those associated with it remained very much a self-contained unit;[169] "the other" contrasted with the established Anglican Church and its place within institutions of government and sites of culture.

[165] Test Act 1871.

[166] Acts "for the Relief of His Majesty's Roman Catholic Subjects" were passed in 1791, 1829 and for Her Majesty's in 1856.

[167] See the very detailed account of this provided by J S Reed in *Glorious Battle: the cultural politics of Victorian Anglo-Catholicism* (Nashville, TN: Vanderbilt University Press, 1996).

[168] For example Ellmann in his biography of Oscar Wilde describes how incidents such as this occurred and the accessibility of Catholic teaching to Oxford undergraduates only 4 years or so after the repeal of the Test Acts, see R Ellmann, *Oscar Wilde* (London: Hamish Hamilton, 1987) pp 51-66.

[169] Mark Bence-Jones' account of the history of the leading English Catholic families makes it clear that marriage amongst the families was inevitable and even junior and impecunious branches of families were included in this, see *The Catholic Families* (London: Constable, 1992) pp 159-83.

The last twenty years or so have seen Catholicism move from the position of being an exception to orthodoxy and the establishment to being in effect the Establishment.[170] Together with Catholicism as a religious statement of belief, its associate figures such as Aristotle and its practices such as its engagement with ritual have also moved to the fore. Catholicism is considered to embody the ancient, the exotic, and the good (not necessarily in that order). This occurs in a variety of ways but perhaps the most significant feature of this rehabilitation is that it avoids, for the most part, direct engagement with issues of religious doctrine. Catholicism has become a cultural statement about individual commitment and virtue. Catholicism's medieval ritualistic heritage of music, candles and incense find a place in contemporary quests for the spiritual. There has been a revival of interest in early and medieval Chant and religious music in general from that period, which, despite its strong liturgical content, has experienced a renaissance both as music on its own terms and as the base for electronically constructed dance music. In several cases performance of this religious music, composed in a period where Catholicism was the only Western form of Christianity, has been undertaken by artists whose gender would have made them rather marginal to the musical life of the medieval Catholic church, for example the plain chant sung by the *Medieval Babes* and the recitals of the *Anonymous Four.*[171] Hildegard of Bingen has become something of a cult figure and not simply for her musical compositions. She is put forward as a figure which allows traditional aspects of religious life to be mingled with new post post-Fordist positions and values.[172] For example she has been presented as "a friend of New Age mystic[s] by stressing the more optimistic, holistic and naturalistic sides of her thought".[173] In 1998, her 900th birthday year, a

[170] M Horsby-Smith, "Into the Mainstream: Recent Transformation in British Catholicism" in T Gannon (ed), *World Catholicism in Transition* (London: Macmillan, 1988).

[171] Women as spiritual leaders within the medieval period are not perhaps as uncommen as we might initially think nevertheless participation in this activity was still very much a male province see C J Mews, "Hildegard and the Schools" in C Burnett and P Dronke (eds), *Hildegard of Bingen: The Content of her Thought and Art* (London: Warburg Institute, 1998) p 89 at p 93f. For a discussion of later developments see N Bradley Warren, *Spiritual Economies* (Philadelphia, PA : University of Pennsylvania Press, 2000).

[172] Some of the contemporary accounts of Hildegard's life and visions are now available in translation, see, for example, *Jutta and Hildegard* (trans A Silvas) (Pittsburgh PA : Pennsylvania State University Press, 1999).

[173] B Newman *Sister of Wisdom: St Hildegarde's Theology of the Feminine* (Berkeley, CA: University of California Press, 1987) p 250.

number of collections of her music were recorded and biographies of her life were published. These gave considerable succour to the idea of suffering and sanctity within her biography[174] and thus they link her to the idea of sacrifice that I set out earlier.

The ancient and the exotic elide into each other in what I term the "Brideshead Phenomenum". In the Autumn of 1981 the nation was gripped each Monday evening by the thirteen part television dramatisation of Evelyn Waugh's novel of 1946 – *Brideshead Revsited.*[175] The precise details of Waugh's story are largely irrelevant.[176] What matters was that the television adaptation of the novel by John Mortimer stressed the grandeur and glamour of the Marchmain family existence but at the same time drew attention to the intellectual and spiritual burden that each family member bore as a result of their Catholic faith. This prime time television exposure pushed the tenets of Catholicism into the public gaze. The impression given was of an exclusive but yet accessible club (Charles Ryder, the only central character who was not originally a Catholic, eventually becomes one[177]) based around ancient aristocratic families[178] in which each generation had struggled with these various dilemmas.

[174] See B Newman, "Three-Part Invention: the *Vita S. Hildegardis* and Mystical Hagiography" in C Burnett and P Dronke (eds), *Hildegard of Bingen: The Content of her Thought and Art* (London: Warburg Institute, 1998) p 189 at p 197.

[175] First published by in 1945 by Chapman and Hall, London. The edition used in the following notes is the Penguin Books reprint of 1962.

[176] For the place that this particular novel of Waugh's occupies within the corpus of "Catholic Novels", see P Sherry, "The End of the Catholic Novel" (1995) 9 *Lit and Theol* 165 and P Allitt, *Catholic Converts* (Ithaca, NY: Cornell University Press, 1997) pp 277-308.

[177] Throughout the novel Ryder views religion and Catholicism in particular as "witchcraft" and "mumbo-jumbo" (at pp 310 and 312 respectively). However it is clear from the epilogue that Ryder embraces Catholicism eventually: "the *art-nouveau* lamp burned once more before the altar. I said a prayer, an ancient, newly-learned form of words, and left . . ." and "Something . . . has come out . . . of the fierce little human tragedy in which I played . . . a small red flame . . . and there I found it this morning, burning anew among the old stones." (pp 330-1).

[178] It is the case that despite the financial hardships incurred as a result of recusancy fines many of the aristocratic Catholic families can trace a lineage back to pre-reformation England. However the Marchmain family were not one of them. It is clear from the narrative that Lady Marchmain was a Catholic and that Lord Marchmain was a reluctant convert who renewed his Catholic faith on his deathbed. For discussion of this and a summary of the views of Waugh's friends, both Catholics and non-Catholics on the novel and its subsequent dramatisation for television, see H Carpenter, *The Brideshead Generation* (London: Faber & Faber, 1989) pp 354-80.

Whereas *Brideshead Revisited* provided the ancient and the exotic and emphasised the accessible, the good came from the tenure of, as Archbishop of Westminster, the late Cardinal Hume. Hume's ministry spanned a period in which Catholicism in the UK re-branded itself from a patriarchal religion, which oppressed women over issues such as birth control and repressed them in respect of issues such as ordination, into a serene and principled religion prepared to try and broker agreements between governments on issues such as Third World Debt. Hume accepted into the Catholic Church those Anglican priests who felt unable to accept the decision of their own Church to ordain women priests without allowing himself or his Church to become embroiled in the controversy. He received the Order of Merit from the Queen who described him as "my Cardinal". A relationship of this closeness between reigning monarch and a Catholic Archbishop had not existed since before the reformation. Hume personally instructed and received into the Catholic Church high profile converts such as the Duchess of Kent. His persona was one of quiet serenity and individual spirituality. This profile plugs into the description of religious experience I have already given of the new relationship that many people seek between *themselves* and their *reflexivity* or *spirituality*. The Catholic Church's position as the Church of those within the Establishment was reinforced by the high level of media coverage accorded to Hume's funeral in June 1999.[179] Several carried the poignant image of Tony Blair, as a non-Catholic and thus unable to receive communion, with his thumb touching his forehead as he signed himself after receiving a blessing.

Catholic Social Teaching and the Third Way

Tony Blair's interaction with Catholicism does not begin and end with attending the funeral of Cardinal Hume. He and his family were parishioners of Hume's and the Blairs' children are being educated at Catholic schools. This leaves Blair as the Prime Minister with the most public involvement with Catholicism that there has ever been. This has done much to not only publicise Catholicism but also to endorse its position and appropriateness as a broad cultural statement. Blair's most recent and most detailed discussion of the Third Way for some

[179] All the broadsheet newspapers carried not only a full obituary and report of the requiem mass but also an order of service, colour photographs and extensive comment. The *Times* on the day following the funeral , Saturday 26 June, drew great significance from the mixing of the old Catholic families with recent converts. The example given was the presence of the Fitzlan-Howards and John Selwyn Gummer.

time was in a speech to the Global Ethics Foundation at Tübingen, Germany.[180] The significance of this lies in the identity of the director of the Tübingen Foundation – Hans Küng. Küng may have had his difficulties with the hierarchy of the Catholic Church, and may now be tenured in the Protestant theology faculty at Tübingen rather than the Catholic one, but he nevertheless remains a Catholic. It was as if Blair was addressing to Küng the foundation stones of his political vision:

> "the inevitability of globalisation demands a parallel of our best ethical values . . . the basic premises of our faiths; solidarity; justice; peace and the dignity of the human person are what we need in the age of globalisation".

In chapter one I made reference to the possible influence that Christian Socialism may have had over Blairite political discourse and concepts such as "community".[181] My point here, which I make whimsically, is that a further influence over the Blairite adoption and endorsement of Third Way politics might be Catholic Social Teaching.

My whimsicality is based on the fact that Blair has made his religious affiliations very clear in the past. He is not a Catholic. He describes himself as an "ecumenical Christian", apparently often confused by differences between Protestants and Catholics.[182] He himself cites the work of Scottish philosopher John Macmurray as an important influence over the formation of his position. Macmurray is an interesting figure to look at in terms of the responses that can be made to the challenges of living in a post post-Fordist world. In religious terms Macmurray, although from a Scottish Calvanist background, remained outside any form of organised religion until he became a Quaker during his retirement years. As a philosopher Macmurray is something of a peripheral figure in the intellectual canon although he did enjoy contemporary populist acclaim.[183] His starting point was as a Kantian believing in practical reason. However over the course of his career he moved to a position which considered emotion not to be irrational and art and religion to be more complete forms of knowledge than science. The most complete statement of Macmurray's philosophy which incorporates this change is found in his Gifford Lectures of 1953 and

[180] 30 June 2000.

[181] For an expansion on this see D Aikman, "He's No Clinton Clone" *American Spectator* July 1997.

[182] Interview with the *Daily Telegraph* Easter 1996.

[183] For example in the 1930s Macmurray was one of the first intellectuals to be involved in radio broadcasting for the BBC along with figures such as A L Rowse.

1954.[184] There Macmurray also provides us with a link to the work of Bauman. For Macmurray:

> "human behaviour carries always, in its inherent structure, a reference to the personal Other . . . . The personal is constituted by personal relatedness. The unit of the personal is not the 'I', but the 'You and I'."[185]

Bauman makes much the same point some 40 years on but circumstances dictate that his position is one of requirement whereas Macmurray's is one of aspiration:

> "a postmodern ethics would be one that readmits the Other as a neighbour, as the close-at-hand-and-mind, into the hardcore of the moral self, . . . an ethics that restores the autonomous moral significance of proximity".[186]

The Third Way has much in common with the broad message of Catholic Social Teaching.[187] By Catholic Social Teaching in this context I mean the material that is contained in *Rerum Novarum*[188] and the encyclicals that follow it. I use the term "broad message" to signal that what I am concerned with is the type of economic system that is being endorsed rather than the specifics of it. In particular the themes of workers' rights and the right to work that occur throughout this teaching are not issues that I wish to engage with. The statement of the Third Way that I used in chapter one was one taken from an October 1998 speech to the Civil Service:

> "It is not the dogma of the old left, concentrating on the means rather than the ends. Nor is it the *laissez faire* of the New Right. Unlike the Old Left we want a market economy. But unlike the New Right we do not want a market society".

[184] See for example *The Self as Agent* (vol 1 of *The Form of the Personal*) (London: Faber, 1957) p 202 and *Persons in Relation* (vol 2 of *The Form of the Personal*) (London: Faber, 1961) at p 26.

[185] *Persons in Relation* (vol 2 of *The Form of the Personal*) (London: Faber, 1961) at p 61.

[186] Z Bauman, *Postmodern Ethics* (Oxford: Blackwell, 1993) p 84.

[187] See R Mathews, *Jobs of our Own* (London: Comerford and Miller; Australia: Pluto Press, 1999). Although much of this book is devoted to looking at the role of distributism within Catholic Social Teaching, it does also draw links to the Third Way. The book's forward is provided by the Rev Peter Thomson, an Anglican priest and mentor of Blair. Given the book's focus this further strengthens the links between Blair, the Third Way and Catholicism.

[188] Leo XIII 15 May 1891.

The central point of *Rerum Novarum* was that the market cannot operate outside of a moral framework or unchecked by regulation but that socialism was equally unacceptable. The link between *Rerum Novarum* and Aristotelian thinking is clear from the sentiment that "the end of civil society is centred in the common good in which one and all in due proportion have a right to participate." The power of the state in Catholic Social Teaching is checked by the principle of subsidiarity set out by Pius XI in *Quadragesimo Anno*.[189] This is the idea that governance of any issue should rest at the lowest level compatible with functionality. The subsidiarity principle is built upon by the present Pope, John Paul II, who stresses the importance of community structures if individuals are not to find themselves squeezed between the state and the market.[190] These structures he describes as "mediating" – presumably the position of the individual – and he may mean trade unions and other groups which hold collective social rights. The idea of subsidiarity within Catholic Social Teaching has much resonance with European Union models of governance and Blairite ideas of Regional devolution through the formation of local assemblies.

All Catholic Social Teaching is to a certain extent situated within the social context of its time. For *Rerum Novarum* it was the unification of Italy and the loss of the Papal States and for *Quadragesimo Anno* it was the rise of fascism[191] in Italy.[192] John Paul II has produced his vision of ideal social and economic relationships from a background of opposition to Communism[193] in an era which has seen the fall of the very same Communist regimes in Eastern Europe and the failure of the New Right

[189] Quadragresimo Anno, 15 May 1931 79-80.

[190] Centesimus Annus 1991 49

[191] P Vallely, "Laying the Foundations: from *Rerum Novarum* to the Second Vatican Council" in P Vallely (ed), *The New Politics* (London: SCM Press, 1998) p 28 at pp 30-7, 41.

[192] This is not to say that these particular components of Catholic Social Teaching are culturally contingent, see for example K Heineman, *Religion and Reform in Depression Pittsburgh* (Pittsburgh, PA: Pennsylvania University State Press, 1999). Heineman ties the influence of Catholic Social Teaching to the rise of employee activism and pressure for social reform in Pittsburgh in the 1930's. The model of Catholic Social Teaching employed was one that was anti-communist, anti-facist and anti *laissez-faire*. The corporate response to this idea of a "Catholic" New Deal or at least a "New Deal" is set out by R Marchand, "Where Lie the Boundaries of the Corporation? Explorations in "Corporate Responsibility" in the 1930's" (1997) 26 *Bus and Econ Hist* 80 at 83-4.

[193] G Weigel, *Witness to Hope: The Biography of Pope John Paul II* (London: Harper Collins, 1999).

to sustain itself as a potential replacement.[194] Like Pius XI, John Paul II also issued an encyclical on the anniversary of *Rerum Novarum*, *Centesimus Annus*. There he set out what was and was not, in the view of the Catholic Church, an appropriate model of capitalism; capitalism is acceptable if it means an economic sector which along with supporting the positive values of business, the market, private property and human creativity also takes responsibility for the means of production and is itself encased within a "strong juridical framework".[195] By strong juridical framework what is meant is governance by the state and other organs in accordance with the principle of subsidiarity and control by society[196] – in other words neither the new right position nor that of the old planned economies of Eastern Europe.

This definition of capitalism was endorsed by the Catholic Bishops' Conference of England and Wales in 1996 in their publication *The Common Good*. This was produced as a document with the aim of influencing public debate, including that taking place within the political arena, about the type of society that it was desirable to (re) create. The actual words used in the document were "the defeat of communism should not mean the triumph of unbridled capitalism." This, they reasoned, could be the result in a situation where "command" economic models were no longer in existence and acting as a break on the operation of capitalism. Their suggestion was that market forces should be corrected if necessary "in the name of natural law, social justice, human rights, and the common good".[197] Expressed like this the position of Catholic Social Teaching and the Bishops' Conference is very similar to that of the Third Way as expressed by Blair and Giddens. Catholic Social Teaching even finds itself fending off some of the same criticisms that are levelled at Third Way politics – is it offering practical solutions or a cultural critique?[198]

[194] The first three pastoral letters of John Paul II – *Redemptor Hominis* (1979), *Dires in Misericordia* (1980) and *Laborem Exercens* (1981) following so soon after his election in 1978 are considered by some as part of a "continuing but unsignalled dialogue with Marxism" I Linden, "People before Profit: The Early Social Doctrine of John Paul II" in P Vallely (ed), *supra* n 191 p 81 at p 89.

[195] *Centesimus Annus* 42. For a detailed discussion of this paragraph see M Novak, *The Catholic Ethic and the Spirit of Capitalism* (New York, NY: Free Press, 1993) pp 127-43.

[196] *Centesimus Annus* 48.-

[197] *The Common Good*, Catholic Bishops' Conference of England and Wales (London: 1996) at paras 50 and 77

[198] See D Finn "John Paul II and the Moral Ecology of Markets" (1998) *Theo Studies* 662 at 666f.

In this chapter my principal aim has been to show the relevance of Aristotelian virtue ethics to both the ability of businesses to perform to the agenda that Third Way politics sets out and to the choices that face individuals in a post post-Fordist world. I have tried to show that virtue ethics places the individual in a process of finding and developing character as opposed to the Kantian alternative of *a priori* ethical positions. Aristotelian thought is very much part of the current intellectual agenda both as an applied philosophy and as a theoretical position. I have tried, albeit briefly, to track the patterns of philosophical thought that have returned it to prominence. In explaining these patterns I have drawn upon changing ideas of cultural reference and discourses around issues such as the self, sacrifice, religion and spirituality. My aim is to show that these ideas can be linked together in a seamless web.

This chapter began with Bauman's suggestion that it might be possible to construct a community of responsible citizens if it was first possible to engage the same citizens in the running of a community and in caring for a community. Here I have set out the Aristotelian methodology for doing this and included corporations as individual actors within this. Aristotle centres on the character of the individual and on the choices that an individual has to make in living through human existence. Choices based upon the virtues Aristotle believes will lead to the creation of a homogenous community. Bauman, on a note of less optimism, asks us to consider a key question for life in the twenty-first century; whether it is possible to make moral choices in a time of such turbulence and uncertainty. For him a prior question is how an individual first negotiates their own potential multiple and multifarious identities. I begin chapter three by examining ways of bringing the ideas of Aristotle and Bauman closer together.

3

Virtue Ethics for the Third Millennium

1. BETWEEN ARISTOTLE AND BAUMAN – ANOTHER JOURNEY BETWEEN CLASHING ROCKS?

Similarities and Differences

In searching for a position for individuals, including corporations, to occupy so that they may face the challenges of post post-Fordism in as comfortable a way as possible I appear to have set in rather stark opposition to each other the views of Bauman and Aristotle. Although both of them begin with the project of the individual, Aristotle's account of the virtues leads ultimately to a universalistic community while Bauman's world is one of individual torment underscored by uncertainty and a lack of guidance. These positions have something of a symbiotic relationship. Bauman explains where the individual is now located, Aristotle gives us part of what is needed by the individual to survive this position. My task at the beginning of this chapter is to find a way to draw Aristotle and Bauman closer together while still preserving the essence of each view. This task is once again not a novel one; a number of contemporary Aristotelians have purported to move Aristotelian thought towards the position occupied by Bauman. This is not necessarily out of a desire to identify with the post modern project but more out of a recognition that Aristotelian dependency on a universalistic *polis* structure for its validity decreases its potential for recognition as a "live" position.

In this context I want to look particularly at the work of Alasdair MacIntyre. My choice of MacIntyre as the contemporary Aristotelian to focus upon stems from the fact that his starting point for critique is similar to the views expressed by Bauman. What is required by both of them is a new settlement for individuals and the collective. The need for this settlement for both of them arises out of their discontents with modernity and the account of human existence presented by liberalism.[1] MacIntyre is also appropriate for the task of this book. As the discussion below demonstrates his work forms part of the canon of literature from which some Business and Society and Business Ethics scholars draw their inspiration in setting out new models of behaviour for business executives and new methods of business practice for corporations. MacIntyre's treatise begins with *After Virtue* published in 1981 and ends with *Whose Justice? Which Rationality?* published in 1988. He views current society as being in moral crisis. Disagreements and disputes within society can not be resolved[2] as those on each side have different positions with no shared human good that can be drawn upon. The argument of each individual may be logical in the sense that it is based upon a premise and follows that premise but what is no longer possible for the individual is to evaluate one premise against another and reach a decision. Instead claims are repeated in the language and thought of emotivism, hence moral debates are irresolvable.

MacIntyre's primary quest then is for an account of a model of justice which derives from the practices of individuals and not from abstract rules or obligations. MacIntyre is using justice in the same way as Aristotle in that justice underpins his account of the virtues. Justice is set up as the fulcrum of a society based upon the virtues rather than laws or other forms of social duty. The contrast that MacIntyre is making is to accounts of liberalism with their dependence upon rights. MacIntyre's ultimate model for the virtue of justice comes from Thomas Aquinas who he identifies as having answered the ethical question posed by Aristotle. My interest in MacIntyre is in his account of how individual life is lived through the virtues and how then individuals lives fit into a community. For MacIntyre our inability to engage in moral debate and only to argue past each other occurred when Northern Europe rejected Aristotelianism in favour of the views of

[1] "At the end of the road modern society has traversed in its pursuit of a Law-like, universally binding code of ethical rules, stands the modern individual bombarded by conflicting moral demands. Options and cravings, with responsibility for actions landing back on her shoulders . . . . Individuals were to be spared the agony of uncertainty in a rationally organised – 'transparent' – society in which Reason and Reason alone rules supreme"; Z Bauman, *Postmodern Ethics* (Oxford: Blackwell, 1993) at p 31. See in particular A MacIntyre "A Partial Response to My Critics" in J Horton and S Mendus (eds), *After MacIntyre* (Cambridge: Polity, 1994) (hereinafter "*Response to* Critics") p 283 at 290–4.

[2] A MacIntyre, *After Virtue: A Study in Moral Theory* (London: Duckworth, 1981) pp 6–7 (hereinafter "*After Virtue*").

post-Enlightenment philosophers. His view of events post the Enlightenment is given in chapters four and five of *After Virtue*. Expressed simply it is that what was promised was an approach to morality anchored in rationality independent of a particular view of human character and independent of the context, both social and historical, in which individuals lived.[3] In MacIntyre's view this was a project doomed to failure as it did not recognise the essentiality of the *telos*.[4] The rejection of Aristotelianism was the rejection of the *telos* – the goal, the end – and so also the rejection of the pursuit of the notional shared good. The individual was no longer working towards what they could be, from what they were but were instead left to determine their own end point.[5] Indeed the consequences for the individual were ones of failing to engage with their own biography and the narrative within which it was situated and engaging instead with rules and principles derived from the ether of impersonality.

Illustrative of the difficulties that modernity finds itself in according to MacIntyre are the identities of its *characters*. *Character* is a central part of MacIntyre's thesis about the consequences of the rejection of Aristotelianism. The label *character* does not just denote a social role such as doctor or chef,[6] instead it indicates that particular moral beliefs and doctrines are both represented and practiced by that *character*. *Characters* are in addition the moral representatives of their culture, the masks worn by moral philosophers. The demands on a *character* are imposed by the way in which others view the *character* in comparison to themselves, they look to the *character* as a moral and cultural ideal. By way of explanation MacIntyre offers us three *characters* which in his view partly define the culture of Victorian England: the *Public School Headmaster*, the *Explorer* and the *Engineer*.[7] Given the link that MacIntyre draws between on the one hand dramatic performance in spheres such as medieval morality plays and the role that stock characters play there in defining the "possibilities of plot and action"[8] and on the other hand the role of representative *characters* within society, it is somewhat surprising that alongside the *Public*

[3] As noted in chapter 2 there is a philosophical school that does not see Kantian ideas of ethical duty and obligation as being so distinctly separate from virtue ethics. This is not MacIntyre's position, see ch 2, n 27.

[4] *After Virtue*, pp 54–5.

[5] *After Virtue*, p 62.

[6] *After Virtue*, pp 27, 28.

[7] *After Virtue*, pp 28, 30.

[8] *After Virtue*, pp 27, 29–30.

School Headmaster et al there is not a figure which demonstrates the undoubted hypocrisy of that age[9] – the music hall actor perhaps or the beadle. The *characters* that MacIntyre identifies as representative of the age or "of our own time" are the *Rich Aesthete*, the *Manager* and the *Therapist.*[10] All three operate in a framework drawn by emotivisim, which means that they treat people as a means rather than an ends. People are no longer being rational and thus the possibility of moral debate is removed. Through this assertion MacIntyre reverses the Kantian imperative of treating people as an end and not a means. For the *Rich Aesthete* this equates to the use of other people to achieve pleasure and relief from boredom. For the *Therapist* this equates to engagement with technical practice only, with the transformation of "maladjusted individuals into well adjusted ones".[11]

The *character* of the *Manager*[12] with its business connotation is of greater relevance to this project than the other two characters to which MacIntyre refers.[13] To explain the character of the *Manager* MacIntyre provides his analysis of the function that bureaucratic organisation undertakes. He sees the exercises of both public (state) power and private (corporate) power by civil servants and corporate managers alike[14] as essentially the function of their own claims to expertise and competence as the directors of scarce resources, both human and non-human, towards the achievement of pre-determined ends. As with the *Therapist* the *Manager's* focus is on technique – the technique of transforming investment into profit and raw materials into finished goods. This picture of the manager as one unable to engage in any moral sense and as one who then resorts to technical processes is similar to the position taken by Bauman. For Bauman the totality of organisations clouds the

[9] A Kenny, "Victorian Values" (1992) 78 *Proceedings of the British Academy* 217 at 224.

[10] The emphasis, through choice of the upper case, is MacIntyre's.

[11] *After Virtue*, pp 30, 73.

[12] *After Virtue*, pp 74-8

[13] For a more detailed discussion of the figure of MacIntyre's *manager* and its plausibility as a description of Weberian management practice and of current management practice, see I Mangham, "MacIntyre and the Manager" (1995) 2 *Organization* 181 and the discussion papers that follow. In the course of rejecting the description and ideal figure of the Manager as having any intersection with the realities of institutional settings of management Paul du Gay provides a very detailed overview of MacIntyre's constitution of the virtues and his use of *character*, see P du Gay, "Alasdair MacIntyre and the Christian Genealogy of Management Critique" (1998) 4 *Cultural Values* 421 and P du Gay, *In Praise of Bureaucracy* (London: Sage, 2000) at pp 14–34, especially pp 28–33.

[14] MacIntyre is not the first to compare corporate management with bureaucracy, see G Frug, "The Ideology of Bureaucracy in American Law" (1984) 97 *Harv LR* 1277.

face of "the other" and prevents the manager from seeing it.[15] For MacIntyre the *Manager* is incapable of seeing the face of the other and so also incapable of engaging in moral debate because his face is set against such a possibility. In his description of the *Manager*, MacIntyre is also describing a broader business culture with an emphasis on efficiency and profit making[16] that could be used to describe both corporate values in the era of the New Right and the attitude of the New Right towards the delivery of public services.[17] MacIntyre and Bauman are both presenting a stereotypical picture of managerialism at its worst as a way of concentrating the gaze upon the impossibility in their eyes of ethical or moral engagement by those practising within a bureaucracy. This calls into question the fate of attempts to suggest that there could a corporate ethical activity. I would suggest that the more likely scenario for corporate internal structures in the third millennium is the one influcenced by the factors that I describe later in this chapter.[18] Given the demise of the New Right that was described in chapter one and the contemporary social and political discourse that was outlined there it is interesting to speculate on what would be MacIntyre's choice of character for now – the era of post post-Fordism. My suggestions to him would be the *social entrepreneur*, the *charity worker* or the *corporate executive for social involvement*. These characters all have the potential to represent a culture of cross sector co-operation and inclusion or efforts to achieve that. They all have a significant part to play in the re-establishment of Aristotelian virtue ethics in modern life.

MacIntyre and Business Ethics

MacIntyre's use of the *Manager* as an emblematic figure in *After Virtue* and his later employment, when explaining his own approach to the discovery of virtues, of examples drawn from corporate/business culture has endeared him to some of those working within the field of business ethics,[19] despite the fact that this, as a topic in itself, is one on

[15] See ch 2, n 41 and the text *infra*.

[16] A MacIntyre, *Three Rival Versions of Moral Enquiry: Encyclopaedia, Genealogy, and Tradition* (Notre Dame, IN: University of Notre Dame Press, 1990).

[17] A Dunsire, "Administrative Theory in the 1980's: A Viewpoint" (1995) 73 *Public Admin* 17 and R Rhodes, "The Hollowing Out of the State: The Changing Nature of Public Service in Britain" (1994) 65 *Pol Quart* 138.

[18] See section 3 later in this chapter.

[19] See J Dobson, "MacIntyre's Position on Business: A Response to Wicks" (1997) 7 *Bus Ethics Quart* 125 and the references contained therein and the observations

which he has written relatively little of a specific nature.[20] The adoption by business ethicists of virtue theory played through the lens provided by MacIntyre is usually presented as a counter point to theories of stakeholding. Kantian notions of obligation and duty – the reverse of virtue ethics, as explained in chapter one, underpin stakeholding. The objective for this type of business ethics is to find a new way for business activity to operate, often irrespective of the need to fit that operation within a larger theory of society. In other words there is no engagement with the possibilities created by premising a society on an Aristotelian structure. The result is a manifesto for revised internal operation of a given business entity, either through exhorting individual businesses to change their way of managing or to advocate conducting business in a way which incorporates particular policies. Both of these suggested methodologies are parochial in the sense that they look almost exclusively towards the treatment of employees within the enterprise, not that this of itself is to be discounted. In relation to individual business executives this is because they can only achieve change within their own immediate working sphere of operation. In relation to calls for a particular business to change the way that it operates in a vacuum, this involves casting the enterprise as a *polis*.

The idea of the corporate actor invoking its own individual action plans in recognition of its status as a *polis* is given merit by MacIntyre's own gloss on Aristotle's ideas; that each community forms and reforms its own virtues relative to its own historical context.[21] This, however, I feel is to take MacIntyre's point out of context. The idea that communities can reshape virtues to match their histories is a central one to the project of finding a position between the ideas of Aristotle and Bauman – the differences between a universalistic community and the barriers to forming community look less formidable if they are mediated by the idea of changing values. Within the idea that the corporation of itself is a *polis* the most conspicuous constituent group is the employees.

contained in J Liedtka, "Constructing an Ethic for Business Practice" (1998) 37 *Bus and Soc* 254. See also C Horvath, "Excellence v Effectiveness: MacIntyre's Critique of Business (1995) 5 *Bus Eth Quart* 499 and the references contained therein.

[20] "Utilitarianism and Cost-Benefit Analysis" in K Sayre (ed), *Values in the Electric Power Industry* (1977) 217; "Power Industry Morality" in *Symposium* (Washington DC: Edison Electrical Institute, 1979) p 94 and "Why are the Problems of Business Ethics Insoluble" in B Baumrin and B Freedman (eds), *Moral Responsibility and the Professions* (New York, NY: Haven, 1982) p 351.

[21] *After Virtue*, pp 146–156, 256–58.

Leaving aside for the moment that, in the main, this business ethics literature, erroneously in my view, treats employees as a homogeneous group with identical concerns and needs, the position of employees within a corporation is clearly a valid if not a valuable concern. However employees are far from the only group with an interest. Using virtue ethics with either the corporation viewed as a *polis* or with individual business managers and executives viewed as agents of cultural change is fundamentally flawed for the reasons that I gave in chapter two. Namely that individual business executives are not in a position to ensure that the corporation continues their ethical stance after the duration of their employment nor can they prevent their moral neutrality from clouding the face of the other. The whole point of placing the corporate entity within a virtue ethics structure and using an Aristotelian framework is to ensure that corporations understand the nature of social contributions and that these contributions are reciprocal.[22] The corporation as a city state is an edifice resulting from political and social contributions. The two positions are entirely different.[23] Additionally these methodologies avoid one of the central questions posed by virtue ethics: without a rule-based structure how can competing interests be assessed and an answer reached? The avoidance of this question in this way does not do justice to the potential of virtue ethics. This is an area that I address later in this chapter.

MacIntyre's Virtue Ethics

MacIntyre's theory of virtue is, as one would expect, similar to Aristotle's in that it describes first virtue ethics within the life of the individual and then uses virtue ethics as a way of relating the life of the individual to that of the larger community.[24] MacIntyre wastes no time in restoring what he sees as one of the principle casualties of the retreat from Aristotelian thought – the background context of an individual's life. Within the life of the individual the background context of every activity is constituted as a "social practice". A "social practice" is a co-operative form, the purpose of which is the achievement of goods internal to that practice rather than external. Internal goods in relation to

[22] J Morse, "The Missing Link between Virtue Theory and Business Ethics" (1999) 16 *J of App Phil* 47.

[23] See ch 2, text accompanying nn 39–42.

[24] J Schneewind, "Virtue, Narrative, and Community: MacIntrye and Morality" (1982) 79 *J of Phil* 653 at 655–61.

any particular practice are goods that can only be achieved by participating in that particular practice.[25] MacIntyre's example is of a chess game; the internal good here is in playing chess well. An external good in the chess example is winning money for becoming a chess champion. The distinction lies in the fact that it is not necessary to be a champion chess player in order to acquire money. Virtue(s) result from ability acquired first through compliance with rules and recognised standards and then enhanced by going beyond that position to achieve internal goods. In the chess example the virtues necessary would be those of justice, courage and honesty. These virtues would be honed through submitting to criticism, learning to accept defeat and keeping to the rules of the game.[26] The term "practice" or "social practice" is also found in the business ethics literature as a term for describing a corporate activity which has a stronger ethical foundation in favour of participation than would normally have occurred in the era of post-Fordism.[27]

It is the case that MacIntyre appears not to accept the relationship within business activity of employees' skills to the products produced as part of his scheme of internal goods and social practices. Rewards within a market economy for employees as part of the production process are driven not by their skill and endeavour but by the success of the business activity itself in producing goods for which there is a demand.[28] His criticism is aimed at the way in which business activity is organised: he sees it as excluding the features of activity that would allow business to be considered a practice. MacIntyre illustrates this through use of his,

25 *After Virtue*, p 175.

26 *After Virtue*, p 191. For a sustained critique of the notion of practices and the games analogy that MacIntyre uses, see D Miller, "Virtues Practices and Justice" in J Horton and S Mendus (eds), *supra* n 1 at p 250–8.

27 Solomon describes the "idea of business as a practice [as] absolutely central to this approach" ie, an analysis based on virtue ethics. See R Solomon, "Historicism, Communitarianism, and Commerce: An Aristotelian Approach to Business Ethics" in P Koslowski (ed), *Contemporary Economic Ethics and Business Ethics* (Berlin: Springer-Verlag, 2000) p 117 at p 122. Solomon bases this essay on his *Ethics and Excellence* monograph (New York, NY: Oxford University Press, 1992). However I am far from certain that Solomon is using "practice" in the same way as MacIntyre. I referred to his work in chapter 2 and made the point that his Aristotelian analysis was hard to follow as he seemed at one and the same time to consider the corporate entity as both a *polis* and an individual member of a *polis*, (see in particular *Ethics and Excellence* p 57). I stand by the critique of this approach that I gave there, see ch 2, n 65 and the text accompanying.

28 A MacIntyre, "Rights, practices and Marxism: reply to six critics" (1985) 7 *Analyse und Kritik* 234 at 245.

perhaps, best known example of the two fishing crews: one is organised as a profit maximising event for each individual employee, manager and owner and the other (the form he favours) is organised as a venture where individuals value each other and consider the impact of events on the surrounding community. To the first crew economic reward is the only value that they are interested in, to the second their concerns, while not excluding the economic, also centre on honing the skill of fishing and committing themselves to a life within a fishing community, whatever the pitfalls. MacIntyre admits that his two fishing crews are ideal economic types. We might critic the first type as crediting employees, even skilled employees, with more economic power than they are ever likely to enjoy.[29] The second crew type does not say enough about the uncertainties of economic life in the era of post post-Fordism to form a useful model for moving forwards. However there is a more basic point to be drawn out of MacIntyre's reasoning and that is that internal organisation of a particular practice is not of itself enough to change a paradigm of behaviour. A practice, if it is to found the virtues, must be institutionalised within a wider society.[30]

So the problem with using MacIntyre in this way is that this is only the first building block in his description of the inculcation of virtue into an individual life and from there into the wider community.[31] MacIntyre's first caveat on how the virtues are acquired – that not all practices are morally acceptable and virtues cannot be seen to emerge from the arbitrary activity of individuals[32] – is of major significance to those who classify corporate activity as a practice. Clearly the internal goods they identify and the virtues that result from them need to be part of a holistic approach. In addition some virtues cannot be tied to a specific practice, for example integrity. To overcome these difficulties MacIntyre turns to look at the narrative of an individual's life. By narrative he

[29] This approach has many similarities in result, if not sentiment, with the contractarian approach to corporate activity. There employees are seen as contracting with their employers in a world where they have equal bargaining power. If they do not like their working conditions the assumption is that they will bring the contract to an end and work elsewhere.

[30] *Response to Critics*, pp 284-8.

[31] As Dobson points out virtue ethics in relation to corporate activity based upon MacIntyre and applied as part of his total scheme places the "firm in a role that is far more active and instrusive than merely creating a contractual structure nexus or a wealth-creating machine": J Dobson, "Theory of the Firm" (1994) 10 *Econ and Phil* 73 at 85.

[32] See *After Virtue*, pp 186–8. Practices that are not acceptable are theft, perjury, bigamy, betrayal and the taking of innocent life.

means an individual's identity and responsibility for past action. Narrative, through intention, is what explains the actions of an individual. Narrative history is essential to explaining a particular act. Every individual's life has a definite narrative form, a narrative unity that the individual lives out. The life of each individual, however, is not a pre-planned project because if that were the case there would be no room for that individual to exercise choice. The role given to choice by MacIntyre echoes Bauman's position on the fate of human kind. MacIntyre presents the role of choice as "life as an unfinished narrative". Each individual has a quest to seek the good and in seeking it the individual will find out more about both the good and their own character.[33] Where MacIntyre departs from Bauman's position is in his assertion that the individual is not entirely alone. Individuals are never more than the co-authors of their own narratives in the sense that an individual plays a part in the narrative of others and vice versa. Sometimes this part is a subordinate one but nevertheless the individual is constrained by this.[34]

The third phase of MacIntyre's account of virtue ethics echoes in part the Aristotelian structure. At this stage the life of the individual meets the life of the community. The virtues carry forward the social fabric of society because an individual brings into the community an identity inherited from the past. As MacIntyre puts it "[t]he possession of an historical identity and the possession of a social identity coincide".[35] The message from MacIntyre is that all living traditions are negotiable through debate and that the virtues are those qualities that sustain traditions as they provide practices and individual lives with their historical context.[36] At this point MacIntyre turns away from the idea of a universalistic community, and indeed a responsive communitarian, one by asserting that no individual is bound by the limitations of the particularities of the society they find themselves in. The individual can, and indeed is exhorted to, move forwards.[37] What is required is that a community is sustained through pursuit of the good. The good is defined, it seems, by those parts of an individual's tradition that the individual is prepared to be at one with. Thus MacIntyre

[33] For an argument that at this stage of his theory MacIntyre is presenting nothing essentially different from "every good bourgeois moralist from Butler to Rawls", see J Schneewind, *supra* n 24 at pp 658–9.

[34] *After Virtue*, p 213.

[35] *After Virtue*, p 221.

[36] This is paraphrased from *After Virtue*, pp 221–3.

[37] *After Virtue*, p 221.

is not suggesting that tradition confers any fixed or firm social identity. Like Bauman he sees the eventual location of this as an individual's choice. Like Aristotle (and thus unlike Bauman) he sees identity as an attainable goal. Above the level of the individual MacIntyre suggests that consensus is impossible to achieve and so desirable instead is "the creation of local forms of community within which civility and the intellectual and moral life can be sustained through the new dark ages which are already upon us".[38] This insistence upon localism as the appropriate locator for community is something that comes to MacIntyre through his reading of Aquinas.[39]

MacIntyre reiterates this proposition in *Whose Justice? Which Rationality?*[40] He emphasises that existence is a shared enterprise by community members: "one cannot think for oneself if one thinks entirely by oneself . . . it is only by participation in a rational practice-based community that one becomes rational".[41] The stress laid on rationality here is the central tenet of *Whose Justice? Which Rationality?* Rationality is distinguished from its enlightenment context by stressing the need for traditions to be presented in their historical context.[42] MacIntyre wishes to explain how different traditions of thought compete with each other with the rational superiority of one over another eventually being established. His account is one that relies on a historical examination of the development of ethical traditions within Western thought from Aristotle to Hume.[43] This search for a primary tradition routed in rationality is not one with which I wish to engage. MacIntyre is important to the intellectual project of this book because he offers a route between Aristotle and Bauman. I am interested in how far his account of virtue ethics moves the Aristotelian position that was the focus of chapter two towards the position of post-modern critique occupied by Bauman.

[38] *After Virtue*, p 263.

[39] P Weithman, "Complementarity and Equality in the Political Thought of Thomas Aquinas" (1998) 59 *Theo Studies* 277.

[40] (London: Duckworth, 1988).

[41] *Whose Justice? Which Rationality?* (London: Duckworth, 1988) p 396.

[42] *Whose Justice*, pp 7–9.

[43] For a summary and critique see J Annas, "MacIntyre on Traditions" (1989) 18 *Phil and Pub Affairs* 388 and M Nussbaum "Recoiling from Reason" (1989) *New York Rev Books*, 7 December, 36.

2. IDEAS FOR CONTEMPORARY VIRTUES

Situating Virtue Ethics

To be able to situate virtue ethics within a framework that acknowledges the progressive nature of society in the twenty-first century is essential if virtue ethics is to bear the significance for human existence that I have given it. MacIntyre's insistence that possession of the virtues must come from the "local and particular"[44] society that an individual is situated within and that the individual can move forwards beyond the position that the particular society offers does much to allow Aristotelian philosophy to speak to the difficulties of life in the third millennium highlighted by Bauman and Giddens. There is no requirement of a universalistic community with a corresponding common good. The common good is now that of a particular society at a particular time. Virtues are relative to each community as that community forms and reforms them.[45] Virtues contain as aspects of an individual's character and each individual's motive in doing an act is what holds the key as to whether that act is virtuous. This is straight from MacIntyre's Aristotelian inheritance. However the cumulative effect of MacIntyre's approach to Aristotelian ethics is to move them significantly towards Bauman's position; gone are stumbling blocks such as the existence of fixed identity and fixed community in either locus or temporality. It is possible to assert that some behaviours can never be virtues and that some virtues, such as integrity, attach to all social roles, irrespective of community.

This picture of the virtues as adaptable to communities and as situated within local communities allows us to envisage a situation in which contemporary virtues might echo the types of values that proponents of both a Third Way and a postmodern morality might suggest. It is this flexibility in establishing and re-establishing the virtues that allows us to locate these in a society which in the fairly recent past reflected the virtues of the New Right. There are likely to be virtues in common between these two societies such as integrity and honesty but also differences such as the nature of self-reliance and the role of trust. From the material in chapters one and two we can link the following general virtues to the positions adopted in response to post post-

[44] *After Virtue*, pp 126–7.
[45] *After Virtue*, pp 256–8.

Fordism. From the political discourse of New Labour there is compassion; the idea that others should not be allowed to feel lonely and helpless. Not being afraid to care in this way comes not only from the political. What was expressed by thousands of people in the first week of September 1997 – the week after the death of Princess Diana – was an approval of and sharing of the way in which she allowed herself to listen to the needs of others. There is an idea of the refreshing of the self here, that the emotional (and therefore the non-rational) can be admitted through the project of self-reflexivity, as can also, on a different level, ideas about issues such as quality of life and work/life balance. Trust and the idea of the individual being able to place trust in another, be it another individual, or some larger collective unit is an integral part of the virtues. The corporation viewed as an individual, in the way I set out in chapter two, is a pertinent example here, as more business relationships begin to advocate trust as a key feature in maintaining stability in their contractual relationships. From Giddens there are the virtues of respect, toleration and the pursuit of social justice. Respect and toleration encourage an interaction with and indeed a veneration of difference not just an embrace of it followed by absorption and ultimately eradication. An idea of social justice in many ways underpins all of these virtues but becomes a virtue in itself through notions of the promotion of social inclusion and participation. Bauman, with his idea of an individual's choice to be moral or not and his description of choice "as fate" makes it clear that pursuit of these virtues is not easy, thus the element of individual aspiration that Aristotle focused upon is still present.

The certainty that Aristotle felt about the suitability of the virtues he identified is demonstrated by his detailed description of how the virtues are both acquired by the young and inculcated in them.[46] His ideas of instruction in the virtues then endured for centuries.[47] MacIntyre does not have a parallel position as such, although his frequent use of examples based upon games would suggest that he sees virtue acquisition as part of a structure built around obedience to laws

[46] S Broadie, *Ethics with Aristotle* (Oxford: Oxford University Press, 1991) pp 103–10; D Carr, *Educating the Virtues* (London: Routledge, 1991) pp 50–60.

[47] Erasmus wrote *Civilite Morum Puerilium* in 1530 in which Aristotelian ideas of how the educational process could be used to produce better citizens imbued with the virtues played a large part. For a discussion of virtues and their use by Norbert Elias in the context of manners see J Minson, *Questions of Conduct: Sexual Harassment, Citizenship, Government* (London: Macmillan, 1993).

and regulations. A theory of moral development based on observation and practice while the individual is situated within a supportive social institution. MacIntyre's one explicit point is that the modern state is totally unfitted to provide any sort of moral education for a community. This comes no doubt from his view that the current age is one of moral bankruptcy. It maybe, as I have suggested before, that MacIntyre would now not be so trenchant in his condemnation. However few would see it as the role of the state, where that state exists as any type of liberal democracy, to act as the primary source of education for the virtues. The choice of what to do, whether to be moral or not in Bauman's terms, remains with the individual. This is an entirely different proposition from the state recognising and promoting particular virtues in a facilitative fashion.[48] For example a DFE Circular was issued in April 2000, entitled *The Citizenship Order*.[49] This made citizenship education in schools a foundation subject from September 2000 and a compulsory part of the curriculum from 2002 onwards. The idea, it seems, is to imbue a level of political and social literacy in school-age children. They are encouraged to participate in school and local projects, to take decisions for themselves while considering other points of view and assessing the implications of their chosen course of action. They are instructed in the workings of the economic and political system and to think of the world as a global community with all the political, economic, environmental and social implications of this. A concern that has been voiced about citizenship education and one which also applies to any identification of certain character traits as virtues, is how does anyone know that these are indeed universal values. The suggestion with regard to education is that any attempts at political and social literacy should be structured around the Human Rights Act 1998 and the Children Act 1988.[50] This itself shows a touching faith in the universal approval of particular legal provisions. There is nothing to indicate that even benign legislation is universally

[48] N Rose, "Inventiveness in Politics" (1999) 28 *Econ and Soc* 467 at 477–8.

[49] The Citizenship Order and its contents was underpinned by the recommendations of the Advisory Group on Citizenship in *Education for Citizenship and the Teaching of Democracy in Schools* (otherwise known as the Crick Report) Qualifications and Curriculum Authority (1998) London. On the Crick Report see N Pearce and S Spencer, "Education for Citizenship: The Crick Report" (1999) 70 *Pol Quart* 219. On the *Citizenship Order* see B Crick, *Essays on Citizenship* (London: Continuum, 2000) at pp 113–21.

[50] H Starkey, "Citizenship Education in France and Britain" (2000) 11 *The Curriculum Journal* 39 at 50–2.

approved of. There are two points to be made here about virtue ethics. The first is that MacIntyre makes it very clear that an individual is not bound by the particularities of any society and is free to make their own way forward. The second is that virtues are entirely aspirational. They are not compulsory; an individual will pursue them if it is their desire to do so. However progress towards a society based on those virtues and sustainment of that society can only occur if the virtues are practised.

Virtue Ethics and Cultural Relativity

Proponents of virtue ethics are likely to be confronted by the charge of cultural relativism on the grounds that although Aristotle was prescribing virtue ethics for a universalistic community his virtues were drawn entirely from Athenian society. Martha Nussbaum, another contemporary Aristotelian, disputes this proposition by ascribing to Aristotle an objective view of society, in that his selection of virtues was based not just on the qualities he admired in his own society of Athens, but on other cultures of which he was aware.[51] Her approach is not uncontroversial within classical studies and philosophical scholarship. However, Nussbaum's position on this point in relation to the application of virtue ethics to contemporary society is compromised by her admission that not only are new circumstances and new evidence relevant to Aristotle's virtues but that the impact of local conditions can also be accounted for in this way. The context in which a decision is to be taken has always been admitted by virtue ethics. Decisions that are reached through the application of virtue ethics are necessarily context-sensitive because the absence of general ethical rules and principles dictates that context has to be taken into account. The context of a particular dilemma is however different to revising the virtues themselves in the light of new circumstances and evidence.[52]

Nussbaum, it would seem, is in no stronger position in relation to charges of cultural relativism than MacIntyre who leaves himself open to this charge because of his advocacy of localism and the entwining of virtue ethics with ideas of local community. Bauman also shares the charge of cultural relativism for rather different reasons. It is the

[51] M Nussbaum, "Non-Relative Virtues: An Aristotelian Approach" (1988) XIII *Midwest Studies in Philosophy*. Her argument on objectivity in Aristotle's virtues is set out in the first part of her article (32–9).

[52] *Ibid*, at pp 43–45

obvious corollary to his view that the choice to be moral or not lies at the level of the individual. This is because the individual is situated in a world in which there is no fixed identity for anyone, where economic flexibility and uncertainty dominate and where judgements of value and morality are made expressly in relation to specific socio-historic contexts.[53] If this pluralism is embraced and valued there can then be no absorption of values and identities into a hierarchy of cultural positions. This leaves us with nothing but potentially contradictory cultural codes. Or perhaps worse still unable to condemn practices which on a personal level we might abhor such as female circumcision for example. Female circumcision is a favourite example of those for whom cultural relativism[54] is problematic but in my view it is a comparatively weak one.[55] It is medically damaging to the women who are subjected to it, it appears to have no offsetting advantages and in addition it is opposed by some who otherwise accept accompanying cultural norms.[56] A "hard case" example, similar to the one used by Hursthouse in relation to abortion and the use of virtue ethics for decision making and cited in chapter two,[57] would be infanticide. By this I mean infanticide practised in cultures where the view is taken that an additional child cannot be supported in terms of food and warmth or a child born with a disability is considered to have no viable future in terms of the medical treatment needed and subsequent quality of life. This example would generate heated debate in many other cultures rather than general approbation.

[53] C Scott, *The Question of Ethics: Nietzsche, Foucault, Heidegger* (Bloomington, IN: Indiana University Press, 1990).

[54] See for example H Steiner and P Alston, *International Human Rights in Context* (Oxford: Clarendon Press, 1996) at p 241.

[55] See K Green and H Lim, "What is the Thing About Female Circumcision? Legal Education and Human Rights" (1998) 7 *Social and Legal Studies* 365 at 368. Green and Lim offer three reasons why female circumcision has become "the example" within universal rights discourse of the consequence of admitting cultural relativism; first it is seen as cruel and primitive: second it is seen as a practice taking one form and so rendering it a simple issue: third it is indicative of the way the West constructs the Other, in this case an African child is constructed as mutilated through the lens of Western notions of childhood and the normal body.

[56] L Kopelman, "Female Circumcision/Genital Mutilation and Ethical Relativism" (1994) 20 *Second Opinion* 55.

[57] See ch 2, text accompanying n 96.

The Role of Legislation and Voluntary Codes

At one level we can speculate on whether it is ever possible to achieve consensus around an all-encompassing set of principles without these principles themselves or their application being either so vacuous as to be devoid of content or falling foul of the charge opposite to cultural relativism – cultural imperialism. If this is indeed the case then there is no reason to condemn virtue ethics and the project of the individual within a local community, which, after all, under MacIntyre's interpretation make no claim to universality. As illustrative of this I offer three rather different examples. These are domestic legislation in the form of the Human Rights Act 1998, codes of corporate conduct issued by international bodies such as the International Labour Organization, the United Nations[58] and the Organization for Economic Co-operation and Development and the Integrative Social Contract theory (ISC) of Donaldson and Dunfee.[59] The Human Rights Act (HRA) 1998 and its progenitors the Universal Declaration of Human Rights[60] and the European Convention on Human Rights contain rights and duties which have no universal agreed meaning, hence the need for a supranational body – the Court of Human Rights in Strasbourg – to act as the ultimate guardian for the development of interpretative standards. This position is not assisted by the activities of the legal academy. It might be expected that a jurisprudence of rights would develop there but while some academics, taking their lead in many cases from American scholarship,[61] have chosen to look at issues of constitionalism and constitutional culture,[62] for many UK legal scholars the

[58] In December 1996 the UN issued the Declaration Against Corruption and Bribery in International Commercial Transactions, as did the EU. On the emergence of mechanisms to deal with bribery and corruption see D Windsor and K Getz, "Regional Market Integration and the Development of Global Norms for Enterprise Conduct" (1999) 38 *Bus and Soc* 415.

[59] T Donaldson and T Dunfee, "Integrative Social Contracts Theory" (1995) 11 *Econ and Phil* 85; "Toward a Unified Conception of Business Ethics: Integrative Social Contracts Theory" (1994) 19 *Acad of Manag Rev* 252; *The Ties that Bind* (Cambridge, MA: Harvard BS, 1999).

[60] See F Klug, *Values for a Godless Age* (London: Penguin, 2000) for an overview of the legislative enactment of the HRA in the UK and some preliminary comments about potential underlying philosophical debates.

[61] See, for example, J Tully, *Strange Multiplicity: Constitutionalism in an Age of Diversity* (Cambridge: Cambridge University Press, 1995).

[62] Probably the best example of this is Murray Hunt, *Using Human Rights Law in Court* (Oxford: Hart Publishing, 1997).

enactment of the HRA 1998 has encouraged them to push positivism to the fore and engage in lengthy exegesis on legal doctrine[63] and concentrate on what needs to be "done" in order to educate justice professionals in the application of rights. Thus the much more fundamental inquiry, into what is required for the transfer of human rights and humanity into legal rights and the legal subject, is ignored.[64]

The corporate codes of conduct suggested by *inter alia* the International Labour Organization and the Organization for Economic Co-operation and Development have been largely unsuccessful. To achieve any degree of consensual support and to be of application in any and every situation of corporate activity these codes are composed in very broad general terms and demand an inoffensively low level of commitment.[65] Codes of this type or rules networks of this type remove the aspirational elements that behaviours built upon individual corporate character and will are more likely to contain. There are, of course, numerous other types of codes of conduct which purport in some way to control global or national corporate behaviour such as codes put

[63] A Lester and D Pannick, *Human Rights Law and Practice* (London: Butterworths, 1999) for example.

[64] The two most interesting texts to date on the enactment of Human Rights legislation in the UK and what this might actually involve are those of Colin Harvey and Costas Douzinas. Harvey's work is an examination of the asylum issue using the structures of dialogic democracy as a way of seeing and hearing the Other, see Colin J Harvey, *Seeking Asylum in the UK: Problems and Prospects* (London: Butterworths, 2000) and "Dissident Voices: Refugees, Human Rights and Asylum in Europe" (2000) 9 *Social and Legal Studies* 367. C Douzinas offers a brilliant engagement with the philosophy of rights through the subject of humanity and the Other, using ideas on the subject drawn from metaphysics and grounded in the ethics of Levinas amongst others. To illustrate his point that rights exist only in relation to other rights Douzinas uses the example of the loss of life caused by the NATO bombing of Kosovo and the subsequent treatment of the ethnic Serbians by the Albanians restored to Kosovo. See C Douzinas, *The End of Human Rights* (Oxford: Hart Publishing, 2000) at p 312 and ch 13. An interesting point of comparison here which illustrates the way in which human rights are popularly conceived of as owned, guarded and delivered by the Western world is provided by the journalist/social commentator Polly Toynbee; "In our political and social culture we have a democratic way of life which we know . . . is far better than any other in the history of humanity . . . Possibly the war in Kosovo was the beginning of the realisation that Western societies have a moral duty to ensure that the political culture of human rights reaches right inside foreign borders where . . . ethnic cleansers think they are safe": P Toynbee, "Who's Afraid of Global Culture?" in W Hutton and A Giddens (ed), *On the Edge* (London: Vintage, 2001) p 191 at pp 196–200.

[65] A Kolk et al, "International Codes of Conduct and Corporate Social Responsibility: Can Transnational Corporations Regulate Themselves?" (1999) 8 *Transnational Corporations* 143 at 161.

forward by national governments, by corporations themselves,[66] by non-governmental organisations and interventions promulgated by some combination of these interests.[67] There are also legislative interventions issued by national governments.[68] The difficulty with this type of involvement is that, as chapter one indicated, additional regulation of corporate activity is likely to be met with a knee-jerk response of non-compliance or minimum compliance by the corporate sector.[69] This can be compared with internationally negotiated agreements around regional and global market integration. This is not the issue of harmonisation of national regulation around business activity but more the negotiation of conditions necessary for transnational economic exchange. The type of negotiations and resulting agreements such as GATT that emerge take place between large actors such as the EU and the WTO. The popular protests against these negotiations that took place in Seattle in December 1999 and in other cities hosting the talks point to the level of interest that these negotiating parties take in attempting to establish international policy around issues such as child labour. The protests themselves may mark a return to a more aggressive social protest against international capitalism than has been observed for many years. The availability of rapid communications technology and access to travel is clearly a factor in its organisation.[70]

[66] This might take the form of single in-house corporate planning in the manner described in the text accompanying notes 82–85 below or a group of companies involved in the same industry. See A Prakash, "Responsible Care: An Assessment" (2000) 39 *Bus & Soc* 183. The author offers an analysis of the Chemical Manufacturers Association Code of corporate behaviour from a variety of perspectives that explain the benefits of membership over non-membership, the weakness of monitoring and enforcement mechanisms and the spin offs in terms of public goodwill. The problem with codes of this type is that their voluntary and self-regulatory nature means that membership is an opportunity to exercise "club" rules over non-members, in other words to push standards to a level that forces non-members out of the market. This does not unfortunately mean that within the club boundaries standards remain high.

[67] For example the CAUX Round Table Principles for Business <www.cauxroundtable.org>.

[68] Consider for example the US position where the Foreign Corrupt Practices Act 1977 exists to regulate the conduct of corporations registered in the US when those corporations are engaged in business activity abroad. The legislation has been much amended over the years and doubts exist about how effectively it is enforced, see J Kaikati et al, "The Price of International Business Morality: 20 years under the Foreign Corrupt Practices Act" (2000) 26 *J of Bus Eth* 213. Sweden is the only other nation state to have enacted similar legislation. It did so in 1978.

[69] See ch 1, text accompanying nn 179–85.

[70] M Fannin et al, "The battle in Seattle: a response from local geographers in the midst of the WTO ministerial meetings" (2000) 32 *Antipode* 215.

Integrative social contract theory is an attempt to arrive at a definition of ethical behaviour specifically in the economic sphere by using a hypothetical social contract which itself is constructed upon the "moral understandings" of individuals operating within existing "economic systems and organisations".[71] This hypothetical social contract is Rawlsian in nature in that its focus is on what rules for economic transactions society members would want applied to them in situations where they were unaware of their position under the rules. This social contract is labelled the macro-social contract and within it there is apparently "moral free space".[72] This moral free space is developed downwards so that contractors can, if they wish, establish for "their economic communities norms more specific than those that can be deduced through general moral rationality".[73] These specific norms are to be regarded as microsocial contracts. Donaldson and Dunfee refute any ideas of relativism within this arrangement by subjecting these norms to three controls: a requirement of consent, the application of hypernorms and the formulation of priority rules to deal with conflicts arising from the application of community norms.

There are numerous difficulties with this structure. As with any structure derived from general principles there are definitional problems: the meaning of "community", discourse problems (and this is additionally so here as Donaldson and Dunfee are suggesting a structure that is driven top down as opposed to applied from the bottom up) in that it is not clear how the micro-social contract would be arrived at and a lack of designation between what can be dealt with at micro level and what must be within the macro level. Hyper-norms add to the definitional confusion. They are fundamental norms; norms by which other norms are to be judged. They are "sufficiently fundamental" to "serve as a source of evaluation and criticism of community generated behaviour".[74] It is not clear whether these hyper-norms are norms to deal with ethical economic behaviour only or whether they are norms of general application. A contractual edifice of this nature would seem more likely to preserve vestiges of cultural relativism than guard against them.[75]

[71] T Donaldson and T Dunfee, "Integrative Social Contracts Theory" (1995) 11 *Econ and Phil* 85 at 86.

[72] *Ibid*, at p 89.

[73] *Ibid*, at p 94.

[74] *Ibid*, at p 96.

[75] M Douglas, "Integrative Social Contracts Theory: Hype over Hypernorms" (2000) 26 *J of Bus Eth* 101. Douglas takes the position that hyper-norms add little to ISCT that

Globalisation and Cultural Relativity

There are also other ways to deflect the impact of the cultural relativity charge upon Bauman's necessarily individualised life and MacIntyre's depiction of virtue ethics. One is to recognise that total relativism is unlikely to exist. It would depend upon the existence of communities or societies that had no links or contacts with any other social group or groups. The globalisation of capital, and for individuals; increased mobility through the availability of travel, forced relocation to seek employment, destruction of local environments through product construction, relocation or ecological damage and the availability of access to technology almost anywhere in the world, have taken away the importance of space[76] and ended insularity. Events and meetings can take place anywhere and be reported everywhere. The focus of information is now at least national, if not extraterritorial, geographically local news, such as there is, is relayed through national and extranational sources. There is now a cluster economy; nodals of activity across the world with relatively flat hierarchical structures. This is the paradox that is globalisation. Electronic communications and global markets will soon diminish the importance of geographical location for corporations except where forum shopping advantages are present. This is certainly the case for individuals with the consequence of insecurity that Bauman identifies[77] and the corrosive effect on personal relationships that Sennett asserts.[78] However mappings of economic activity demonstrate the cluster effect. Areas such as Silicon valley, both the US and UK version, for example, show a concentration of innovation and creation of firms in that locality. This is an issue that I return to when looking at regional development policies and how corporations fit or could fit their activities into these.[79]

a more detailed set of priority rules could not. With this caveat he remains broadly convinced of the utility of the theory.

[76] Z Bauman, *The Individualized Society* (Cambridge: Polity, 2001) at pp 37-8 and M Poster, *Cultural History and Postmodernity* (New York, NY: Columbia University Press, 1997) at pp 38–41.

[77] Z Bauman, see ch 1, text accompanying nn 51–6.

[78] R Sennett, see ch 1 text accompanying nn 51–6.

[79] M Porter, "Clusters and the new economies of competition" (1998) 76 *Harv Bus Rev* 77. The use of cluster as a term within regional development geography has been mapped and given several meanings to denote particular types of cluster. My preference for a descriptor is "linkages between economically related activities in spatial agglomeration". For discussion of this and other descriptors see A Lagendijk and J Cornford, "Regional institutions and knowledge-tracking new forms of regional development policy" (2000) 31 *Geoforum* 209 at 214–215.

The globalisation of capital in which I include, over and above electronic banking and the emergence of a global finance system, the creeping advance of issues such as efficiency, methods of production, and wage labour into previously subsistence level agricultural economies,[80] has had profound effects such as the dispersal of people into urban environments and the arrival of different forms of non-local cultural milieu into previously closed fora.[81] Capitalism is not a closed monolithic force that undermines and eradicates local economies. My point is rather that the issues it raises, as a force, opens up these economies to both horizontal and vertical cross-fertilisation of new ideologies and new methodologies. Thus the triangular relationships between individual actors, the state and the economy are unlikely to stay the same. As chapter one hinted at there are differing national and regional versions of capitalism.[82] Recognition of these variations by inward investing corporations often results in corporations putting together their own individual codes of conduct that they then seek to impose on their own employees or on other business ventures in the supply chain. The purpose of these codes is not necessarily to deliver any message of respect for regional or national sensibilities.[83] Instead they might be drafted as a defensive mechanism[84] to indicate to

[80] N Mouzelis, "Towards a Transcultural Value System: A New Perspective on Relativism" (2000) 10 *Responsive Community* 11.

[81] Giddens in his Reith Lectures of 1999 provided the example (true) of an anthropologist who arrived in a remote village in Africa to commence research and found the video of *Basic Instinct* playing there before its release in London, see A Giddens, *Runaway World* (London: Profile Books, 1999) at p 6.

[82] See R Heilbroner and W Milberg, *The Crisis of Vision in Modern Economic Thought* (Cambridge: Cambridge University Press, 1995) at p 109 and M Yang, "Putting Global Capitalism in Its Place" (2000) 41 *Current Anthropology* 477. Both take as their theoretical reference point the work of J K Gibson Graham, see ch 1, text accompanying nn 39–45.

[83] See T Donaldson, *The Ethics of International Business* (New York, NY: Oxford University Press, 1989): "a multinational must not be tempted to make all societies in its own image but must balance this against the risk of forgetting ethics altogether." See also with regard to the differences in business cultures between states, Z Su and A Richelieu, "Western Managers Working in Romania: Perception and Attitude Regarding Business Ethics" (1999) 24 *J Bus Eth* 133 and T Donaldson, "Values in Tension: Ethics Away from Home" (1996) 74 *Harv Bus Rev* 48. From the perspective of design and implementation of codes see V Sandborg, "Developing Global Environment Health and Safety Principles" (2000) 17 *Corporate Environmental Strategy* 170.

[84] See the material presented in C McCrudden, "Human Rights Codes for Transnational Corporations: What can the Sullivan and MacBride Principles Tell Us?" (1999) 19 *OJLS* 167 especially n 12 at 169.

potential investors, NGOs positioned geographically elsewhere or to potential customers that the corporation does not intend knowingly to participate in social dumping activities.

This appears to be particularly true of corporations in the retail sector where brand image whether in design or in labour standards may provide a competitive advantage. National governments may welcome these types of initiatives from inward investing corporations as it may relieve pressure on them to regulate business practice and yet at the same time allow them to improve/project their public image in order to capture additional investment or aid opportunities.[85] The difficulty with firm-specific codes of conduct that are imposed on employees and other corporations that are or that wish to be involved in the supply chain is generally the way in which their cultural presence is promulgated. Code provisions encourage aspirations but not necessarily ones that lead to virtuous conduct. There are likely to be rewards for code compliance in terms of contract awards or employee bonuses but these of themselves do not necessarily require either employees or other corporations to act virtuously or practice acquiring the virtues. This is particularly the case when codes are drafted so as to prohibit altogether some types of behaviour and to support others. This removes, or at least dulls, the thinking process that virtue ethics demands. A code to assist in the inculcation of virtue ethics into corporate culture must make clear what virtues an employee or corporation is to practice and allow decisions to be made within that spectrum. It must allow those within its remit to elect to act virtuously if they wish and not drive them to act only in pursuit of financial reward or other workplace recognition.

The impact upon individual lives of shared cultural experiences is perhaps a further way to combat the charge of cultural relativism. This is something that Nussbaum promotes. She identifies within Aristotle what she describes as an attempt by him to objectify the virtues. This he achieves apparently when he refers to experiences common to all humanity, for example death, bodily appetite and the need to distribute resources. While individuals may not have the same position with regard to these issues, they nevertheless will have a position and thus virtues can be "fixed by the sphere of experience".[86] Nussbaum terms

[85] J Diller, "A Social Conscience in the Global Market Place? Labour Dimensions of Codes of Conduct, Social Labeling and Investor Initiatives" (1999) 138 *Int Labour Rev* 99.

[86] M Nussbaum, "Non-Relative Virtues: An Aristotelian Approach" (1988) XIII *Midwest Studies in Philosophy* 32 at 36.

these shared experiences as "grounding experiences". She identifies eight such experiences varying from death to humour which she feels will exist in all cultures even if they do not "provide . . . a single language – neutral bedrock on which an account of virtue can be straightforwardly and unproblematically based".[87]

Elsewhere in her work[88] Nussbaum suggests a model of citizenship, world citizenship even, based upon the education in cross-cultural studies and pluralistic modes of thinking that are being offered in a number of American educational institutions. The idea of world citizenship can be linked to "grounding experiences" as further refutation of the relativist charge. As Nussbaum's work in this context is specifically concerned with issues of curriculum content in the Higher Education sector it would be wrong to criticise her conception of world citizenship as one open only to those able to participate in this elite sector. However the model that she puts forward for this sector is open to criticism. Nussbaum's idea of "citizens of the world" and the appropriate education to produce citizens of the world would seem to be one that is orientated towards the production of US citizens with a more enlightened view of the world than perhaps exists at the moment. There is certainly no interest in a model of Higher Education that could be applied to the typical age cohort of its participants no matter where in the world they studied. The suggestions are towards creating two bodies of knowledge – a knowledge of us and a knowledge of them.[89] Where is the world of postmodernity in this?

A Way Forward?

I think that the idea of postmodernity and within it the possibilities for personal development for the individual hold the key to presenting another argument to challenge those who see virtue ethics as a statement of cultural relativity only. The idea of "grounding experiences" that Nussbaum puts forward involves looking back to both events and

[87] *Ibid*, p 46.

[88] M Nussbaum, *Cultivating Humanity* (Cambridge, MA: Harvard University Press, 1997). This a volume in support of curriculum reforms in US universities to broaden the education that is offered away from traditional exposition of the humanities towards more liberal conceptions of the philosophical and cultural.

[89] *Ibid*, at p 295 "We do not fully respect the humanity of our fellow citizens . . . if we do not wish to . . . appreciate the differences between their lives and ours . . . We can acquaint them [ie students] with some rudiments about the major non-Western cultures and minority groups within our own."

to institutions which are likely to bear a far greater cultural significance than she ascribes to them. This is because either in the case of events long past they have acquired a folklore of their own, or, in the case of institutions, (and I would class mortality and what follows it for the deceased person, near kin and wider society as an institution) they are steeped in a rich cultural construction and value set[90] that makes it impossible to isolate anything but superficial similarities. It is not sufficient, I think, to assert that because death is something every culture experiences that makes it a feature of common humanity.[91]

Not withstanding my comments above about how no society is likely to be totally isolated from another and how globalisation in all its manifestations has worked to ensure this, it is still the case that entrenched rituals surrounding particular beliefs persist long after the beliefs themselves have been abandoned by many members of that society. In the UK it seems that few people opt out of the burial rites provided by the various religions even if they have not been practising members in their adult life. Much more likely to provide grounding experiences are recent unique and significant events, with no history of their own and beamed around the world via extranational news media. The novelty of these events allows each individual to create their own historical bond with them and their own response from their own history while the grounding or unifying feature perhaps is the event itself. The form that news delivery takes means that many people experience such events as literally as well as figuratively a solitary figure. Examples of the sort of events that I have in mind are the explosion of the spacecraft Challenger in January 1986 and the Millennium celebrations of 31 December 1999–1 January 2000. For this last event the technology of global media made it possible to see the reactions and celebrations respectively of other cultures in their time frame, to share, to acknowledge, and to accept the validity of their experiences. It seems to me that these types of events are more likely to produce cross-cultural knowledge and at the

[90] D Davies, *Death Ritual and Belief* (London: Cassell, 1997) pp 81–92. No more than a glance at this type of text is needed to explain that thoughts of the meaning of death, the afterlife and the purposes of mortuary ritual vary hugely across cultures.

[91] M Nussbaum, "Non-Relative Virtues: An Aristotelian Approach" (1988) XIII *Midwest Studies in Philosophy* 32 at 46–7: "When we read Sophocles' *Antigone*, we see a good deal that seems strange to us; and we have not read the play well if we do not notice how far its conceptions of death, womanhood, and so on differ from our own. But it is still possible for us to be moved by the drama, . . . to regard their debates as reflections upon virtue that speak to our own experience, and their choices as choices in sphere of conduct in which we too must choose". Who here is the "we"? Who is the "they"?

same time to allow an individual to work on their own biography. Through this individuals shape their social identity, in MacIntyre's terms, which combines with a received historical identity to contribute to community life. Even historical identity is subject to renegotiation in the context of "anniversary replays" of unique events. For example the recent replays of the Challenger accident on the occasion of the fifteenth anniversary of its explosion caused individuals to reflect on their original memory of the event and perhaps then to reassess and to re-evaluate their experience in the light of more current experiences and discourses. Likewise the death of John Kennedy Junior had the potential to result in the recycling of memories and emotions held from the assassination of his father in 1963. On John Junior's death, the images of him as a small boy – Jonjo – saluting the national flag of America, in which his father's coffin was draped, were replayed and projected around the world.

3. THE CORPORATE ENVIRONMENT FOR CORPORATE SOCIAL INTERVENTION

Setting the Scene

Corporate Social Intervention is the term that I intend to use to describe what is perhaps more familiarly called corporate community involvement or corporate social responsibility. Corporate social intervention is a term that in my view more accurately denotes what it is that corporations are doing when the decision is taken to distribute profits more widely than to shareholders alone. As I explained in chapter one, any corporate social intervention that is to answer the question raised about corporate legitimacy has to be a strategic one in the sense of strategic to the needs of society. In other words an intervention that at the very least does not impose additional burdens on other assistance orientated organisations and one that is broadly sustainable, if it is to capture the aspirations of the virtues. The premier driver behind corporate social intervention should be a desire to do what is required to be a virtuous corporation in both the planning and execution of any intervention. If corporate social intervention is to be virtuous then it has to be done for its own sake or as part of a holistic business strategy that itself reflects the virtues, not one that is orientated towards seeking competitive advantage. This, as chapter one explained, does not involve a complete rejection of the profit motive or the adoption of a very different redistribution system, it demands a re-assessment of the underlying purposes of corporate activity and a complete re-thinking of how those purposes might be achieved. However it is important to recognise that there are other drivers that might shape the environment in which all corporate activity, including social intervention, takes place. Some of these such as government-inspired regeneration strategies and work practices in the era of post post-Fordism were touched upon in chapter one in the context of the need for corporations to participate in such ventures in order to re-establish their legitimacy. In this section I want to look at regeneration strategies and other drivers from the standpoint of how they construct an environment for corporate activity. Excluded from this analysis is any consideration of the legal regulation surrounding corporate activity. I take legal regulation and compliance with legal regulation to be a given baseline; the rules of the game as Friedman so famously put it.[92]

Corporations do not operate within a vacuum, like all organisations they align themselves to their environment; social, political and economic.[93] The idea of a strategy shaped by external and internal factors is not a new one.[94] It is against this background that proponents of the learning organisation paradigm have formulated their theory. In its simplest form this theory is that in an environment of rapid and unpredictable change the only corporations that survive are those that can learn and then leverage that learning within the organisation.[95] Much of the learning organisation literature is focused on issues such as Total Quality Management and leadership structures. However it is possible to map developments in corporate social intervention against the social and political landscape that was set out in chapter one to demonstrate the impact of corporate learning and the development of responsive strategic thinking in this area. The early 1980s were characterised by discretionary corporate donations usually in the form of cash gifts to the favoured causes of influential executives free from notions of sustainability that would come with more extended project support.

[92] M Friedman, *Capitalism and Freedom* (Chicago, IL: University of Chicago Press, 1962) at p 133.

[93] B Husted, "A Contingency Theory of Corporate Social Performance" (2000) 39 *Bus and Soc* 24 at 29.

[94] R Miles and C Snow, "Fit, Failure and the hall of fame" (1984) 26 *Calif Manag Rev* 10 at 11.

[95] P Senge *The Fifth Discipline* (New York, NY: Doubleday, 1990).

The idea that corporate social intervention should become part of corporate life and integrated into corporate strategy began to evolve in the late 1980's.[96] This drive towards integration has continued throughout the 1990's with the development of cause related marketing programmes allowing corporations to identify themselves with particular public campaigns.[97] These developments fit neatly with the eras of the New Right and unrestrained profit-taking for immediate investor gain, the corporate collapses of the late 1980s and early 1990s and the changed political and economic map of the late 1990s.

It is also possible to overlay these developments in corporate social intervention with developments in the theory of the firm. This has moved from the idea of the firm as a nexus of private contracts in which regulatory issues were settled by the market or use of the market,[98] to a wider conception of corporate responsibility extending to those groups that, whilst affected by corporate activity, stand outside the matrix of immediate property interest.[99] This model of wider interest is one that is framed as "the stakeholder issue". A contractual relationship is not necessary to be a stakeholder, with "contractual" here denoting not just legally enforceable arrangements but also more loosely those of contract in an administrative sense of the word. To reverse a classic proposition, it is status that is of greater importance.[100] In chapter one I made my position on the bankruptcy of the stakeholder device as a tool for analysis in the context of legal reform of company law very clear.[101] Later in this chapter I deal, again from a negative standpoint, with its use in the context of corporate social intervention specifically. I suggest, instead, a model that identifies needs through use of needs audits and expresses responses to these

[96] T Mescon and D Tilson, "Corporate Philanthropy: A Strategic Approach to the Bottom-Line" (1987) 29 *Calif Manag Rev* 49.

[97] C Fleisher and R Hoewing, "Strategically Managing Corporate External Relations: New Challenges and Opportunities" (1992) 5 *J of Strat Change* 287.

[98] Otherwise known as the Law and Economics approach, this is dealt with in more detail in the introduction to this book.

[99] D Young and D Burlingame, "Paradigm Lost: Research toward a New Understanding of Corporate Philanthropy" in D Young and D Burlingame (eds), *Philanthropy at the Crossroads* (Bloomington, IN: Indiana University Press, 1996).

[100] The proposition in question "from status to contract" belongs to Henry Maine, *Ancient Law* (London: Routledge & Sons, 1905) at p 141. The original edition appeared in 1861. The point that Maine was making with this proposition was one of progression – the progression from relationships based upon agreement being structured through governance of the family to these relationships being based upon contract.

[101] See ch 1, text accompanying nn 101–12.

needs through care plans. Thus my reference to "status" and "contract" and the reversal of these positions is made precisely to denote relationships within the corporate sector that are based on the personal and on the model of needs and caring for needs rather than on the more rights-based notion of stakeholding.

Competitive pressure on profit-making is a significant factor in the corporate environment. There is more consumer choice exercised between products as a result of the availability of consumer information and consumer mobility. The initial Third Way bargain for corporations between themselves and the state that was referred to in chapter one[102] has been augmented by other Government agendas. Corporate social responsibility has become a portfolio raised to Ministerial level and Regional development is a major part of Government Policy. The first of these is obviously directed at corporations, the second not so obviously but nevertheless it opens up exploitation opportunities and with these come corresponding duties. These external factors also have an impact within the corporation itself. The corporation stands in relation to those outside it as a social unit in and of itself. It is also a self-reproducing unit as it is assured of perpetual succession for as long as it wishes. Corporate employees are not hermetically sealed within the corporation. They have identities outside the workplace. These identities are exposed to the political and social discourses identified in chapter one, their behaviour in response to these helped shape the issues of character put forward as virtues. Employees both shape and are shaped themselves by the corporation.[103] They bring with them their own life narratives that add to that of the corporation and in exchange the corporation adds to these narratives. This idea of life narrative is one that derives from my earlier discussion of MacIntyre. Equally it is a concept that the business ethicist William Frederick calls the "X" factor; the unknown beliefs that each employee brings to the employment role that may or may not influence corporate activity.[104] Employees are not a homogenous group with identical interests and concerns. They may have different perspectives on a variety of issues borne out of differences of race, sexuality, religious persuasion and other major life issues. Additionally they are also likely to be divided by

[102] See ch 1, text accompanying nn 129–32.

[103] E Schoenberger, *The Cultural Crisis of the Firm* (Oxford: Blackwell, 1997) at p 116.

[104] W Frederick, *Values Nature and Culture in the American Corporation* (New York, NY: Oxford University Press, 1995) at pp 23, 101–33.

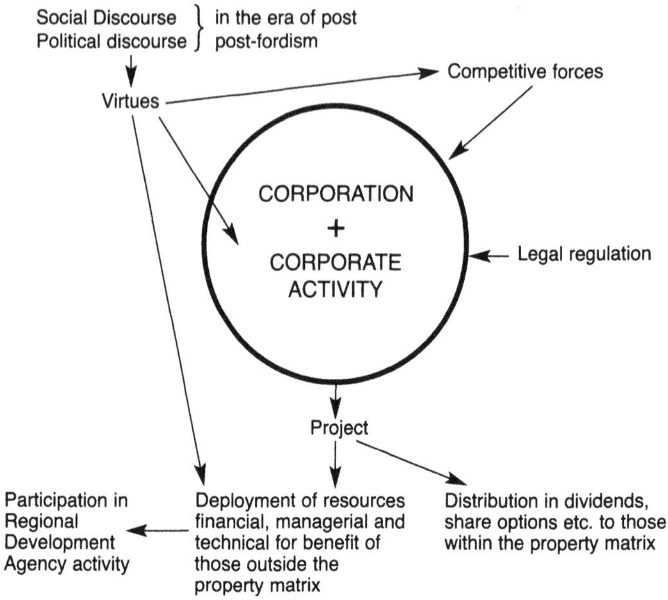

Virtues govern business activity with corporation, employee behaviour within corporation, deployment of resources and also structure how competition is pursued.

Figure 3.1

economic and care issues. Main earners and second earners, primary child carers or elderly relative carers and single wage earners have different concerns and leading on from that perhaps different expectations of their employers.[105] Employees also face the issue of competing loyalties: loyalty to trade union agendas, to their professional values or perhaps to environmental concerns.[106] These loyalties have an ongoing role in life narratives and may have some input into internal practices within the corporation. In addition specific political policies, such as those around the work/life balance, designed to assist those in employment or those who wish to become employed and more general policies around the regeneration of particular geographical areas will cut into the relationship of employee and employer.

[105] It is this failure to recognise difference through dialogue strategies that formed the basis of my criticisms of works councils in ch 1, see the text accompanying nn 191–3.

[106] Whistleblowers now have their interests safeguarded by the Public Interest Disclosure Act 1999.

Agendas for Regional Development and the Corporate Role

Regional Development Agencies (RDAs) were launched in eight English regions in April 1999, with a ninth (London) following in July 2000. This policy step was the result of the synthesis of a number of different determinants.[107] As chapter one touched upon, the idea of a "Europe of the Regions" has been driven from the EU policy making organs downwards for some time. This downwards drive is likely to continue as the European Union urges on not only economic development and regeneration of Europe's regions but also a new Social Agenda. The Commission Communication on the new Social Agenda called for action to be underpinned by:

> "an improved form of governance. This means providing a clear and active role to all stakeholders and actors . . . . All actors, the European Union institutions, the Member States, the regional and local levels, the social partners, civil society and companies have an important role to play".[108]

Regional structures in the UK have been informally created so that there can be participation in the distribution of European Structural Funds.[109] Partnerships at local level between public and private sector actors were also a key feature of these EU policy initiatives.[110] At national level successive Conservative governments echoed this strategy of informal regional development and partnership structures, although the emphasis then was on specific areas of urban regeneration through the use of Urban Development Corporations and the City Challenge Project, set up in 1991.[111] Business in the Community was launched by Government in 1981 to support these ventures followed by

[107] M Jones and G Macleod, "Towards a Regional Renaissance? Reconfiguring and Rescaling England's Economic Governance" (1999) 24 *Trans Inst Brit Geog* 295.

[108] Communication from the Commission to the Council, the European Parliament, the Economic and Social Committee and the Committee of the Regions: Social Policy Agenda COM (2000) 379 final at para 3.2.

[109] It is also possible to obtain European Social Fund grants for "new approaches to Corporate Social Responsibility including awareness raising, extension to include small and medium sized enterprises and exchanges of best practice under ESF Regulations EC 1984/1999 Art 6.

[110] For example Comission of the European Community, "Medium-term Social Action Programme" 1995–1997 *Social Europe* 1/95 DGV.

[111] An overview of Conservative urban regeneration and development policy can be found in A Adair, et al "Evaluation of Investor Behaviour in Urban Regeneration" (1999) 36 *Urban Studies* 2031 at pp 2031–4.

Training and Enterprise Councils.[112] Programmes such as the Single Regeneration Budget Challenge Fund demanded partnership structures as a prerequisite to funding allocation.

In an altogether different sphere from the economic, constitutional developments within the union state of the UK from the beginning of the 1997 Parliament onwards have created a rather different climate for regionalism. Leaving aside the issue of a form of devolved governance for Northern Ireland as this involves rather different issues, the current Labour administration has seen the passage of both the Scottish and Welsh devolution legislation. Scotland and Wales now have elected assemblies, albeit with rather different powers from each other, with development agendas.[113] At times English regionalism has been seen as a non-existent tradition or "the dog that never barked".[114] That was certainly true in a formal sense from 1979 onwards as the attacks on regional planning structures by the Thatcher Government demonstrate. There also has been little documented backlash against Scottish and Welsh devolution in terms of a call for an "English" Parliament. Nevertheless regions at the extremities of England – Cornwall and the North East for example – have long argued that their physical distance from London has disadvantaged them. The final card in the regional development game has been the recognition that the weakening of the nation state in the face of globalisation makes a stronger, more reflexive regional policy the only way to promote economic restructuring.[115] As the Secretary of State for Trade and Industry phrased it:

> "In the modern economy we can not build a strong economy, a strong nation, if we have a tail of under-performing regions. We need all of our

[112] The Conservative Election Manifesto 1992 described Training and Enterprise Councils as "the most significant partnerships between government and industry this century. Urban Development Corporations were designated the flagship of 1980s urban policy, see B Robson et al, *Assessing the Impact of Urban Policy* (London: HMSO, 1994).

[113] For a detailed analysis of these constitutional developments see J Tomaney, "End of the Empire State? New Labour and Devolution in the UK." (2000) 24 *Int J of Urban and Regional Research* 675 at 686f.

[114] C Harvie, "English regionalism: the dog that never barked" in B Crick (ed), *National Identities: The Constitution of the UK* (Oxford: Blackwell, 1991). For a different view of regional pressure for devolution see P Lynch, "New Labour and the English Regional Development Agencies: Devolution as Evolution" (1999) 33 *Reg Stud* 73.

[115] M Storper,"The Resurgence of regional economies, ten years later: the region as a nexus of untraded dependencies" (1995) 2 *Euro Urban and Regional Studies* 191 and M Rocco, "Competition, Collaboration and the New Industrial Districts: Examining the Institutional Turn in Local Economic Development" (1999) 36 *Urban Studies* 951.

regions firing on all cylinders .... In order to enjoy increasing prosperity in our country we need strong economic growth in all our regions".[116]

Notwithstanding the emphasis within EU policy, rhetorically at least, on the linkage between social exclusion and regional economic regeneration,[117] the statutory *raison d'être* that was given to each of the nine RDAs was almost entirely economic; the furthering of economic development, the development of skills relevant to employment, the promotion of business competitiveness and efficiency and the promotion of sustainable development and employment. Each RDA was tasked with "provid[ing] a business-driven direction for its region's economy" on the basis that "the overall aim of each RDA's Regional Strategy [would] be to improve the competitiveness of each region".[118] RDAs will have considerable budgetary autonomy within their ring-fenced funding and together will be responsible for the spending of more than two billion pounds of public money. Social exclusion appears only as a secondary consideration – a mere passing acknowledgement of the fact that it may have something to do with varying economic performance between regions and that it may need to be addressed as a result. The apparent subordination of the social to the economic in this way is unfortunate in the sense that it may raise concerns about the control of labour and other players in civil society by business interests. The DETR places considerable emphasis on the establishment and facilitation of collaborative networks within regions.[119] The composition of these networks is left to the individual agencies but the advice of the DETR is that local authorities and other regional players such as Chambers of Commerce, Universities and the Voluntary Sector be included. If these networks function as inclusive mechanisms[120] then fears of business domination may be allayed.

[116] S Byers Speech to the LGA Economic Regeneration Conference, Liverpool, 21 November 2000.

[117] *Regeneration from Within* (Dublin: European Foundation for the Improvement of Living and Working Conditions, 1997).

[118] DETR Supplementary Guidance to Regional Development Agencies (1999) at ch 2 pp 1-3.

[119] Supra at ch 2, p 13.

[120] The RDA for Yorkshire and the Humber (Yorkshire Forward) provides a useful example in this context. The nine universities in the region have formed an alliance with the RDA the purpose of which is to increase business start-ups and to attract inward regional investment through offering the research and technical strength of regional universities to potential investors, see <www.yorkshire-forward.com>.

RDAs are to build upon existing work that identifies regional needs and potential regional policies rather than duplicate it. Each RDA has a regional chamber, not as a body to which it owes accountability, but more, it seems, as a body that reflects the collaborative networks referred to above. Echoing this there is no prescriptive mechanism for chamber composition across RDAs aside from the insistence upon a dominant local authority element and a role for "regional economic stakeholders".[121] This last term is not defined and it can support a number of different meanings in this context. One is that it refers to major employers in the area and groupings representing smaller business interests. Another is that it should involve all those who contribute to the accumulation process: trade unions and other representatives of labour. This helps to reveal a potential debate around the question of democratic deficit – regional chamber members are not elected and even if they were RDAs would not be accountable to them. It also further demonstrates the poverty of the word "stakeholder" as an explanatory tool. My interest in the constitutional factor behind the creation of RDAs is a passing one in the use of quasi-constitutional mechanisms to further economic development. It is not my intention to address issues of civic participation other than as they arise in the context of corporate intervention.

Thus what emerges from the RDA framework is the importance of subsidiarity within the state's use of spatial selectivity as a mechanism for regeneration and the relative freedom thereafter to create a new institutional space.[122] RDAs and regional chambers are a new regional ordering of space that cut across existing levels of more local activity pursued by local actors – local authorities and existing regeneration partnerships for example. This ensures that the space will be non-neutral, possibly contested space: local actors will not wish to see local priorities abandoned in favour of solely regional initiatives.[123] Nor for that matter will indigenous business interests wish to see inward

[121] More detail on chamber composition across the regions can be found in A While, "Accountability and Regional Governance" (2000) 14 *Local Economy* 329 and A Harding et al, "Regional Development Agencies and English Regionalisation: the question of accountability" (1999) 17 *Enviro and Planning* C 669.

[122] M Jones, *New Institutional Spaces* (London: Jessica Kingsley, 1999). Jones develops a theoretical framework for the spatial selectivity of the state around TECs, see pp 237–53.

[123] I Deas and K Ward, "From the 'new localism' to the 'new regionalism'? The implications of regional development agencies for city-regional relations" (2000) 19 *Pol Geog* 273 at 275–82.

investors being awarded advantages not available to them.[124] The task for the RDA is to arrive at balanced compromises. The task for the corporate sector is to ensure their involvement within this space preferably as members of the RDA itself.[125] The attraction for corporations on structuring social intervention through the RDAs is that it makes it easier to identify those corporations whose response to the crisis of legitimacy that corporations find themselves in is to indulge in free riding. It is easier to assess corporate participation across the nine RDA's than it is to engage in a company by company search at national level.[126] The absence of a clear agenda for social side intervention can, for the corporate sector, be fulfilled in part by the new Business and Society strategy issued by the DTI in March 2001.[127] This strategy document presents both good practice in corporate social intervention and the worst aspects of corporate community involvement or corporate social responsibility. The strategy is framed in terms of an informal exhortation to participation with a trade-off of a potential enhancement in corporate profits. This is the basis of the competitive corporate social conscience and unstructured largesse that I described in chapter one. Case studies are supplied of what is considered to be successful corporate community involvement with no mention of values that might lie behind that involvement, the reasons for its selection or its sustainability. Corporations are urged to look at commercial materials on forming a "responsible" profile and those offered by Business in the Community. Without exception the message delivered by these interest groups is that what corporations should do is to select an initiative and then project themselves outwards and use "show and tell" mechanisms for publicity, rather than looking outside the corporation first and then devoting resources to what appears appropriate in terms of outside

[124] There is scope for any RDA to make its position on the desirability or not of inward investment clear in its Regional Strategy. However the likelihood of any Regional Strategy not including the attraction of inward investment with the consequent employment opportunities as a priority is remote. See D MacKinnon and N Phelps, "Regional Governance and Foreign Direct Investment: The Dynamics of Institutional Change in Wales and North East England" (2001) 32 *Geoforum* 255 at 264f.

[125] This has already begun to happen; the North East RDA for example has 3 members with commercial sector interests and several others with backgrounds in business.

[126] The US adopts a regulatory approach to the free rider issue through use of its tax levy policy in Business Improvement Districts. Interestingly the same misgivings around questions of democratic deficit and control of the public sphere by private corporations still arise, see R Briffault, "A Government for Our Time? Business Improvement Districts and Urban Governance" (1999) 99 *Col Law Rev* 365.

[127] <www.societyandbusiness.gov.uk>.

needs and sustainability. In this vein a rather more appropriate test for corporations planning a social intervention would be that of a risk assessment calculation in a Research and Development project of a similar size.[128] Research and Development projects are likely to contain assessments of sustainability and viability – questions that are missing from the Business and Society strategy document.

On a more positive note the areas in which the strategy document highlights corporate involvement as desirable – improving in adult literacy and numeracy skills and investing in deprived communities – are framed by the language of bargain and partnership between government and the corporate sector. There is to be a shared challenge around corporate sector contributions and the response of government. Although participation in the Business and Society agenda does not have the air of formality that the RDA structures have, taken together these strategies are a way of creating a third way alternative to the market/state dichotomy so often presented in regional planning at the level of Central Government.[129] The stress laid by the DETR on RDAs as a single actor created from different component parts is crucial to the consideration of long standing problems requiring sustained strategic intervention rather than the provision of quick-fix, short-term shore-ups that are nevertheless high profile.[130] RDAs have the potential to collate information from different members and use it to develop new policy initiatives.[131] Useful in this collation and recalibration of information from a variety of different sources to identify regional priorities and methodologies for tackling them will be Geographic Information Systems (GIS). In the US and in South Africa this type of approach has already played a role in generating "community" level participation in urban regeneration and development projects.[132] The debates and difficulties around first the construction of community and second the

[128] C Letts et al, "Virtuous Capital: What Foundations Can Learn from Venture Capitalists" (1997) 70 *Harv Bus Rev*, March/April.

[129] A Amin, "An Institutional Perspective on Regional Economic Development" (1999) 23 *Int J Urban and Regional Research* 365.

[130] S Waddock and M-E Boyle, "The Dynamics of Change in Corporate Community Relations" (1995) 37 *Calif Manag Rev* 125.

[131] For a contrary view see B Knight, "Community Politics" in D Campbell and N Lewis (eds), *Promoting Participation: Law or Politics?* (London: Cavendish, 1999) p 175.

[132] E Sheppard, "GIS and Society: Towards a Research Agenda" (1995) 22 *Cartography and Geographic Information Systems* 5; R Ghose, "Use of Information Technology for Community Empowerment: Transforming Geographic Information Systems into Community Information Systems" (2001) 5 *Transactions in GIS* 141.

concept of community participation are examined in more detail in the material which follows. The final evaluation report from the City Challenge Project demonstrates that it is possible for cross-sector partnerships to deliver what actors acting singularly cannot.[133] However there is evidence to suggest that partnerships between sectors can often be problematic for a variety of reasons. In the material that follows I try to identify how some of the stumbling blocks might be overcome through the use of a virtue ethics framework.

Inside the Corporation

In addition to these external factors there are specifically internal factors that structure the business environment for corporate social intervention. These factors are difficult to disaggregate of themselves. Technological advances have driven forward large scale corporate restructuring. Internal workplace hierarchies have flattened out as layers of middle management have been phased out. Non-core functions have either been out-sourced or sold off. Corporate strategy has become more tightly focused and as a result activity under the heading of corporate social intervention has been drawn closer to both remaining managers and employees. Employees under their internal identity are ambassadors for their corporate employer, in their external identity they are potential beneficiaries of corporate largesse. In this way employees see their personal and work lives converging. There are also other issues that add to this convergence such as the amount of flexibility around work time and re-skilling that is demanded of them. It is not then surprising that employees should expect, as part of the exchange relationship, their corporate employers to have knowledge of and to support the sort of issues that they support themselves.[134] The flattening of hierarchies has lead to some devolvement of general decision-making into the hands of those employees who interface directly with

[133] DETR, *What Works – Learning the Lessons: Final Evaluation of City Challenge* (London: DETR Publications, 1998). This was an independent evaluation by KPMG. Interestingly Knight's pessimistic view of the success of partnerships in urban regeneration, supra n131, was based on an earlier (1994) DETR report.

[134] B Altman, "Corporate Community Relations in the 1990's" (1998) 37 *Bus and Soc* 221 at 224. Knowledge of employees interests in some third sector activities can be gleaned through their participation in the "pay-roll giving scheme". If financial support to registered charities is given under the Payroll donation scheme a further 10% is added by Government.

suppliers, customers and other client groups.[135] Decision-making and the attendant responsibility that goes with it in this arena is likely to be traded off in demands by employees for increased participation in the formulation and delivery of corporate social intervention. While corporations see this type of involvement as a way of building corporate loyalty it is also an ideal opportunity for a corporation to develop a holistic approach to corporate activity, corporate social intervention included, based upon the virtues.

In chapter one I referred to the different forms of working structure that were available in the era of post post-Fordism in terms that indicated the decline of traditional patterns of work life (the nine to five day). Changes in family structure are tied into these changing forms of work as individuals try to juggle the demands of work life and the demands of life outside work. The net effect of these changes is that the relationship between employer and employee within the corporate setting is altered. The area of work-life balance is one in which there has been both government intervention and initiatives by various corporations. Government intervention has concentrated on enhancing the basket of statutory rights for particular groups of people. The agenda for this is the encouragement of work-based economic contributions by those groups who might otherwise have been disadvantaged in the labour market by their tie to, for example, child caring responsibilities.[136] Those in need of assistance are considered to be dual income/two parent households with children requiring care. Single parents are afforded little in the way of express recognition of their needs. In some ways this intervention, despite its limited view of which groups require assistance,[137] is still a step forward. At least it is recongnised that those families with two adult members are likely to be juggling at least two jobs between them.[138]

[135] It would be unwise however to view service sector employment, so characteristic of the post post-Fordist economy, as all "hearts and flowers", see V Belt et al, "Women's Work in the Information Economy: The Case of Telephone Call Centres" (2000) 3 *Information, Communication and Society* 316.

[136] Highlights include the introduction of the national minimum wage, extension of maternity rights, new rights for part-time workers on pay, pension entitlements, training provision and holidays.

[137] For some of the complex family arrangements that emerge around the care of elderly relatives see J Barnat et al, "Generational Ties in the 'New Family': Changing Contexts for Traditional Obligations" in E Silva and C Smart (eds), *The New Family* (London: Sage, 1999) p 115. In an aging population this type of care is likely to become a significant issue in the future.

[138] 62% of couples with dependant children are in work, 66% of mothers return to

Corporate recognition of work-life balance issues appears on one level to be more enlightened. A grouping of large corporations calling themselves Employers for Work-Life Balance have begun to issue a number of position papers and best practice guidelines around not only the offering of different types of work form, such as working from home and short-fat working weeks, but also dealing with employees' health and well-being. Their suggestions embrace those employees with and without caring responsibilities. The rational for this is apparently that as employers they feel it is their responsibility to their employees to offer them the means to have fulfilled lives outside work. Mitigating against this positive attitude are a number of questions which, if answered by future research, will provide a much clearer picture of the value and extent of corporate policies on this issue. For example it is not clear if all employees working at every level are included in these policies nor is it clear that employees working in the few remaining heavy industries as opposed to "clean hands" industries will have these policies offered to them. Just as chapter one tracked the emergence of competitive social conscience outside the corporation in areas like cause related marketing and environmentally friendly products, so it is not at all unlikely that flexible working policies could be used to recruit and retain staff in key areas.[139] Corporations would compete against each other to offer the most attractive packages. Adoption of such policies on this basis is certainly not virtuous conduct.

4. STEPS TOWARDS EFFECTIVE CORPORATE SOCIAL INTERVENTION

Needs Audits and Care Plans

My intention in this section is not to provide a manual for corporations on how to execute corporate social intervention but rather to point to its distinctive features and thus make clear how it differs from other types of socially related activity that corporations may have been involved in or may be presently involved in. The essence of the intervention that I am advocating is that it be a genuine advancement of corporate

work after maternity leave, women represent 33% of the full time work force and 81% of the part time work force. Statistics taken from the 1998 and 1999 Labour Force Surveys.

[139] L McKee et al, "'Family Friendly' Policies and Practices in the Oil and Gas Industry: Employers' Perspectives" (2000) 14 *Work Employment and Society* 557 at 563–5.

assistance to those outside the usual matrix of property distribution in the form of dividends or share options. There may of course be elements of double benefit receipt; employees for example may benefit through what is paid as dividends to institutional shareholders if those shareholders themselves comprise part of their pension fund portfolio and they may also benefit from corporate social intervention in the locale surrounding their workplace, but that is merely a fortunate spin-off for those concerned. The point of the advancement of corporate assistance is not for corporations to indulge in altruistic behaviour or to ensure that the intervention is cost-free because of increased product sales rather it is for corporations to secure a middle way that allows them to retain/recover legitimacy in a world that is structured through the virtues of compassion, reconstruction of selfhood, respect, trust and the others that were identified earlier in this chapter.[140] The intervention is made not out of duty or obligation but out of a desire to be an individual intent on aspiring to a virtuous existence.

To achieve this an intervention needs to be structured so that it supplies the appropriate tools to achieve its purpose. In the past corporations have been content to donate money, match funding raised from other quarters or donate some of their own used infra-structure equipment such as computers without caring whether the end result was achieved or even achievable.[141] This approach does not accord with corporate social intervention that looks to be viewed as virtuous. Corporations need to inform themselves of the landscape in which intervention will take place by ascertaining needs and matching those needs against the skills and resources that they have at their disposal. I see this taking place in the form of an audit of needs.[142] Audit is an ideologically charged term[143] and it is used deliberately in this context

[140] See the text accompanying nn 44–6.

[141] R Moss Kanter, "From Spare Change to Real Change" (1999) May/June *Harv Bus Rev* 122.

[142] What I go on to suggest as the dimensions of needs' audits bears some similarities in terms of creation and on going maintainence to the model of Constructive Corporate Citizenship put forward by Vidaver-Cohen, see D Vidaver-Cohen, "Public-Private Partnership as a Strategy for Crime Control: Corporate Citizenship Makes the Difference" (1998) 100/101 *Business and Society Review* 21. The differences between our models lie in what we see as a desirable outcome. For Constructive Corporate Citizenship it is the improvement of the competitive edge of participating corporations, for needs audits it is the opportunity to become a citizen pursuing the virtues.

[143] For a discussion of what the term "audit" has come to mean in general terms, see M Power, *The Audit Society* (Oxford: Oxford University Press, 1997) at pp 1–9 and A Cooper, "The State of Mind We're In" (2000) 15 *Soundings* 118.

to emphasise not just the drawing together and collection of existing information but the centrality to corporate existence that intervention strategies should have. What I am advocating is a recasting of corporate social intervention; one that is undertaken as a result of an engagement process – not a simple unilateral decision or a selective consultation exercise – a genuine attempt at listening, rather than assuming what would be beneficial as is often currently the case. In some geographic areas there will be an abundance of information already accumulated that corporations can tap into, in others there will be very little. The execution of an audit-type exercise affords corporations opportunities to link with RDA members, other corporations, business representative bodies, third sector organisations and other voluntary groups. All these organisations are potential future partners in intervention projects, some may already be partners in existing corporate community involvement (CCI) ventures. Activities under this heading and others such as cause-related marketing, for example, are still perfectly permissible. They represent part of the range of typologies of interests that corporations can have in their social, political and economic environment. However there has to be a recognition that many of these activities, without amendment, do not qualify as corporate social intervention.

Under the framework of virtue ethics this type of audit exercise involves the articulation and interpretation of needs rather than rights. The phenomena of rights conflicting with each other is well known. However it is also the case that "needs" range across contested territory. Nancy Fraser in her work on state welfare regimes makes a series of important observations about the nature of needs and the articulation of needs.[144] Some of these are germane to corporate audits of needs and beyond that into interpretation of needs by RDAs and other bodies such as local authorities, despite the fact that in Fraser's work these observations are being used to isolate policy options at an altogether higher level. First there have to be adequate and fair forums in which needs can be articulated and interpreted. Otherwise the more rehearsed and organised are at an advantage. Second the identity of the needs' interpreter is a politically charged question – this is something that is particularly pertinent to the formation and maintenance of partnerships and it is examined below. Diminishing hierarchies within corporations make the process of listening to needs accounts more

[144] N Fraser, *Unruly Practices: Power, Discourse and Gender in Contemporary Social Theory* (Cambridge: Polity, 1989) at p 164.

egalitarian. It should be possible to build into the audit process an acknowledgement that needs will conflict with each other. This is something that CCI and stakeholder models of the corporation never articulated; that by satisfying one need, others in need might be disadvantaged. Models promoting stakeholding would find it difficult to acknowledge conflicting or diverging interests without also accepting that these differences exist not just between the apparently clear and entirely separate categories of interest they promulgate but also within those interest groups.[145]

Fraser's answer to her own question about the nature of the forums in which needs are articulated is a Habermasian one – that there needs to be a "dialogical, particpatory process of need interpretation".[146] This certainly resonates with the debates around welfare provision with which she is engaging and it is also an obvious place to employ Habermas's discourse model with its emphasis on the public sphere. In one way employing it around corporate audits of needs is an attractive proposition as it emphasises the quasi-public nature of this activity. It prevents what Fraser calls the "reprivatization of needs"[147] – one of her examples of this is particularly apposite in the corporate context – the claim that a factory closure is an issue only for those able to deal with it as a legitimate exercise of the privilege of property ownership. In another way this model of communication assumes a formality that may not in fact be present. In the Habermasian model of discourse, communicative activity in the private sphere feeds the lifeworld constructed through governmental and non-governmental institutions.[148] The private sphere consists of circles of friends, neighbours and work colleagues.[149] The presence of groups at this lower level of structural evolution needs to be acknowledged and a forum appropriate to them also adopted. Urban neighbourhoods, for example, are likely to be a loose affiliation of individuals and families with only one apparent shared interest, perhaps poor housing conditions[150] – the classic limited

[145] For a welcome advance in bringing these points within stakeholder theory, see M Winn, "Building Stakeholder Theory With a Decision Modeling Methodology" (2001) 40 *Business and Society* 133.

[146] *Supra* n 144 at p 157.

[147] *Ibid*, at p 172.

[148] J Habermas *Between Facts and Norms* (Cambridge: Polity, 1997) at p 363.

[149] *Supra* n 148 at p 365.

[150] Mohan makes the point that pockets of deprivation are concentrated at ever smaller spatial levels, see J Mohan, "New Labour, New Localism?" (2000) 4 *Renewal* 56.

liability community.[151] For them to project this need into something like Habermas's lifeworld a rather different strategy may have to be employed.

It is important to recognise here that what is missing is a workable notion of community which would allow us, if it existed, to assume that all instances of need would be articulated through the institutions that make up Habermas's lifeworld. It maybe that in Fraser's world of large scale issues within models of state welfare provision the assumption that concentric multiple identities within large pressure or interest groups are either temporarily suspended or adequately protected can be made. However at the level of corporate needs audits this assumption can not be made. In chapter one I explained the ways in which community was being used as a signifier for a particular political position and in the case of corporations as a designation of a particular activity. Neither of these is of any assistance in providing an answer to the question of how individuals with needs not articulated by the lifeworld can nevertheless be assisted. A problem with drawing attention to this potential accounting deficit is that it can be taken to invest notions of community with idealistic qualities they perhaps do not have and have never had.[152] This aside, there would appear to be two potential ways forward both of which corporations, with the skill base that exists within them, are likely to be able to assist, at least, in facilitating. One is the setting up of a project that is entirely neutral for all participants, if such a thing can be conceived.[153] Through the execution of this project, barriers between individuals would be broken down and needs articulated. The other is to set up neighbourhood Freirian type culture circles. Freire is more usually associated with his work on adult literacy[154] however within that work his political project of empowerment at the level of the individual has a much wider application.[155] It offers a

[151] A Muniz and T O'Guinn, "Brand Community" (2001) 27 *Journal of Consumer Research* 412.

[152] S Szreter, "A New Political Economy for New Labour" (1999) 7 *Renewal* 30. Szreter makes the point that traditional communities, often ones drawn on geographic lines, prevent rather than encourage the formation of social ties as they are often hierarchical and authoritarian.

[153] S Lowe, "Creating Community: Art for Community Development" (2000) 29 *J Contemp Ethnog* 357.

[154] P Freire, *Pedagogy of the Oppressed* (New York, NY: Herder and Herder, 1970); "The Adult Literacy Process as Cultural Action for Freedom" (1970) 40 *Harv Ed Rev* 205; "Cultural Action and Conscientization" (1970) 40 *Harv Ed Rev* 452.

[155] P Taylor *The Texts of Paulo Freire* (Buckingham: Open University Press, 1993).

model of communication that is dialogical, interactive and anti-authoritarian.[156] These circles would involve critically aware co-ordinators that would, while preserving the autonomy of individuals, enter into group dialogues. In Freire's methodology there are three stages involved; the naming stage which involves the positing of a particular problem, the reflection stage which examines why a particular issue is a problem and the action stage which identifies what can be done to change the situation.

The next stage in formulating corporate social intervention is the construction of a care plan. The rationale for a care plan is to make clear a corporation's intervention strategy. The arbiters of the efficacy of this plan will be individuals within the *polis*: those who actively contest corporate legitimacy, potential partners both inside the RDA and outside it and those who receive care under the plan. In another sense the plan's efficacy depends on the motives and intentions of the corporation; is it the intention to pursue the virtues or not? A virtuous outcome, without being prefaced by an appropriately virtuous motive, does not satisfy the aspirations of virtue. Care plans would indicate which needs the corporation felt that it could best meet with its resources and skill base, how it intended to care for those needs, how care would take place on an operational level, and how those receiving care would feedback their experiences.[157] Care plans would indicate the communication strategies that corporations would put in place to ensure that their interaction with those benefiting was a participatory dialogue.

Care plans are less ambitious than stakeholder management when the latter is considered as an option in theoretical terms only. On the level of stakeholder implementation however this position is reversed. Care as a descriptive term does not imply any universality of subject. It does not, without more, suggest who is within the ambit of care nor does it suggest a hierarchy of relationships that should be singled out for care. Care is not meant to convey demeaning notions of inequality in terms of "you can't, so we will" but rather it is a recognition that inequalities do exist and can be addressed through notions of meeting needs through care.[158] Stakeholding in its most sophisticated form

[156] McClaren, "Paulo Freire's Legacy of Hope and Struggle" (1997) 14 *TCS* 147 at 150–1.

[157] This four stage conceptualization of the care process is taken from B Fisher and J Tronto, "Toward a Feminist Theory of Caring" in E Abel and M Nelson (eds) *Circles of Care. Work and Identity in Women's Lives* (Albany, NY: SUNY, 1990) p 38.

[158] J Tronto, *Moral Boundaries: A Political Argument for an Ethic of Care* (London: Routledge, 1993) at p 145. See also the text accompanying n 179 below.

divides its interest groups into primary and secondary stakeholders[159] or stakeholders necessary for the survival of the corporation and the rest.[160] Having done this, however, as a theory it then seems to draw no substantive distinction between the two groups. It does not stress the need for dialogue structures still less advocate notions of partnership with other actors, stakeholders or not. Ventures organised under the canopy of stakeholder management may give no clue as to their sustainability. Stakeholding has no conflict resolution dimension to it. Care on the other hand is a concept which can resolve conflict through its interaction with the virtues. Corporations indicate their priorities for social intervention through their care plans. Competing needs are examined through pursuit of the virtues; this ensures that corporations have a structure that will assist them in making choices.

The Terminology of Care

The choice of the term "care plans" is a deliberate one. Possible substitute terms for the activity described above suggest themselves such as action plans and intervention goals but these substitutes do nothing to describe the nature of the corporate activity that is being undertaken. In particular they say nothing about the nature of the corporation's relationship to others over and above that which I described in chapter two and elaborated upon earlier in this chapter:- an individual situated within a host of other individuals, each with their own life narrative augmented by their shared inheritance from society, seeking to improve the quality of their existence and so incidentally that of the broader collective by reference to the virtues, which themselves are tied to changing perspectives of the shared good. To this, care as a terminology emphasises the importance of the relation between the individual and the larger collective rather than seeing these terms in opposition to each other.[161]

Care as a descriptive term has a history that has seen it at times described as a feminist ethic and as a result of this, then, as an ethic that stands in opposition to the ethic of justice.[162] Much of this history

[159] M Clarkson, "A Stakeholder Framework for Analyzing and Evaluating Corporate Social Performance" (1995) 20 *Acad Manag Rev* 92.

[160] See ch 1, n 187.

[161] S Sevenhuijsen, "Caring in the Third Way: The Relation Between Obligation, Responsibility and care in *Third Way* Discourse" (2000) 20 *Crit Soc Pol* 5 at 9.

[162] Noddings is probably the leading exponent of this position, see N Noddings *Caring: A Feminine Approach to Ethics* (Berkeley, CA: University of California Press, 1984) at pp 40–3 for a worked example illustrating this approach.

is developed from the Gilligan/Kohlberg[163] controversy first articulated around issues of moral development in children. It is a history that is well documented and one with which I do not intend to engage[164] save for the points that are relevant to the themes of this book.[165] Gilligan herself disavows any gender connection for her work.[166] Indeed a much broader frame for her work can be found in those commentators who point not to a specifically gendered turn within her work but more generally to her disavowal of Kantian notions of rational individuals[167] bound together by loose notions of respect, equality and due process and the liberties *inter alia* of free speech, association and assembly but with not necessarily any notion of the interpersonal relationships required to make the exercise of these rights any thing other than a very minimal foundation for the most basic of civil societies.[168] A description more accurate for the results of Gilligan's experiments in moral psychology is that she found the existence of an ethics that was anti-principlist in focus, one that recognised the importance of context, of narrative and of relationships to others.

Gilligan's work has found its way into numerous areas within the social sciences and the "caring" sciences such as medicine where it is often used as a way of labelling an oppositional voice to a predominant culture without necessarily offering an alternative paradigm. This is

[163] Carol Gilligan, see *In a Different Voice* (Cambridge, MA: Harvard University Press, 1982) and L Kohlberg *Essays in Moral Development vols 1 and II* (New York, NY: Harper and Row, 1981, 1984).

[164] In addition to views which take one side of the debate or the other there is also a literature coming from both psychology and philosophy that denies even the efficacy of this type of research, see O Flanagan, *Varieties of Moral Personality: Ethics and Psychological Realism* (Cambridge, MA: Harvard University Press, 1991) at pp 196–252 and M E Ross, "Feminism and the Problem of Moral Character" (1989) 5 *Journal of Feminist Studies in Religion* 59.

[165] For a fuller discussion see L Nicholson, *The Play of Reason* (Buckingham: Open University Press, 1999) at pp 17–28.

[166] C Gilligan, "A Reply to my Critics" in M Larrabee (ed), *An Ethic of Care* (London: Routledge, 1993) p 207 at p 209 and "Moral Orientation and Moral Development" in E Kittay and D Meyers (eds), *Women and Moral Theory* (Totowa, NJ: Rowman and Littlefield, 1987) p 19 at p 20.

[167] On Gilligan and Kant see G Nunner-Winkler, "Two Moralities? A Critical Discussion of an Ethic of Care and Responsibility versus an Ethic of Rights and Justice" in W Kurtines and J GeWirtz (eds), *Morality, Moral Behavior and Moral Development* (New York, NY: John Wiley, 1984) p 348. For a discussion of the Kantian voice within Kohlberg's work see S Benhabib, *Situating the Self* (Cambridge: Polity, 1994) at pp 148–77.

[168] A Baier, "The Need for More than Justice" (1987) 13 (supp vol) *Can J of Phil* 41.

certainly the case within the scholarship on legal structures for corporations. There is an emerging literature that describes itself as taking a feminist approach to the corporation, while drawing upon Gilligan's work.[169] It is cited by some of those who object to the influential market orientated and neo-classical economic paradigm of the firm that I referred to at the beginning of this book.[170] It is presented as an oppositional voice to what can best be described as the "gung ho, never mind human needs and frailties" approach of law and economics.[171] The major weakness of this oppositional voice is that it fails to present a picture of what a corporate structure and corporate activities would look like under an agenda built around the ethics of care that it cites. It would be unfortunate if this voice was to contribute nothing more positive to the theory of the corporation than a rejection of a current popular position.

My own view, despite assertions to the contrary in the past, is that a picture of corporate behaviour and aspirations which genders care, particularly when that picture is also overlain with familial roles, is unhelpful. As I explained above the use of care plans allows a corporation, guided in its behaviour by the virtues, to identify those within the parameters of its care. Application of a mother/child paradigm[172] for example would not permit this but would not necessarily result in the idea of corporate care spreading more widely. It also suggests that conventional ideas of the family are still very much at play; that children will be cared for primarily by someone occupying the role of "mothering person".[173]

[169] See for example T Gabaldon, "The Lemonade Stand: Feminist and Other Reflections on the Limited Liability of Corporate Shareholders" (1992) 45 *Vand L Rev* 1387; K Lahey and S Salter, "Corporate Law in Legal Theory and Legal Scholarship: From Classicism to Feminism" (1985) 23 *Osgoode Hall LJ* 543 and A Belcher, "Gendered Company: Views of Corporate Governance at the Institute of Directors" (1997) V *Feminist Legal Studies* 57.

[170] See T O'Neill, "The Patriarchal Meaning of Contract: Feminist Reflections on the Corporate Governance Debate in F Macmillan (ed), *Perspectives on Company Law 2* (London: Kluwer Law, 1997) Kluwer 27.

[171] Possibly the best description of this sort of scholarship, which emphasis its rhetorical power and dependence on conceptual simplicity is provided by Mary Joe Frug; "singular, daunting, rigid and cocksure". See M Frug, *Postmodern Legal Feminism* (New York, NY: Routledge, 1992) at p 116.

[172] See for example both W Frederick and R Derry whose work is influenced by that of Virginia Held, W Frederick, *Values Nature and Culture in the American Corporation* (New York, NY: Oxford University Press, 1995) and R Derry, "The Mother-Child Paradigm and its Relevance to the Workplace" (1999) 38 *Bus and Soc* 217.

[173] Held attempts to gender neutralise her concept by referring to the "mothering

For many families these sorts of roles no longer exist in this way.[174] This model gives the impression of a corporation prepared to indulge in self-sacrificing behaviour. This type of behaviour is unlikely to lead to a strategic corporate social intervention as the existence of trading profit is essential for intervention. The corporation seen as a father figure again runs into the problem of family construction and moreover suggests a patriarchal monolith operating a hierarchical structure from which unstructured largess is dispensed on a whim.[175]

The counter-position of the ethic of care to an ethic of rights or justice with the two viewed as incompatible comes from Gilligan's initial work. The idea of justice is orientated towards a universality of general principles located in the public sphere. Care on the other hand is seen as confined to the private sphere with an emphasis on the importance of context and of maintaining relationships.[176] These two perspectives have gradually been elided not least by Gilligan herself.[177] Significantly Onora O'Neill from her perspective of Kantian universalism decides not that care alone is not enough but that justice cannot stand on its own.[178] Tronto presents the most forceful case for resituating the ethic of care. Her reason for not only pushing the ethic of care beyond ideas of gender but also for it "to be connected to a theory of justice" is primarily a political one. In her view only if this occurs can the idea of care be pushed beyond the private sphere into a public democratic process. She points to the potential power imbalance that may otherwise result between care giver and care receiver and the possibility of "parochialism" creeping into the distribution of care giving.[179] This last point is perhaps better explained by Mendus:

person", whether this succeeds or not is debatable but it still raises spectres of traditional family roles, V Held, *Feminist Morality: Transforming culture, society and politics* (Chicago, IL: University of Chicago Press, 1993) at pp 195–8.

[174] M Howard and M Wilmott, "The Networked Family" in H Wilkinson (ed), *Family Business* (London: Demos, 2000) p 45.

[175] H Schwartz, "The Sin of the Father: Reflections on the Roles of the Corporation Man, the Suburban Housewife, Their Son and Their Daughter in the Deconstruction of the Patriarch" (1996) 49 *Human Rels* 1013.

[176] For a more detailed breakdown of the differences between these two perpectives see E Porter, *Feminist Perspectives on Ethics* (Harlow: Longman, 1999) at pp 12–16

[177] J Dean, "Discourse in a Different Voice" in J Meehan (ed), *Feminists Read Habermas* (New York, NY: Routledge, 1995) p 205 at pp 208–11.

[178] O O'Neil, *Towards Justice and Virtue* (Cambridge: Cambridge University Press, 1996). See also D Smith, "How Far Should We Care? On the Spatial Scope of Beneficence" (1998) 22 *Progress in Human Geog* 15.

[179] J Tronto, *supra* n 158 at p 171.

"unsupported by considerations of justice and equality, care may simply not extend reliably beyond the immediacy of one's own family, or group, or clan, to the wider world of unknown others".[180]

The importance of Tronto's work in shaping an ethic of care so that it can also incorporate a justice perspective necessary for it to be a public theory of democracy does not end there. She returns us to the anti-Kantian stance first taken by Gilligan and asserts that the care perspective is a contextual moral theory in that it is situated in the behaviours of particular societies and addresses the "broader moral capacities of actors." From the capacities of individuals any contextual moral theory must be able to describe the ways in which these individuals progress to exhibit concern for others. Tronto's claim is for the ethic of care to develop itself as such a contextual moral theory. She does acknowledge that Aristotelian ethics is just such a contextual theory.[181] For my purposes I would posit Aristotelian virtue ethics and the modifications made to it by MacIntyre as the obvious contextual moral theory in which or alongside which the care ethic might sit quite comfortably. Like Aristotelian ethics[182] an ethic of care incorporates emotion.[183] Its dominant values are ones of reciprocity, equality, trust, respect for difference, and the promotion of self-respect.[184] These are values similar to those that I have identified as virtues. The difference between these values as part of a virtue ethics structure and these values as an ethic of care is that as part of a virtue ethic structure they place the corporation in a particular role within society and in a particular relationship with other individuals. I see the ethic of care as pushing these values into an operational structure but not necessarily grounding them within a larger picture.

The major stumbling block to situating the concept of care alongside Aristotelian virtue ethics is if care is considered to be a feminist ethic. Despite my rejection of care being categorised in this way it is impossible not to engage at a basic level with this criticism. The argument is

[180] S Mendus, "Different Voices, Still Lives: Problems in the Ethics of Care (1993) 10 *J App Phil* 17 at 21.

[181] J Tronto, "Beyond Gender Difference to a Theory of Care" (1987) 12 *Signs* 644 at 657–9.

[182] Emotion is incorporated through the mean of the virtues and also through the idea that one should derive pleasure from doing the right thing, *NE* 1177a24.

[183] B Koziak, *Retrieving Political Emotion* (Pittsburgh, PA: Pennsylvania State University Press, 2000) at pp 164–78.

[184] R Lister, *Citizenship: Feminist Perspectives* (Basingstoke: Macmillan, 1997) p 102.

that the Aristotelian position is misogynist and anti-feminist.[185] Virtue ethics are heavily dependent on tradition and tradition in the past has operated largely to the detriment of women. Aristotle's position on women was that he barely acknowledged their existence; most of his references to the position of "man" are in opposition to that of slaves and animals. There is a strong sense of the peripherality of women to Aristotelian thought. This does not mean that virtue ethics has to remain static on this point. The section at the beginning of this chapter on the work of MacIntyre makes the point that tradition and societies change and alongside them the virtues will also change. Indeed there is an argument that where Aristotle does recognise the presence of women he affords them respect. For example in *NE*[186] he refers to the fact that men should hand over the running of matters which befit women to women and thereafter not interfere, for to do so would be to disregard the respective worth of the parties.[187] Possibly there is a message for corporations here; that they should not, in the name of care, inclusiveness or anything else, confer rights and identities on the parties they deal with that that those parties may not want. Recognition should be based on respect and a valuing of what is done.

Partnership Issues

Starting Positions

In many ways partnerships represent the very essence of corporate social intervention under the Third Way. The actors involved essentially

[185] E Fraser and N Lacey, *The Politics of Community: A Feminist Critique of the Liberal-Communitarian Debate* (Toronto: University of Toronto Press, 1993). Indeed Annette Baier (*supra* n 165) makes a similar point in relation to the inheritors of the Aristotelian position "But when we transcend the values of the Kantians, we should not forget the facts of history – that those values were the values of the oppressors of women. The Christian Church, whose version of the moral law Aquinas codified, in his very legalistic moral theory, still insists on the maleness of God . . . (at p 51). For a contrary view see C Freeland (ed), *Feminist Interpretations of Aristotle* (Pittsburgh, PA: Pennsylvania State University Press, 1998) and in particular the discussion in R Groenhout, "The Virtue of Care: Aristotelian Ethics and Contemporary Ethics of Care" 171 therein.

[186] *NE* 1160b19.

[187] The contrary position on this point is taken by Selma Sevenhuijsen who argues that this particular division around household management has resulted in the evolution of political tradition which places care in the private sphere and politics as an activity in the public sphere whereby the individual is freed of the concerns of care. The essence of our disagreement is evidenced above, see S Sevenhuijsen, *Citizenship and the Ethics of Care* (London: Routledge, 1998) at pp 130–1.

negotiate a compromise which involves each in the suppression of some interests and the articulation of others. Actors from each sector come to the idea of partnership imbued with their experiences under the economic, social and political ideals of the New Right and, in some cases, wary also of the expectations placed upon them by the new Third Way regime. This was certainly the case for the voluntary sector. The third sector had not undergone the root and branch reforms that the public sector had with the introduction of Next Steps Agencies, Charters, Compulsory Competitive Tendering and such like. In fact it had been treated only to piecemeal reforms in its legal and taxation regime.[188] Nevertheless it found itself fragmenting in the effort to provide services across the burgeoning gaps that were created by the retrenchment of the welfare state.[189] Thus it was somewhat unprepared to be pushed into the spotlight and acclaimed as a key resource for active citizenship and crucial to civil society.[190] The corporate sector for its part had seen periods of high growth and profits interspersed with periods of deep recession and now found itself existing within a market of global competitiveness.

Partnership Structures

Partnerships between sectors, as the previous section made clear, were not invented under the auspices of the Third Way, but they were given a new impetus. It appears that what this has done at the operational level is to create a proliferation of new partnership arrangements on top of existing ones thus exacerbating governance and structural problems that already existed.[191] What is becoming clear despite the fact that it is too soon in a temporal sense to evaluate the effectiveness of delivery under individual partnerships is that the maximum degree of flexibility

[188] J Kendall, "The Mainstreaming of the Third Sector into Public Policy in England in the Late 1990s: Whys and Wherefores" (2000) 28 *Policy and Politics* 541.

[189] C Ashworth, "Changing Cultures and Building Shared Ownership" (2000) 15 *Local Economy* 256.

[190] Speech by Gordon Brown, "Civic Society in Modern Britain" 17th Arnold Goodman Charity Lecture, 20 July 2000. The third sector found itself the subject of a Treasury Tax Review in 1997, the lynchpin of the Active Community Unit based at the Home Office and involved in a compact with Government that emphasised their separate but also complimentary positions around service delivery, *Getting it Right Together.* Compact on Relations between Government and the Voluntary and Community Sector in England, Cm 4100 (HO Nov 1998).

[191] B Jupp, *Working Together* (London: Demos, 2000) at p 25, P 6 et al, *Governing in the Round: Strategies for Holistic Government* (London: Demos, 1999).

in partnership structure is required.[192] In some instances the partnership members want to operate on the basis of network and loose alliance, in others they want a much tighter structure.[193] This mirrors the statutory brief given to RDAs. However for partnerships to be able successfully to negotiate issues of structure and the subsequent management of that structure there need to be shared objectives and shared ways of reaching these objectives. The most obvious tension here is between the corporate sector with its experience of competitive corporate community involvement and the third sector with objectives that are potentially very broad as third sector involvement often means in reality a loose alliance of a number of small organisations.

The partnership members need to address issues of trust between themselves and following on from this the differences in their organisational structures, for example, the role of adversarial debate, consensus management and majority rule. Reference to the virtues at the stage of objective setting should place the partnership in the position of achieving a virtuous act by means of performing through the virtues. Performing through the virtues pushes virtue ethics into the performance of the venture so that each partner treats the other in a virtuous manner as well as regarding the venture as something to be achieved through the virtues. Advocating the virtues in these circumstances may seem like a panacea that is just too simplistic, however, given that the problems partnerships encounter are based around dimensions such as the regulation of power and the establishment of a common discourse,[194] and dilemmas around questions of leadership, accountability and infrastructure capability, the virtues provide remembrance of a neutral starting point. From this neutral starting point it then becomes easier for each member of the potential partnership to deal with key points of concern; for example for the third sector this might

[192] NCVO Press Release Wednesday 26 July 2000, M Taylor, "Communities in the Lead: Power, Organisational Capacity and Social Capital" (2000) 37 *Urban Studies* 109.

[193] For a discussion of the types of legal structure available see I Leigh, "The Legal Framework for Community Involvement" in A Dunn (ed), *The Voluntary Sector, the State and the Law* (Oxford: Hart Publishing, 2000) p 9 at pp 15–20.

[194] There are of course more sceptical ways in which to view the whole idea of partnership. One is that it disempowers discourses of dissent by enveloping them within these structures which are then used to provide legitimacy for capitalist discourse, see M Taylor, "Partnerships: insiders or outsiders" in C Rochester and M Harris (eds), *Voluntary Organisations and Social Policy: Perspectives on Change and Choice* (Basingstoke: Macmillan, 2000).

be its independence as a service provider from local authority and central government concerns.[195]

Community Participation in Partnerships

Partnerships return us to a central question that resonates with the era of post post-Fordism – Can we identify "community"? How, then, can "community" be included in these ventures as an active participant or even recipient if it cannot be identified? These questions arise specifically in this context because of the importance that has been placed by post-1997 political rhetoric, not just on the general idea of "community" which was looked at in chapter one, but specifically on community involvement in partnerships. This involvement is a new addition to previous incarnations of partnership ventures.[196] Local people and community groups are to be the key to successful development and regeneration partnerships[197] and yet communities stand as deeply fragmented publics. They are fragmented not by selfish individualism but by the rise of self-reflexivity leading to the recognition of individual desires, fears and ultimately identity. Third sector organisations can no longer be considered as analogous to or representative of "community". This is a separate point from the issue of their independence. Rather it concerns the pressure in a competitive sense that has been put upon the Third Sector to obtain its funding under contracts with Central and Local Government for service delivery and the involvement with cause related marketing that has been on offer for larger organisations. Smaller third sector organisations either do not have the infra structure to become part of this culture or in order to do so are forced to abandon a narrow, often locality based, focus.[198]

[195] D Morris, "The 'Contract Culture' as Dependency Culture for Charities?" in A Dunn (ed), *supra* n 190, p 123 at pp 126–7 and M Smerdon et al, "William Beveridge and Social Advance: Modern Messages for Voluntary Action" in B Knight et al (eds), *Building Civil Society* (West Malling: CAF, 1998) p 13 at p 20.

[196] P Foley and S Martin, "A New Deal for the Community? Public Participation in Regeneration and Local Service Delivery" (2000) 28 *Policy and Politics* 479 at 482–5.

[197] M Taylor, "Maintaining Community Involvement in Regeneration: What are the Issues? (2000) 15 *Local Economy* 251.

[198] For a general theoretical discussion of these phenomena see S Smith and M Lipsky, *Non Profits for Hire: The Welfare State in the Age of Contracting* (Cambridge, MA: Harvard University Press, 1993) at pp 22–40. For a specifically UK discussion see D Morris, "Charities in the Contract Culture: Survival of the Largest?" (2000) 20 *Legal Studies* 409.

Individuals have certain shared pasts and presents in the local sense that MacIntyre describes. Third Way discourse seeks to build on this through the establishment of community forums, focus groups, and citizens' juries. The model for these mechanisms is broadly one of participatory democracy. The nature of the fault lines in these fragmented publics demand that for these mechanisms to have legitimacy they must address at some length questions of inclusiveness, accountability and accessibility with their end point as engagement rather than consultation. The suggestions that have been offered to augment these mechanisms are social brokers, facilitators and even a narrow version of social entrepreneurship. These offices are similar to the role of co-ordinators in the Freirian type culture circles that I suggested that corporations should adopt. Just as needs auditors' may use GIS technology to inspire the articulation of needs so this technology may be of use in encouraging fragmented publics to take part-ownership of partnership ventures. GIS implementation brings together technical, social and scientific perspectives. It highlights differences and shared conceptions.[199] Depending on the nature of the planned venture it should be possible to at least secure valid community consensus around broad spectrums of spatial interest, leaving other issues to more detailed negotiations.[200] What results then is not reconstituted community but individuals recognising opportunities to pursue limited shared objectives

In this chapter I have used the work of Alasdair MacIntyre to broaden the conceptual base of virtue ethics so that it admits a component of locality in all senses of this word and thus fits better into a postmodern world. The result of that is that virtue ethics can accommodate both ideas of the individual and ideas of individuals living in communities that share common features. I have set out my vision of corporate social intervention in a setting that is structured not by the balance between state and market that is engineered by one political ideology or another but by ideas of a new settlement based upon virtue.

[199] F Harvey and N Chrisman, "Boundary Objects and the Social Construction of GIS Technology" (1998) 30 *Environment and Planning A* 1683.

[200] D Howard, "Geographic Information Technologies and Community Planning: Spatial Empowerment and Public Participation" (1998) <http://www.ncgia.ucsb.edu/varenius/ppgis/papers/howard.html>.

4
Conclusion

In this final section I will draw together and review the main points of my argument. Chapter one began by looking at the role of national structures in the shaping of corporate behaviour in an era when, for many commentators, the only discussion that there can be is around the implications of globalisation. In chapter three some of the paradoxes of globalisation are illustrated by the discussion about the importance of local structures in a political climate where the EU as a supra-national body promotes regional development and notions of subsidiarity.[1] These ideas of subsidiarity link to the comparison I make between Catholic social teaching and Blairite political in chapter two. The intention of chapter one was to demonstrate why corporations both felt, and indeed should feel, the need to (re)legitimise themselves within society. There I provided material which examines the current position on corporate community involvement alongside my plea for this to develop into a much more structured intervention within society, thus replacing the idea of social intervention as part of the competitive agenda between corporations[2] or social intervention as constituted by purely altruistic acts. A number of inter-connecting factors were suggested as underscoring the need for change in terms of the way in which corporations relate to wider concerns outside the immediate narrow issue of market driven accountability to shareholders. Capitalism has undergone significant changes in an era that has seen the decline of the overt market liberalism of the New Right and the so called "high trust" capitalism of the Tiger states of the Far East. In the same time frame many Marxist regimes have collapsed and the economies of these countries have begun attempts to move towards some sort of market economy.

[1] On the European consciousness and subsidiarity see the discussion in C Turner "Open Behind: Myth and Politics" in R Fine and C Turner, *Social Theory after the Holocaust* (Liverpool: Liverpool University Press, 2000) 235 at pp 251–4.

[2] For an example of how social intervention can be used to mask the true nature of corporate behaviour see J Frynas "Corporate and State Responses to anti-oil protests in the Niger Delta" (2000) 100 *African Affairs* 27 at 44–9.

The decline of traditional capitalism has resulted in the end of long-familiar workspaces and patterns. An individual has now to value mobility and communication skills over fixed durable property.[3] Anxiety and insecurity are rife and the life journey for the individual has become fraught with difficulties. Individuals and Government are confronting issues such as the work/life balance. For example, technological advances now make home-working a distinct alternative to work attendance at a fixed geographical location. The positive aspect of this is that it allows greater flexibility in the designation of time as family time or work time. More difficult to navigate around are the problems raised by the lack of full-time and traditional-hours employment, for example, loss of status for former breadwinners.[4] There has been a retreat from acquisitive individualism towards a recognition that the way forward is a collective response based upon common desires to avoid common problems.

Giddens provides part of the political response. Political discourse of recent years has coalecesed around the idea of a Third Way. This is essentially a political position which is not clearly influenced by the ideas of either the Right or the Left. The Third Way is varyingly described as "modernisation" or "traditional values in a changed world". Giddens has intellectualised this as a desire for renewed social democracy and as the creation of policies to offer citizens a way through the dilemmas of the world identified above while still maintaining a concern for issues of social justice. The mobility of capital in the age of globalisation does

[3] See Z Bauman, *Liquid Modernity* (Cambridge: Polity Press, 2000), especially at pp 148–55. "Liquid Modernity" is the term that Bauman offers for the state of the world we live in now as contrasted with the solid modernity that preceded it. This text offers a theorisation in these terms of many of the types of scenarios that Richard Sennett describes in his *Corrosion of Character* (New York, NY: Norton, 1998). Indeed Sennett is Bauman's most cited source in this volume. Those of us who feared that post modernity as a descriptor had left Bauman's vocabulary are pleased to see it referred to with approval on p 76.

[4] Beck very incisively sees much of the current concern around the shape of family life as a rhetoric which seeks to explain by means of biographical narrative, the systemic concerns of our age: "The tension in family life . . . is . . . that equality between men and women be created in an institutional family structure which presupposes their inequality. In personal relationships conflicts are also initiated when possibilities of choice are opened up: in conflicting needs over careers, in the division of housework and childcare . . . . Lacking institutional solutions, people are having to learn how to negotiate relationships on the basis of equality. So the entire structure of family life has come under pressure from individualization . . .", "Interview with U Beck" (2001) 1 *J of Consumer Culture* 261 at 264.

not exempt corporations from these concerns. Consumer groups are more informed than ever before about the nature of corporate activity and increased interest in ethical investment means that corporate activity is no longer monitored only around the issue of profitability.

Ideas of civic renewal through the device of "community" are a recurrent theme of the political discourse that surrounds the Third Way. I try to offer a meaning for community which connects with virtues and which recognises that a major difficulty for individuals is in constructing larger units of reference for themselves in a society where traditional perceptions of community, based upon specific identities, have largely broken down. Bauman goes some way to resolving this difficulty with his observation that what is possible for individuals depends upon their willingness to participate in, and engage with, a larger project. In using the idea of community as a locus for corporate social intervention to take place I try to take something positive from each of the pre-existing definitions; social, geographical and political. Thus I seek to distinguish myself from those who have portrayed the idea of community as only an expression of equal distrust of the politics of both right and left.[5]

The first part of my reconstruction for society comes from an examination of Aristotelian virtue ethics and the structures for living life through the virtues that Aristotle suggested. The guiding virtues for life post the millennium, I put forward in chapter three. These are compassion, recognition of and care for the needs of others and trust – in sum, the pursuit of a model of social justice that incorporates respect and toleration.[6] It is suggested that these virtues can support a project of self-renewal based upon an engagement with emotion. My concern for much of chapter two was to answer the question "Why Aristotle?" The answer, in short, is that, in my view, virtue ethics capture more accurately the spirit of the age than other forms of ethical expression irrespective of the fact that they might be more familiar. In addition, Aristotelian political thought deals with many of the issues that confront the individual in the search for a larger unit of reference. I matched the intellectual renaissance of virtue ethics and the increased general interest in Aristotelian ideas to a growing flirtation

[5] G Rose, *Mourning Becomes the Law* (Cambridge: Cambridge University Press, 1996) at pp 15–20.

[6] S Roseneil "A Moment of Moral Remaking: the Death of Diana, Princess of Wales" in F Webster (ed) *Culture and Politics in the Information Age* (London: Routledge, 2001) p 96 at pp 110–11.

with Catholicism. My principal argument was that just as the Enlightenment had ended interest in Aquinas and thus also by dint of association Aristotle, so a growing contemporary fascination with the trappings of ritual and a desire to control science has rekindled interest in Catholicism and those whose philosophical positions are associated with it. The use of classical thought to shed light on contemporary problems is a device that has been used on previous occasions and to evidence this I refer, albeit very briefly, to the ideas of T H Green and the British Idealists.

There is work within business-ethics scholarship that has for some years identified Aristotelian virtue theory as a way of remoulding the behaviour of corporations. My use of Aristotelian theory differs from this in that I suggest that the corporation should be integrated into an Aristotelian-type community as an individual actor in its own right. Thus it becomes an entity which is required to perform according to these virtues if it is to be part of a reconstructed society in the era of post post-fordism. The focus will be on the creation of corporate culture in which the virtues are inculcated rather than on the delivery of a particular type of behaviour by individual corporate executives.

With this as a backdrop, I used chapter three to set out my ideas for corporate behaviour in a society structured around the ideas of the Third Way. This I see not as a duty based society, despite some of the political rhetoric that has been couched in terms of "no rights without responsibilities",[7] but as a values- or even virtues-based society. In a world which for the individual is one of uncertainty and also bewildering choice, these values can be seen as the virtues of character that each individual possesses to some degree or another. The pursuit of these virtues ensures that there are, in very loose terms, common trajectories and goals. Virtue ethics can be distinguished from Kantian ethics and utilitarianism through its focus on the individual's values and motives. Character developed by pursuing the virtues is what produces the framework for actions and decisions not rules and principles.[8] Thus virtue ethics can only ever be a guiding hand which offers a range of possible courses of action in relation to a particular issue.

Pursuit and application of the virtues are in danger of being stretched between two positions which if not exactly at opposite ends of the spectrum then are certainly a long way apart – Aristotle's univer-

[7] T Blair, *The Third Way* (London: Fabian Society, 1998) p 1.

[8] W Spohn "The Return of Virtue Ethics" (1992) 53 *Theological Studies* 60.

salistic community and Bauman's warning of the struggle that the individual faces. Aristotle's scheme for the inculcation and application of the virtues as a guide to living centres around the construction of the *polis* in which the aristocracy (those citizens prepared to involve themselves in the running of common affairs) will form a governing body. Aristotle's community was a universalistic one in that each individual had a place albeit, in some instances, a place of little or no regard. Within the *polis*, debate was supposed to flow freely among those permitted to make a contribution and who wished to do so.[9] This is in sharp contrast to the position taken by responsive communitarians[10] such as Etzioni. I outlined their authoritarian stance towards the construction and adoption of community positions in both chapters one and two. While responsive communitarianism raises interesting questions about dialogic structures between groups, the results it seeks to achieve from these structures would seem to be far from constructive.[11] In chapter three I looked at how corporations might undertake what I

[9] On one level this comment does nothing more than point to the role of oratory and debate within Greek society. However on another it is of much more significance. It touches upon a major difference in view between two contemporary Aristotelians; Martha Nussbaum and Alasdair MacIntyre. They offer different interpretations of the role of tradition and agreement around the virtues in Aristotle's *Nicomachean Ethics*. For MacIntyre views of *eudaimonia* in Arisotelian Athens would have been based around a set of fundamental agreements. For Nussbaum views of *eudaimonia* would have emerged based on discussions around shared human experiences.

[10] The label "responsive" in front of "communitarian" is an important one. It is perfectly possible within philosophical communitarian thought to take a position which is neither authoritarian or has the potential to legitimise intolerance. See A Cohen, "Communitarianism, 'Social Construction' and Autonomy" (1999) 80 *Pac Phil Quart* 121. Within this piece Cohen specifically refers to Alasdair MacIntyre as a communitarian. This is a label that MacIntyre himself disavows any notion of within his work, see A MacIntyre, "A partial response to my critics" in J Horten and S Mendus (eds), *After MacIntyre* (Cambridge: Polity, 1994) p 281 at pp 302. Given the way in which he defines communitarianism there this is an avenue open to him.

[11] Responsive communitarianism has many advocates and manifestos some orientated towards the intellectual and others towards the practice of the everyday. It seems that underpinning all of them are a set of positions from which it is presumed that responsive communitarianism may arise. Consider the following example: "One source of moral truth . . . is religious belief . . . . [M]ost religious believers need little encouragement to avoid behaviour that is hateful, hurtful or destructive . . . they are forbidden from violence or killing, not because there is a law against it, but because of a divine sanction against it that they violate at the risks of their own souls", D Eberly, *America's Promise* (Lanham, MD: Rowman and Littlefield, 1998) at p 205. This as a position is Christo-centric and thus exclusionary. Even as a Christo-centric proposition recent events in Northern Ireland and parts of central Europe would point to its inaccuracy.

described as an "audit of needs" of all the constituent groups within society in an effort to structure their interventions in a more coherent fashion. One of the aims of this type of exercise based upon listening is to avoid the sort of marginalisation that could occur within responsive communitarianism.

Bauman's view of contemporary society is that "individualism is a fate not a choice".[12] The result of this is that individuals do not come together to negotiate the meaning of *summa bonum* – the common good – and common principles of conducting life.[13] This position is in direct contrast to that of Aristotle and comes from Bauman's most recent work, *The Individualized Society*, where he sounds a greater note of pessimism than that taken in earlier work. The influence of Ulrich Beck's ideas on living within a "risk society" are evident here and Bauman thus concludes that individuals instead coalesce together in communities of fear to address shared worries and anxieties. These communities would then become, presumably, ones of risk management where short term solutions are found to current problems. Chapter three locates a meeting place for Aristotle and Bauman in the work of Alasdair MacIntyre. MacIntyre offers a bridge between Aristotle and Bauman by introducing the idea that in engaging in a life structured by the virtues the individual stands not alone but alongside others. MacIntyre positions the life of the individual within the life of a localised community. This localised community helps to sustain the individual and the individual brings to the community an identity inherited from tradition and history. The individual is not constrained by any bounds of this community, indeed individual identity is a fluid construct as are community virtues which form and reform over time.

This type of analysis, with its appeal to localism taken from MacIntyre and its endorsement of the individual transfixed by a fast changing world in which there is no such thing as a certain identity taken from Bauman, is open to the challenge of cultural relativism. I defended my analysis against this in chapter three. Ways out of cultural relativism, while still pursuing an ethical foundation to life, are provided ostensibly by devices such as voluntary codes, standard setting legislation and hypothetical social contracts purporting to embody propositions capable of universal recognition. These approaches all fail to find a balance between cultural imperialism and content so thin

[12] Z Bauman, *The Individualized Society* (Cambridge: Polity, 2001) at p 46.

[13] *Supra* at p 50.

as to be vacuous in meaning. They fail because they seek to impose a rights-based structure in a world that has yet to recognise or perhaps, if one is to be optimistic, to remember its ethical commitment to the other.[14] Notions of relativism depend upon the existence of societies that are isolated from each other. Post globalisation of the image, the musician and coca cola this is likely to be the case in very few, if any, instances.

The majority of chapter three is devoted to setting out how corporations might operationalise their relationship with corporate social intervention to make the most effective input into an environment structured by the virtues. This involves corporations not in abandoning their profit motive but in making alongside it an intervention that has the intention of pursuing the virtues. My suggestion is for corporations to structure their intervention through engaging with the possibilities offered by membership of and co-operation with Regional Development Agencies. Participation in this level of local governance offers an opportunity for cross-sector partnership and concentration in structural intervention rather than the "show and tell" mechanisms that are advocated by much of the professional management literature and recent government policy documents. Cross-sector partnerships, in my view, encapsulate the very essence of Third Way behaviour in that such structures involve engagement and discussion, suppression of some interests and the promotion of others. Engagement with RDAs will allow needs audits – listening exercises – undertaken by corporations to build upon existing information. Audits of needs result in the articulation of needs and the subsequent requirement that these needs be interpreted. This could be done, I suggested, through the use of Freiren methodology.[15]

I advocate the establishment by corporations of care plans and I also explain how at an operational level these plans offer a stronger platform for sustained and targeted intervention than stakeholding. The choice of the term "care" is a deliberate one to demonstrate the nature of the corporation's relationship to the other – a relationship

[14] See Costas Douzinas' Hegelian tour de force, *The End of Human Rights* (Oxford: Hart Publishing, 2000).

[15] Since the time of writing this I have become aware of the work of Kathleen Weiler in which she presents a powerful feminist critique of Freire's pedagogy. Careful consideration of Weiler's work may have lead me to present my argument on this point rather differently. See K Weiler "A Feminist Pedagogy of Difference" (1991) 61 *Harv Ed Rev* 449 and "Myths of Paulo Freire" (1996) 46 *Ed Theory* 353.

structured through the virtues, of which care is one, marked by a desire to participate in the shared good. I distinguish care in this context from the way in which it is used in debates around feminist ethics. The anti-Kantian stance of Gilligan's original work on the emergence of "care" ethics and Tronto's more recent work underscore a general conception of care as the ideal operational partner to the contextual moral theory based upon Aristotle and MacIntyre that I developed earlier in the book.

Third Way ideals as a response to the political and social events of recent years require corporations to relegitimise themselves. Adoption of a modified virtue ethics structure as a means of grounding corporate activity and positive engagement with society through strategic social intervention represents the ways in which the relegitimisation project can be accomplished.

EPILOGUE: POST SEPTEMBER 11, 2001

In chapter one, the first draft of which I wrote in the winter of 1999, I commented that:

> "[T]here is a sense in which events such as globalisation have taken away the need for national policies to be founded upon concerns like common security and thus there is a space to look at other issues such as disabled and gay rights".[16]

One has only to remember the events of September 11, 2001 and to examine the response led by the Anglo-American task force, for want of a better word, to see that this prediction/wish was somewhat wide of the mark. While the response to September 11 demonstrates the paranoia that surrounds apparent immediate threats to security, it also demonstrates the emergence of new fault lines in global politics. It seems that right and left political positions have indeed been abandoned. At the fore instead is a perceived hostility between a different character of paired belief systems: Islam and Christianity. However, to express the nature of the conflict in these terms is to ignore the very deep concern with the politics of cultural imperialism and aggressive support of other state powers hostile to Islam by certain very powerful Western actors. What has Third Way political discourse offered as a

[16] Chapter 1, text accompanying note 77.

response to a conflict framed in this way? The answer seems to lie in an extension of the idea of community; an international community with "an active and interventionist role in solving the world's problems".[17] One expression of this has come through a reworked conception of the underpinning idea of social justice,[18] another suggestion is a campaign to end world poverty.[19] However, in the absence of a strong social dialogue to accompany these ideas they are likely to remain as statements of political rhetoric.

[17] Tony Blair, Speech at the Lord Mayor's Banquet, 12 Nov 2001.
[18] Tony Blair, Speech to the Labour Party Conference, 3 Oct 2001.
[19] Gordon Brown, Speech to Federal Reserve Bank, New York, 16 Nov 2001.

Index

Page number followed by "n" indicates a note reference.

www.ingramcontent.com/pod-product-compliance
Ingram Content Group UK Ltd.
Pitfield, Milton Keynes, MK11 3LW, UK
UKHW020123290926
15471UKWH00003B/253

9 781901 362633